RARE BIRDS
IN BRITAIN AND IRELAND

Rare Birds
in Britain and Ireland

by J. T. R. SHARROCK & E. M. SHARROCK

WITH ILLUSTRATIONS BY

Robert Gillmor

P. J. Grant

R. A. Richardson

D. I. M. Wallace

Ian Willis

T. & A. D. POYSER
Berkhamsted

First published in 1976 by
T & A D Poyser Ltd, 281 High Street,
Berkhamsted, Hertfordshire, England

ISBN 0 85661 014 3

Text set in 11/12 pt Photon Times, printed by photolithography,
and bound in Great Britain at The Pitman Press, Bath.

Suddenly, as rare things will, it vanished . . . .

Robert Browning

Contents

Introduction

In a previous book, *Scarce Migrant Birds in Britain and Ireland*, the patterns of records of two dozen species were displayed and discussed at length. This present book now takes the birds rarer than those, and over 8,000 records of 221 species are illustrated in such a way that it is easy to see at a glance how many, where, when and how regularly each one appears in Britain and Ireland.

Most birdwatchers are fascinated by rarities. To some, the occasional rarity is an unexpected but welcome excitement in the course of a normal year's birding, but to others the finding of rare birds becomes the *raison d'être* of their hobby. Once known as tally-hunters, tick-hunters or tickers, these rarity seekers are now known colloquially as 'twitchers'. Willing to travel hundreds of miles to see a single rare bird and covering perhaps thousands of miles each year in this pursuit, twitchers undoubtedly include among their number some of our most skilled and energetic field ornithologists.

Even 'serious' ornithologists, who consider that projects such as the Common Birds Census, the Ornithological Atlas and the Register of Ornithological Sites* are of far greater importance and value than the search for rare birds, will admit that the discovery of a rarity gives them a thrill of excitement, and many choose to take their holidays at bird observatories† where an element of the attraction is the chance of seeing rare birds. There is no doubt that, for the majority of us, rare birds add some spice to our hobby. While a single rarity record has minimal (some would say nil) scientific value, the *patterns* shown by analysis of accumulated data have value to the student of migration and, in many cases, changes in vagrant status may reflect changing numbers and distributions in the breeding and wintering areas.

In this book, records before 1958 are summarised or listed but those for the 15 years 1958–72 are analysed in detail. These years are referred to as 'the period' or 'our period'. In the cases of extreme rarities, records subsequent to 1972 are also listed. The 8,000 records for 1958–72 have been extracted from the journal *British Birds,* the *Irish Bird Report* and (for Pectoral Sandpiper *Calidris melanotos* and Richard's Pipit *Anthus novaeseelandiae*) the British

---

* For details of these and other projects, write to British Trust for Ornithology, Beech Grove, Tring, Hertfordshire, HP23 5NR.

† See *Bird Observatories in Britain and Ireland* edited by R. F. Durman.

county and regional bird reports, where records of rare birds are published annually. This is, however, the first time that the patterns of these records have been displayed as maps and figures, as distinct from lists of individual records. Every published accepted record is included in this book, which, therefore, provides a complete documentation of rare birds in Britain and Ireland for a 15-year period. A very small number of observers refuse to co-operate with the national or county assessment bodies, but the few missing records (certainly less than 1%) would not significantly alter the general patterns, although it should be noted that rather more records may be missing from Northern Ireland than from other areas.

The records included here have all been carefully assessed and accepted by national or regional panels of experts: all 1958–59 records and British records since 1960 by the *British Birds* Rarities Committee, 1960–70 Irish records by the editor of the *Irish Bird Report* (at that time, Major R. F. Ruttledge) and independent referees with specialist knowledge of individual species, and Irish records since 1971 by the Irish Records Panel. Pectoral Sandpiper and Richard's Pipit were dropped from the list of species considered by the *British Birds* Rarities Committee from 1963 and 1970 onwards, respectively, and subsequent British records of these species were assessed by the county or regional report editors or records committees. The first record of each species in Britain and Ireland was always additionally examined by the Records Committee of the British Ornithologists' Union*. No assessment of records can ensure 100% accuracy. Accepted records undoubtedly include a few biras which were misidentified and it is probable that a greater number of genuine records were rejected, usually because of inadequate documentation. However, taking into account the hundreds of rare birds which must occur here annually but which are never seen by ornithologists, the accepted records provide us with a relatively unbiased sample of the vagrants reaching our shores. Birdwatchers owe a great debt to those whose idea it was to set up the national reviewing bodies, thus providing uniform methods of collection and treatment of rarity records from the whole of Britain and Ireland.

The *British Birds* Rarities Committee, consisting of ten members with extensive field experience and knowledge of rare birds and of vetting rarity records, was set up in 1959, largely at the instigation of I. J. Ferguson-Lees and P. A. D. Hollom. Under the chairmanships of P. A. D. Hollom (1959–72) and D. I. M. Wallace (since 1972), and with the honorary secretaries G. A. Pyman (1959–61), C. M. Swaine (1961–63), D. D. Harber (1963–66), F. R. Smith (1966–75) and J. N. Dymond (since 1975), this voluntary committee has thrived, despite an ever-increasing volume of work. Eighteen other members

* Since this book includes records of all extreme rarities seen up to 31st December 1975, there are inevitably a few species new to Britain and Ireland which have not yet passed through all of the rigorous vetting procedures. We consider that readers will prefer us to include them all, rather than omit species, most of which seem likely to be added officially to the British and Irish list in due course. The fact that such a record is still under review is always noted.

served on this committee during the 15 years: H. G. Alexander, D. G. Bell, A. R. M. Blake, P. E. Davis, R. H. Dennis, I. J. Ferguson-Lees, P. J. Grant, A. Hazelwood, R. J. Johns, H. P. Medhurst, Prof. M. F. M. Meiklejohn, Dr I. C. T. Nisbet, R. A. Richardson, Major R. F. Ruttledge, Dr. J. T. R. Sharrock, K. D. Smith, R. Wagstaffe and K. Williamson. An assessment of the committee's achievements in its first ten years is to be found in *British Birds,* 63: 113–129.

A parallel committee, the Irish Records Panel, dealing with records from the whole of Ireland, was set up in 1971, its members being K. Preston (secretary), T. Ennis (1971–73), F. King, O. J. Merne and Dr J. T. R. Sharrock.

Some of the main field-characters of each species are given at the start of each account in this book, but only very briefly. The various field guides which are now available provide a very good grounding to the identification of most of the birds dealt with here. The number of species, however, dictates that the space devoted to any one is very small. The art of field identification is now such that more specialised books (such as *Flight Identification of European Raptors,* by R. F. Porter, Ian Willis, Bent Pors Nielsen and Steen Christensen, and the three BTO field guides to the warbler genera, *Identification for Ringers,* by Kenneth Williamson) have become essential. Many important identification features are still hidden away in papers and notes in various ornithological journals, however, and we therefore draw attention to some of these under each species heading. It is hoped that this handy reference to detailed notes will be a useful service to the ornithologist wishing to trace a fuller description of a bird he has seen than is given in the field guides. In many cases, these references will themselves lead the searcher to further ones. The references are abbreviated, and only the first page number is given.

As M. D. England and T. P. Inskipp have shown (*Brit. Birds,* 67: 177–197 and *All Heaven in a Rage*), there is now a very considerable problem for the field-ornithologist provided by birds escaping from aviculturalists' collections. With the exceptions of divers, grebes, most seabirds, nightjars, swifts and hirundines, almost any species seen in Britain and Ireland could now be such an escape, and not a genuine vagrant. It is usually not possible to assess escape likelihood in individual instances, but the overall patterns of occurrence of most of the species in this book suggest that the majority are wild birds. In cases of doubt, we have included all records rather than 'doctor' the picture by omitting some which do not fit the vagrancy pattern.

The histograms and maps in this book are intended to convey, visually, all the important information about the records of each species: at what time of year they occur, in which years most have been seen (and how regular occurrences are) and where in Britain and Ireland most have been observed. To these ends, we have attempted to give uniform treatment, listing the records when these number one to three and providing diagrams and maps when they exceed three. Any uniform treatment is bound to suit some patterns better than others. We have usually split records into spring and autumn and, unless there was an obvious reason for doing otherwise, have taken the end of June as the dividing line.

FIGURE 1. The counties of Britain and Ireland. The boundaries and names are those used during the period covered by this book.

10	Aberdeen	89	Donegal	41	Lancashire	62	Radnor
48	Anglesey	84	Dorset	112	Laoighis	24	Renfrew
13	Angus	94	Down	54	Leicester	101	Roscommon
91	Antrim	107	Dublin	98	Leitrim	6	Ross-shire
15	Argyll	33	Dumfries	116	Limerick	31	Roxburgh
95	Armagh	17	Dunbarton	42	Lincoln	54	Rutland
26	Ayr	37	Durham	76	London	87	Scilly
8	Banff	22	East Lothian	90	Londonderry	32	Selkirk
65	Bedford	70	Essex	105	Longford	1	Shetland
77	Berkshire	93	Fermanagh	102	Louth	53	Shropshire
28	Berwick	18	Fife	100	Mayo	99	Sligo
67	Brecknock	46	Flint	103	Meath	79	Somerset
66	Buckingham	106	Galway	51	Merioneth	50	Stafford
27	Bute	75	Glamorgan	76	Middlesex	16	Stirling
49	Caernarvon	73	Gloucester	23	Midlothian	64	Suffolk
3	Caithness	83	Hampshire	96	Monaghan	81	Surrey
56	Cambridge	63	Hereford	74	Monmouth	82	Sussex
61	Cardigan	71	Hertford	52	Montgomery	4	Sutherland
114	Carlow	57	Huntingdon	7	Moray	111	Tipperary
68	Carmarthen	11	Inverness	9	Nairn	92	Tyrone
97	Cavan	39	Isle of Man	55	Norfolk	59	Warwick
45	Cheshire	87	Isles of Scilly	58	Northampton	118	Waterford
20	Clackmannan	88	Isle of Wight	30	Northumberland	21	West Lothian
110	Clare	80	Kent	43	Nottingham	104	Westmeath
119	Cork	120	Kerry	109	Offaly	38	Westmorland
86	Cornwall	108	Kildare	2	Orkney	117	Wexford
36	Cumberland	115	Kilkenny	5	Outer Hebrides	113	Wicklow
47	Denbigh	12	Kincardine	72	Oxford	35	Wigtown
44	Derby	19	Kinross	29	Peebles	78	Wiltshire
90	Derry	34	Kirkcudbright	69	Pembroke	60	Worcester
85	Devon	25	Lanark	14	Perth	40	Yorkshire

Such a split has occasionally appeared to be rather meaningless (as when there is a scatter of records from April to September with no marked spring or autumn peaks), but at least the method may show whether there is any difference in the patterns for early and late records; similarly, with winter records, whether there is a difference between those at the end of the year and those at the beginning.

Throughout this book we have treated a single bird as one record, regardless of how long it stayed or whether it moved around the country. Thus, birds that stayed for long periods are counted once only—on the date they were first seen. In species where long stays are regular, we have usually commented to this effect.

With over 8,000 records, it was quite impracticable to pinpoint each sighting at its exact locality. The counties of Britain and Ireland, though irregular in shape and size, provide a perfectly adequate basis for distribution mapping of vagrants which, in many cases, have travelled hundreds (or even thousands) of miles before reaching us. Most birdwatchers also have a feeling of loyalty towards their home county (hence the tales of twitchers chasing birds over county boundaries!) and the county distribution, therefore, may be of intrinsic interest to readers. The counties utilised in this book are those in existence during the period under review and still adopted as recording units by most bird clubs and societies. In time, no doubt, the new counties which came into existence on 1st April 1974 (England and Wales) and 16th May 1975 (Scotland) will be adopted for recording, but we have not pre-empted such developments by using them here. For the convenience of future and foreign readers, the counties are shown in fig. 1. It should be noted that we have treated the Isles of Scilly, the Isle of Wight and the Outer Hebrides as distinct counties, but have included Rutland with Leicestershire and Middlesex with London.

Birds seen at localities on county boundaries are shown in only one county. We usually made the arbitrary decision of showing them in the county coming first in the alphabet (e.g. birds at a locality on the Bedfordshire/Huntingdonshire border would be shown only in Bedfordshire). When the same individual bird was seen in several counties, however, it was usually mapped only in the county in which it was first seen.

The seasonal distribution diagrams use seven-day periods as their basis, to eliminate the considerable weekend-bias in the data (*Brit. Birds,* 59: 556–558). The 52nd period is, of course, an eight-day period.

The number of active birdwatchers has increased markedly; membership of the British Trust for Ornithology, for instance, rising 2½-fold in the 15 years, from 2,641 in 1958 to 5,994 by the end of 1972. (The comparable figures for the Royal Society for the Protection of Birds were 7,500 in 1958 and almost 118,000 in 1972.) The influence of this increase is discussed in the Summary (p. 323) but is mentioned here as it must be constantly borne in mind when viewing the annual totals of each species.

The source of the greatest bias, however, is the uneven distribution of observers in Britain and Ireland. There are far more birdwatchers in midland and southeast England than elsewhere and very few indeed in parts of Scotland and, especially, Ireland. This pattern (shown in fig. 2) must be taken into account when viewing the distribution maps.

This is not a book on identification, but the line drawings accompanying each species account are far more than mere decoration. As well as being artists of international renown, the five illustrators of this book are also expert field ornithologists and the drawings show each species in a typical stance, conveying not only the identification marks of the plumage but also the bird's jizz. Each group of species is drawn by one artist (e.g. the herons by Robert Gillmor, the gulls by P. J. Grant, the warblers by D. I. M. Wallace), to facilitate comparisons between closely-related birds. Each artist has illustrated those groups with which he is most familiar. We feel sure that readers will find this collection of vignettes of rare birds of great value as an identification aid, in conjunction with a field guide containing more stereotyped illustrations.

The vernacular names, scientific names and sequence of species in this book

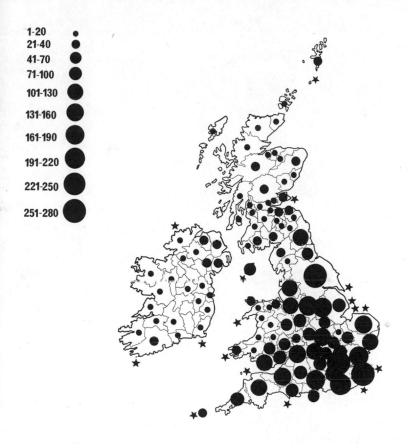

1-20	•
21-40	•
41-70	●
71-100	●
101-130	●
131-160	●
161-190	●
191-220	●
221-250	●
251-280	●

FIGURE 2. Distribution by counties of observers in Britain and Ireland. The dots show the actual or estimated number of contributors to the 1967 county or regional bird report. The stars show bird observatories which were in operation for a significant part of the 15 years 1958–72 and which, because of the presence of a resident warden or through drawing largely on observers from outside the county, effectively boosted their county's recording potential.

follow *A Species List of British and Irish Birds* by Robert Hudson (BTO Guide 13). The make-up of the book necessitates some accounts being out of sequence, but such instances are always indicated boldly in the correct position.

We have taken every care to ensure that the information in this book is accurate. But we are human, and errors may have crept in. We would be most grateful if any reader spotting such a slip would inform us of it, so that future editions can be corrected. Please write to the authors, c/o T. & A. D. Poyser, 281 High Street, Berkhamsted, Hertfordshire.

Acknowledgements

We are delighted to express our gratitude to D. I. M. Wallace, the present Chairman of the *British Birds* Rarities Committee, for his encouragement and help. K. Preston and J. N. Dymond, the secretaries of the Irish Records Panel and *British Birds* Rarities Committee, respectively, were both most generous with their time in providing details of late records and answering our queries. We are most grateful to L. Cornwallis for his detailed comments on the identification notes relating to the wheatears. Our publishers also gave quite exceptional assistance.

Certain books are an invaluable source of reference and we, like all ornithologists, owe a debt to their authors: *The Handbook of British Birds* (1940–41; H. F. Witherby, F. C. R. Jourdain, N. F. Ticehurst and B. W. Tucker); *A Field Guide to the Birds* (1947; R. T. Peterson); *The Pocket Guide to British Birds* (1952; R. S. R. Fitter and R. A. Richardson); *A Field Guide to the Birds of Britain and Europe* (1954; R. Peterson, G. Mountfort and P. A. D. Hollom); *The Birds of the Palearctic Fauna* (1959, 1965; C. Vaurie); *The Popular Handbook of Rarer British Birds* (1960; P. A. D. Hollom); *Atlas of European Birds* (1960; K. H. Voous); *Birds of North America* (1966; C. S. Robbins, B. Bruun and H. S. Zim); *The Status of Birds in Britain and Ireland* (1971; British Ornithologists' Union); and *The Birds of Britain and Europe with North Africa and the Middle East* (1972; H. Heinzel, R. Fitter and J. Parslow).

We also wish to thank all those who supplied unpublished records of Pectoral Sandpipers and Richard's Pipits or who helped in other ways: K. Allsopp, K. Atkin, M. Blindell, P. F. Bonham, D. A. Christie, F. R. Clafton, Dr J. P. Cullen, G. M. S. Easy, Robert Hudson, J. R. Mather, N. R. Phillips, C. W. N. Plant, J. Stafford, I. F. Stewart, R. Stokoe and C. Winnington-Ingram.

White-billed Diver

Gavia adamsii

Breeds Arctic, from western Russia to Canada.

Resembles Great Northern Diver *G. immer,* but bill never has dark culmen ridge and is usually held pointing upwards, like Red-throated Diver *G. stellata.* *Brit. Birds*, 64: 519; 67: 257.

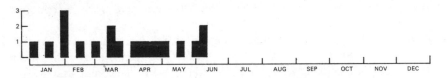

The 19 records in 1958–72 were all in late winter/spring, from January to June, with no pronounced peak, suggesting a small wintering population.

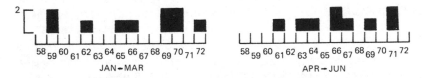

Though the numbers seen increased during the course of the 15-year period (four in 1958–62, seven in 1963–67 and eight in 1968–72), this matches, and probably merely reflects, the increasing number and vigilance of observers. There were 19 records during 1958–72, compared with only 18 prior to 1958. The identification problem makes it difficult to draw conclusions from these figures. One may expect an increasing number of records as a result of the recent paper in *British Birds* on the identification of the species.

The winter (January-March) and spring (April-June) records show distinct patterns, with a much more northerly bias in spring. Together with the late winter arrival, in January, this suggests a westerly mid-winter movement across the North Sea from Norwegian waters, but a northerly departure in spring.

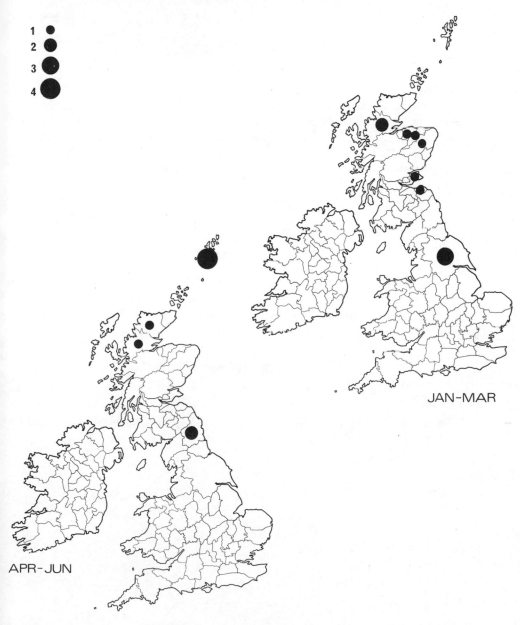

JAN-MAR

APR-JUN

19

Pied-billed Grebe
Podilymbus podiceps

Breeds North, Central and South America.

Slightly larger than Little Grebe *Tachybaptus ruficollis* but with thick, short, stubby bill; mostly grey-buff, darker above than below; in summer plumage the pale bill has a vertical dark central bar, and the throat is black. *Brit. Birds,* 58: 305; 60: 290, 295.

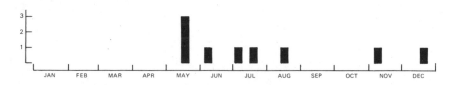

Though nine records are shown, these (the first in Britain and Ireland) probably relate to only three individuals. Two of the birds stayed for long periods and one returned to the same localities in several years.

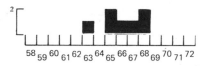

The 1963 bird was probably the same as one in 1965–68, with two other singles in 1965 and 1968.

The Somerset records probably relate to one individual, at Blagdon Reservoir and Chew Valley Lake, on 22nd December 1963, 17th August–23rd October 1965, 15th May and 22nd July–2nd November 1966, 14th May–2nd October 1967 and 14th May–5th June and 4th–5th July 1968. The Yorkshire bird was at Beaverdyke Reservoir on 9th June–24th November 1965 and the Norfolk one at Welney on 9th–12th November 1968.

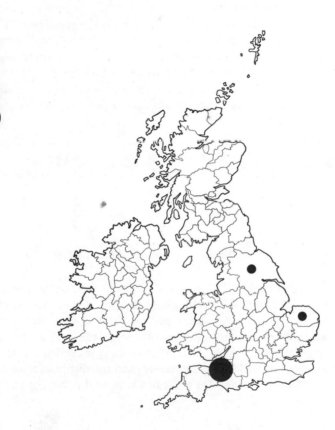

Black-browed Albatross
Diomedea melanophris

Breeds islands of southern oceans.

Larger than a Gannet *Sula bassana* and shaped like a huge Fulmar *Fulmarus glacialis,* fat-bodied, with a short, thick neck and short tail, with very long, narrow wings and powerful gliding flight. Adults identified by brownish-black underwing with white central stripe, wholly white head (except for black 'brow') and yellow bill; immatures have head and neck grey, less white on underwing and bill dark grey or yellow with dark tip. *Brit. Birds,* 57: 179; 59: 376; 61: 22.

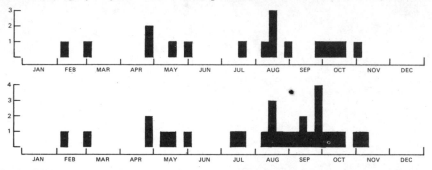

61% of the albatrosses recorded in our period were identified as this species, and almost all of the others were also probably Black-browed. The records of those specifically identified are shown in the upper and those of all albatrosses in the lower histograms. The main concentrations of records were in late April to early June and July to early November. Most sea-watching is carried out from late March to May and July to October, however, and the distribution of records may result partly from this bias. One adult Black-browed Albatross frequented

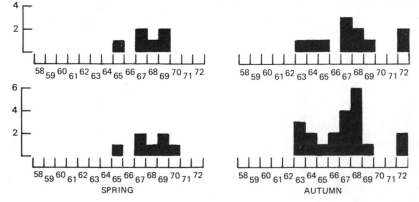

22

the gannetry on the Bass Rock (East Lothian) during May–September 1967, April–July 1968 and April–May 1969, and was also seen in Berwick and Fife. (In June–August 1974, one frequented the gannetry on Unst, Shetland.)

The 28 records in our period compare with three prior to 1958—inland records of Black-browed Albatrosses in Cambridge in July 1897 and Derby in August 1952, and an unidentified albatross in Shetland in May 1949. Though there was probably some duplication of records, there is no doubt that several different adults and immatures were concerned during 1963–72, and the sudden increase in records was not wholly due to the increase in the amount of sea-watching carried out from about 1959 onwards. One of the Cork records (26th August 1968) concerned two together: all other sightings were of single birds.

Though the Bass Rock in East Lothian was the base for an adult during the summers of 1967–69, most passage albatrosses were seen off the coasts of Co. Cork (seven of them off Cape Clear Island) and Yorkshire (four localities). The maps show all records during 1958–72, including unidentified albatrosses.

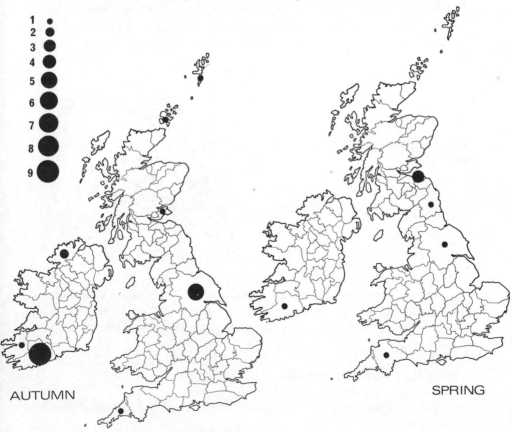

AUTUMN

SPRING

23

Bulwer's Petrel

Bulweria bulwerii

Breeds islands of North Atlantic and Pacific, between 40°N and 10°S.

Size of Little Shearwater, but almost wholly black, with long, wedge-shaped tail, and very fast, swooping flight. *Cape Clear Bird Observatory Report,* 7: 13.

One record in the period:
Cork: Cape Clear Island on 26th August 1965

The two previous records were in Yorkshire (May 1837 and February 1908). This species may be more regular than the records suggest, for fishermen based in southwest Ireland have reported single all-dark petrels in several recent years.

Soft-plumaged Petrel

Pterodroma mollis

Breeds islands of Indian and Atlantic Oceans, north to Madeira.

Gad-fly petrel the size of Manx Shearwater *Puffinus puffinus* but with uniformly blackish underwing; brownish-grey upperparts, ear-coverts and wing-coverts darker than rest; white underparts, sometimes with dusky breast-band. *Ibis,* 99: 182.

None in the period, but one since:
Cork: Cape Clear Island on 5th September 1974

This is the only record; it is still under review for admission to the British and Irish list.

Wilson's Petrel
Oceanites oceanicus

Breeds Antarctica and islands of southern oceans.

Small, square-tailed, round-winged storm-petrel with long legs, which extend beyond the tail in flight or are dangled as the bird skips with slightly raised wings over the surface of the sea. Though difficult to see, yellow webs to the feet are diagnostic. Compared with Storm Petrel *Hydrobates pelagicus,* white rump patch larger, and extends more round body; stronger and more direct flight, skimming back and forth over waves; lacks white bar on underwing. *Sea Swallow,* 14: 12; 18: 69.

Three records in the period:
Cork: Cape Clear Island on 3rd August 1969
Cornwall: St. Ives Island on 29th October 1967
St. Ives Island on 20th October 1970

The four previous records were also all in the west in autumn (Cornwall in August 1838 and Argyll, Fermanagh and Down, all in October 1891).

Magnificent Frigatebird
Fregata magnificens

Breeds on islands in tropical Atlantic and east Pacific.

Huge, fork-tailed seabird with eight-foot wing-span and wonderful powers of flight, gliding and skimming food from surface of sea. *Brit. Birds,* 47: 58, 59.

There were no certain records of this species in the period, but one record of an unidentified frigatebird:
Aberdeen: Forvie on 20th August 1960
and one other since:
Cork: Cape Clear Island on 24th August 1973

The only other fully accepted record is of a Magnificent Frigatebird at Tiree, Argyll on 9th July 1953. Though not generally accepted, a record of an unidentified frigatebird off Filey Brigg, Yorkshire, on 15th October 1966 is regarded as valid by several seabird experts.

Cory's Shearwater
Calonectris diomedea

Breeds Mediterranean and North Atlantic islands north to Azores.

Distinguished from Great Shearwater *Puffinus gravis* by lack of dark cap contrasting with white side-neck and by yellowish instead of dark bill. In calm weather, glides on bowed wings; in rough weather, towers: but Great Shearwaters and Fulmars *Fulmarus glacialis* may behave similarly. At distance, appears to have rather rounded gull-like wings. *Brit. Birds*, 61: 163, 571; *Cape Clear Bird Obs. Bull.*, 9: 66.

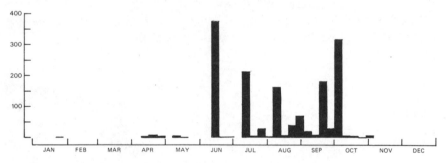

Apart from one in January (dead, Norfolk 1966), the pattern was of tiny numbers in April–May and occasional huge movements at any time in June–October, probably dependent upon weather conditions and movements of fish-shoals bringing the birds within sight of land. June records are here regarded as referring to the autumn.

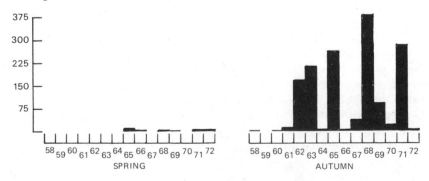

26

There was only a handful of records prior to 1958, apart from an influx of several thousand large shearwaters (at least two, and perhaps many, of which were this species) in Dingle Bay, Co. Kerry in September–November 1854. This compares with 1,498 during 1958–72 (plus many hundreds of individuals too distant for identification beyond Great/Cory's). Large movements probably occur every two or three years in western Ireland and it is likely that the change in status is due to the virtual lack of sea-watching there prior to 1959 (see *The Natural History of Cape Clear Island*). The chance of witnessing a large movement of this species, such as those documented in *Brit. Birds*, 56: 189–190, 57: 200–202, provides the spur to many keen sea-watchers. The 1968 peak is largely due to two rafts totalling 374 birds off Cape Clear Island, Co. Cork on 16th June.

The 18 April–May records were all of birds seen from sites in western Ireland or the English Channel coast. Autumn records were more widespread, including the North Sea coast, but 79% were in Co. Cork, and no other county exceeded 6%.

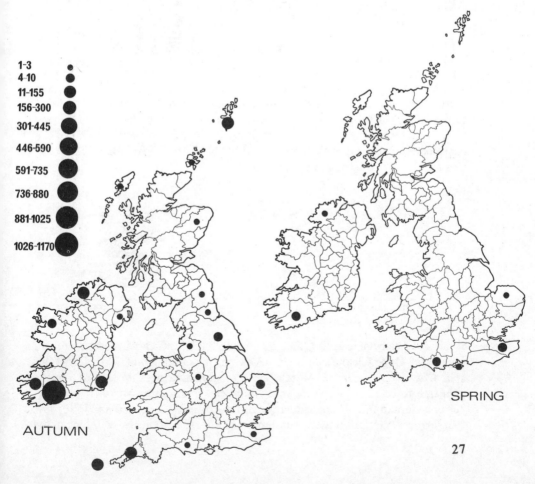

1-3
4-10
11-155
156-300
301-445
446-590
591-735
736-880
881-1025
1026-1170

SPRING

AUTUMN

Little Shearwater
Puffinus assimilis

Breeds islands of Atlantic, Pacific and Indian Oceans south of 32°N.

Resembles a very small Manx Shearwater *P. puffinus,* but black cap extends only down to eye (not below it) and the wing-beats are far more rapid, giving a fluttery, auk-like appearance. *Brit. Birds,* 51: 393; 58: 189; *Irish Bird Report,* 13: 13; 14: 13; 15: 17; 16: 16.

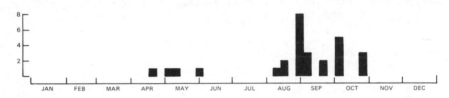

Though there are only 28 records, these clearly show a small spring passage in April–early June and a larger autumn passage in August–October. In addition to the 28 fully-accepted records, a further 20 small shearwaters with a fluttery flight were seen during 1958–72, the pattern of occurrences fitting that of the accepted records, and these were probably also Little Shearwaters. This contrasts with only five records prior to 1958.

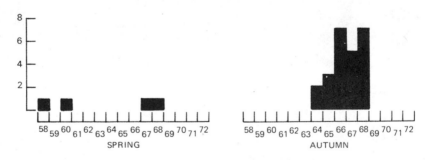

While still a vagrant in spring, the concentrated efforts of sea-watchers in Ireland (mostly at Cape Clear Island, Co. Cork and Brandon Point, Co. Kerry), inspired by the Atlantic Sea-watch Scheme sponsored by the Seabird Group, appeared to be showing by the mid-1960s that this species was of regular occurrence in autumn. Then, suddenly, the flow of records ceased and in the last four years of our period there was none! The effort spent on sea-watching in the early 1970s was certainly less than in the mid-1960s, but the change was not sufficient, nor sudden enough, to explain this cessation, and, indeed, there were six more records from Cape Clear Island in 1973.

The spring birds in Cheshire and Norfolk were both dead or dying storm-driven vagrants of the Madeiran race *P. a. baroli.* The two other spring records and all but one of those in autumn were seen during sea-watches from recognised sea-watch stations in the west of Ireland. No less than three-quarters of all the birds were seen from Cape Clear Island or Brandon Point.

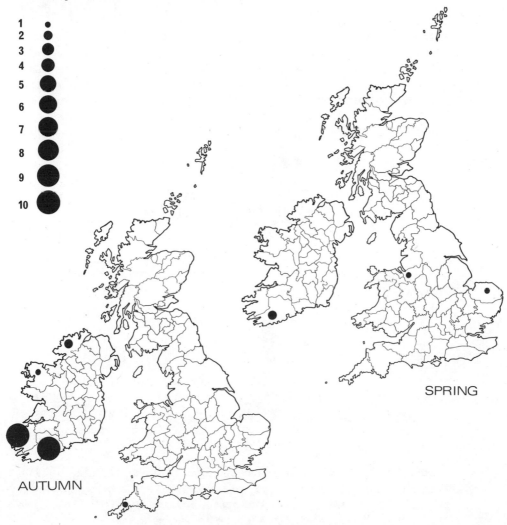

AUTUMN

SPRING

Wilson's Petrel *Oceanites oceanicus,* see page 25.
Magnificent Frigatebird *Fregata magnificens,* see page 25.

Purple Heron

Ardea purpurea

Breeds from Netherlands, Iberia and northwest Africa eastwards to Manchuria and Indonesia; also southern Africa.

Slightly smaller, with slenderer neck, than Grey Heron *A. cinerea*; general colour darker, with less contrast in wings, and vinous underparts in adult; in flight, legs and large feet extend beyond tail and folded neck curves down below body-level. *Brit. Birds,* 45: 331; *Cape Clear Bird Observatory Report,* 9: 67.

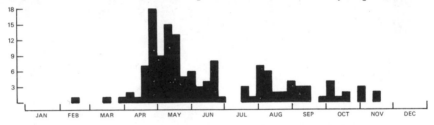

More than two-thirds of the records were in spring, with a marked peak at the end of April and in early May. The less obvious autumn peak came in early August.

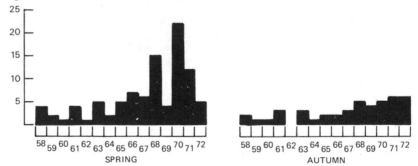

There were 139 records in the period, compared with about 85 prior to 1958. With peak numbers in spring 1968, 1970 and 1971, and a steady increase in autumn numbers, there is a striking recent increase (19 in 1958–62, 36 in 1963–67 and 84 in 1968–72). With up to five at a time at one locality (Minsmere, Suffolk on 23rd May 1968), regular occurrence there, and in the Stour valley in Kent, and some extended stays in late spring, hopes were expressed that breeding would occur, but this has not yet been recorded.

The strong south-easterly bias to the records at both seasons suggests that most of the birds seen here originate from the Netherlands, rather than from southern Europe. This is confirmed by two ringed Dutch birds being recovered (Fair Isle, Shetland in May 1969 and St. Mary's, Isles of Scilly in May 1970). The four south-eastern counties from Norfolk to Kent accounted for 37% of the spring birds and 50% of those in autumn, whereas the comparable figures for the five south-western counties from Somerset and Dorset to the Isles of Scilly were 22% in spring and 9% in autumn. This suggests that some south European birds may occur (especially in the west) in spring.

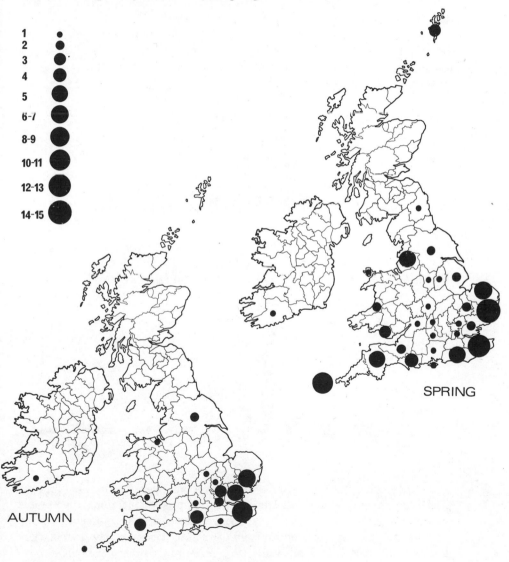

31

Little Egret
Egretta garzetta

Breeds from Iberia and northwest Africa through the Mediterranean eastwards to southern Asia and Australia; also southern Africa.

Small, snowy-white heron, with black legs and yellow feet, which extend beyond the tail in flight. In breeding plumage has long drooping crest and scapular plumes. (Indistinguishable in the field from Snowy Egret *E. thula* of the Americas.) *Brit. Birds*, 46: 252, 256.

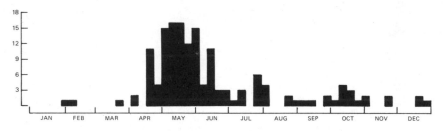

Most occurred in spring, with 42% of all the records in May. A number stayed for long periods, however, with several instances of overwintering on quiet estuaries (e.g. October 1969–April 1971 in Pembrokeshire).

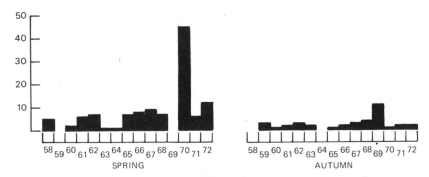

Prior to 1952 only 12 Little Egrets had been recorded here and by 1957 the total had risen to only about 25. The 153 in our period, therefore, represent a staggering increase for a conspicuous species such as this. The absence of spring records in 1969, the unprecedented numbers in the fine warm autumn of 1969 and then the phenomenal influx in spring 1970 are the most striking features.

32

The spring records were concentrated on the south coast, as one would expect of a south European species, with 55% in the ten counties from Cork to Kent (or 68% including those in East Anglia), but a scatter north to Shetland. The fewer autumn records had a westerly bias, with 51% in southwest England, Wales and Ireland, and not one in southeast England.

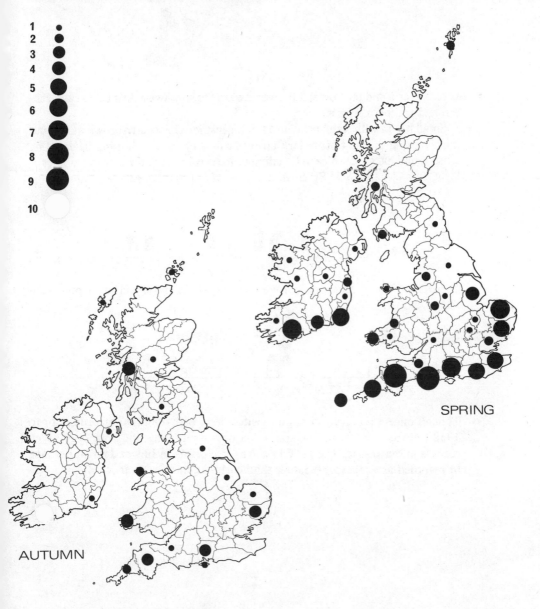

Great White Egret *Egretta alba*, see page 58.

Squacco Heron
Ardeola ralloides

Breeds Iberia and northwest Africa eastwards to southwest Asia; also east, central and southern Africa.

Small heron with small head and thick neck, looking sandy-brown at rest but mainly white in flight, with dark stripy head. Legs greenish (pink in breeding season) and bill green (blue in breeding season) with black tip. Looks stubbier in flight than elegant Little Egret. *Brit. Birds,* 45: 278; 52: 185.

There is no clear pattern, but four were in May–June and two in late September–early October.

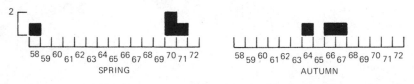

Though once a relatively common visitor here, with about 90 records prior to 1958 (mostly pre-1914), this species is now a rare vagrant, with only seven records in our period. The 1966 bird was in Norfolk in July and might perhaps be regarded as a late spring rather than early autumn occurrence.

The scattered records were all in the southern half of Britain and Ireland.

1●

SPRING

AUTUMN

35

Cattle Egret
Bulbulcus ibis

Breeds Iberia and northwest Africa, and very discontinuously eastwards to Japan and Australia, southwards to southern Africa; colonised the Americas earlier this century.

Half the height of Grey Heron *Ardea cinerea*, with short, thick neck, altogether stockier than Little Egret; white apart from buff on crown and shoulders (mostly lost out of breeding season); bill yellowish and legs dusky, except in breeding season, when both reddish; 'pouch' under bill gives heavy-jowled effect. *Brit. Birds,* 45: 317; 56: 293.

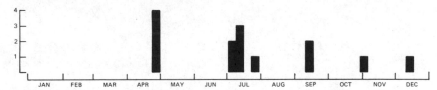

Though 12–15 Cattle Egrets occurred during 1958–72 (treated here as 14 records), the species is resident in southern Europe and vagrant records north of the breeding range are rare. Most British records (there is none for Ireland) are, therefore, considered to refer to escapes, since the species is commonly kept in captivity. The four in April refer to a party in Sussex in 1962 (and a single bird there at the same time may have been a fifth individual), and these are considered to have been genuine vagrants. Three of the six July records were in 1964 (Dumfries, Lancashire and Westmorland) and may have related to a single bird. Even four in one month of the year is remarkable, however, and may perhaps suggest that a pattern of early autumn vagrancy is emerging. It is clear that all occurrences should be put on record and not summarily dismissed as escapes.

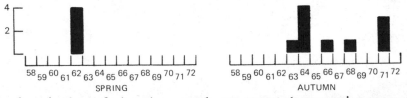

The four (perhaps five) spring records are accepted as genuine vagrants, whereas all recent autumn records have, to date, been dismissed as escapes from captivity. Of past occurrences, only two others are accepted as genuine vagrants, both in October (1805 in Devon and 1917 in Norfolk).

36

The spring birds in Sussex relate to a single party (1962). The autumn scatter perhaps lends support to those who interpret the records as referring to escapes from captivity, since the counties concerned are mostly not particularly favourably placed for receiving southern vagrants.

AUTUMN

SPRING

Night Heron

Nycticorax nycticorax

Breeds Iberia, northwest Africa, France and Netherlands eastwards to Japan; also southern Africa and the Americas.

A small, compact heron, with short neck and legs and crepuscular habits. Adult has black crown and back, grey wings and tail and white or greyish-white underparts; immature is dark brown above, boldly spotted with buffish-white, and greyish below, with dark streaks; legs yellowish (reddish in breeding adult, greenish in immature). *Brit. Birds,* 47: 340.

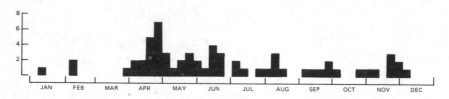

The 65 records in 1958–72 included occurrences in every month of the year, but 54% were in April–June, with a distinct peak at the end of April.

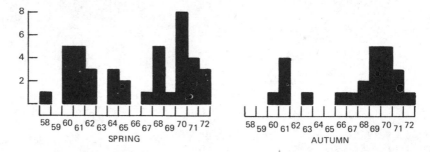

There were spring peaks in 1960, 1961, 1968 and 1970, and autumn peaks in 1969 and 1970. Taken together, the records show a distinct decrease during 1963–67, compared with the previous and subsequent five-year periods. The 65 records compare with about 160 prior to 1958.

38

There is a free-flying breeding colony at Edinburgh zoo (*Scottish Naturalist*, 69: 32–36) and the possibility that British and Irish records derive from this source has clouded discussions for more than two decades. The spring records came under less suspicion than autumn records of immatures but, even though occurrences from the immediate vicinity of Edinburgh zoo are seldom put on record, the published occurrences include only four birds in the 15 years within 200 miles of the zoo. It seems only logical to conclude that the majority of autumn immatures, as well as the spring adults, are wild birds. Those in the east of England are perhaps most likely to derive from the Netherlands and those in the west, particularly in spring, from southern Europe.

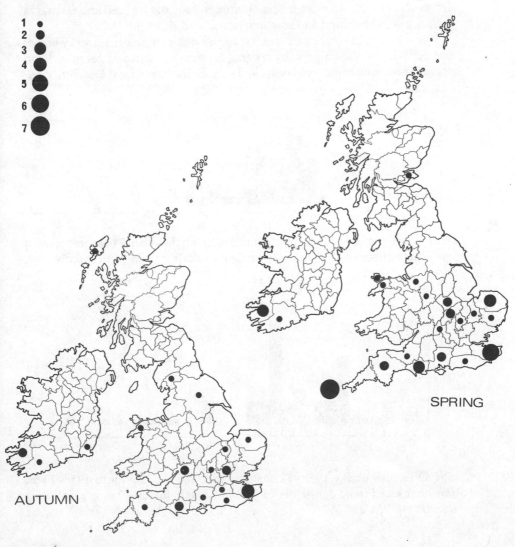

SPRING

AUTUMN

Little Bittern
Ixobrychus minutus

Breeds most of Europe (except Scandinavia, Britain and Ireland) and eastwards to Sinkiang; also central and southern Africa and Australia.

Tiny heron; male black and creamy; female duller; immature streaky brown and buff: but all show pale wing coverts, forming conspicuous patch in flight, which is low, with rapid wing-beats and long glides; green legs. *Brit. Birds*, 46: 138, 450.

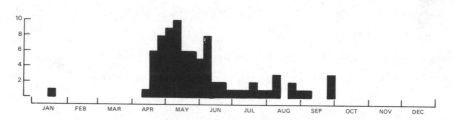

Apart from one in January (Norfolk in 1968), all the other 81 records were in April–September and 71% were in the eight weeks from mid-April to early June, with a peak in early May.

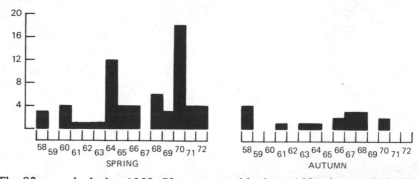

The 82 records during 1958–72 compare with about 150 prior to 1958. There was no marked trend during the 15 years, the main features being large spring influxes in 1964 and 1970.

40

The spring records were mostly on the south coast—in all but two counties from Cork to Kent—and in East Anglia. This is a skulking species, easily overlooked, but nevertheless some have been noted staying in large reedbeds during the summer. It is possible that breeding has been attempted, though this has yet to be proved here. Some 'autumn' records may refer to such summering birds being belatedly located, though the three in autumn 1967 (after none in the spring) and the rather different geographical distribution (mostly East Anglia and southeast England, with hardly any in the west—18%, compared with 42% in spring) suggests that most are new arrivals, from the east rather than the south.

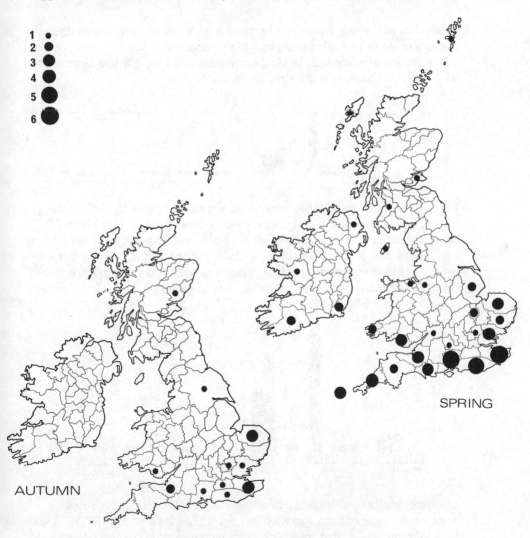

SPRING

AUTUMN

American Bittern *Botaurus lentiginosus*, see page 58.

White Stork
Ciconia ciconia

Breeds discontinuously Iberia and northwest Africa, northeast France through central Europe to Iran, Turkestan and Manchuria.

Unmistakable; white with black flight feathers and red bill and legs; unlike herons, neck extended in flight. *Brit. Birds*, 65: 4.

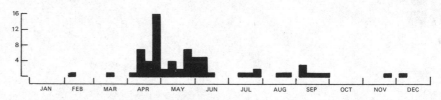

Though scattered through the year, most were in spring, with 77% of the 70 records in April, May and early June. Two of those in April (Norfolk in 1967) stayed throughout the summer and, since display was frequently observed, there were hopes that breeding might take place, for the first time since the only previous British breeding record, in Edinburgh in 1416. This did not occur, however, and one was killed by hitting an overhead cable in December; the other bird stayed until May 1968.

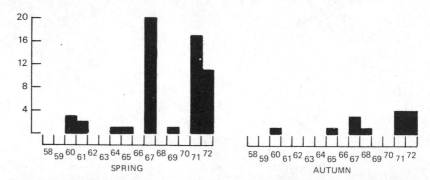

The small numbers of single birds in the early 1960s were under suspicion of being mostly escapes from captivity, but the striking influxes in 1967, 1971 and 1972 certainly concerned wild birds, and were probably the largest recorded arrivals here, there being only about 70 records prior to 1958.

It is not easy to eliminate duplication due to individuals wandering within Britain. As far as possible, birds are included only in the county in which they were first recorded. Spring arrivals were mainly from the east, with a concentration in southern England and East Anglia, and records north to Orkney. The autumn records in 1971 included three ringed as nestlings in Denmark, one of which eventually reached Madeira, while another fell down a chimney and was kept in captivity until August 1972 (*Brit. Birds,* 65: 4, 303). The subsequent movements of this second bird confuse the 1972 picture. One in Norfolk in December 1961 to February 1962 had been held in captivity in Denmark over the 1960/61 winter and is not included here.

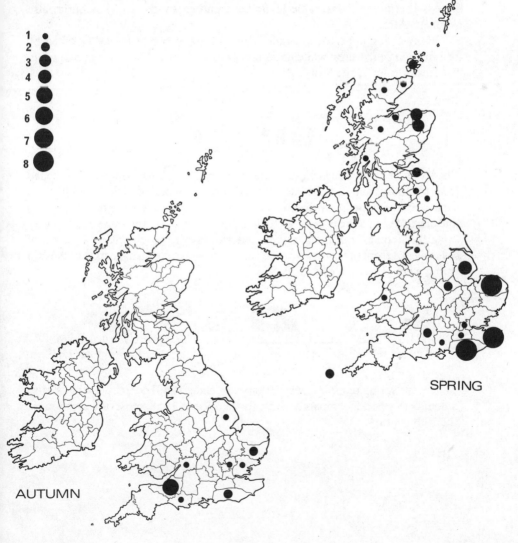

Black Stork
Ciconia nigra

Breeds Iberia and from Baltic to Balkans and eastwards to Manchuria; also southern Africa.

Glossy black upperparts, head, neck and upper breast (black replaced by brownish in immature); white underparts and axillaries; bill and legs red; wing-beat faster than White Stork. *Brit. Birds,* 59: 147.

The six records have all been suspected of referring to birds which have escaped from captivity, and at least one other record in the period was traced back to such a source. One in Norfolk in May 1969 (six days after the one in Suffolk) and one in Hampshire in May 1970 (five days after one in the same county) may bring the actual total to eight. The pattern—five to seven within a period of seven weeks from the end of April to early June—strongly suggests that those in spring were genuinely wild birds.

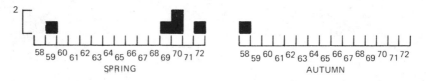

SPRING   AUTUMN

The recent spring records (four, perhaps six, since 1969) constitute what almost amounts to a flood, compared with only 26 prior to 1958, most of which were in the 19th century.

The few records, if they do refer to wild birds, suggest arrival from the east. (A Norfolk and a second Hampshire bird are omitted from the spring map, since they may represent duplication.)

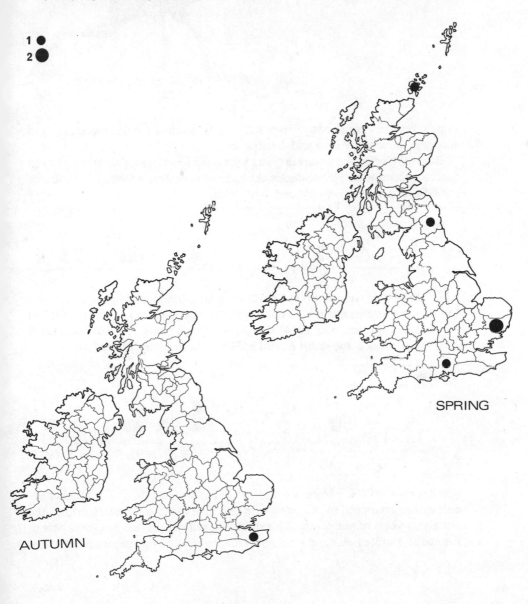

1 ●
2 ●

SPRING

AUTUMN

Glossy Ibis
Plegadis falcinellus

Breeds very discontinuously from Balkans to southern Asia, Indonesia and Australia; southern Africa and Caribbean.

Shape of Curlew *Numenius arquata* with black/dark brown plumage, glossed bronze, green and purple; white streaks on head in winter; in flight, head and legs extended and wings very rounded. *Brit. Birds,* 45: 278.

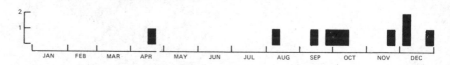

Nine of the ten records in 1958–72 were in autumn and winter, August–December. There may have been only eight individuals, for records in Devon (21st November–19th December 1964), Cornwall (31st December 1964 to 28th March 1965) and Sussex (22nd–23rd April 1965) may have related to one bird.

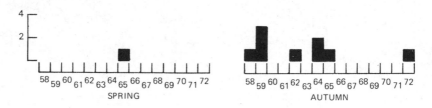

Small parties of Glossy Ibises were formerly fairly regular here. The number occurring has continued to decrease, with only one in the last seven (perhaps the last eight) years of our period. This doubtless reflects the declining numbers in Europe and, indeed, some of those now recorded may be escapes from captivity.

46

The records are scattered from Cornwall and Sussex north to Sutherland. The concentration on the English south coast may be erroneous, since one of the Devon records and those in Cornwall and Sussex may have related to one individual, in 1964/65.

1 ●
2 ●

SPRING

AUTUMN

Black Duck

Anas rubripes

Breeds North America.

Resembles dusky female Mallard *A. platyrhynchos* but purplish-blue speculum lacks broad white margins and the underwing is silvery-white, giving striking contrast with dark underparts. *Brit. Birds,* 48: 341, 342; 54: 324; 60: 482.

The only record prior to 1958 was in Co. Kilkenny in February 1954. Thus, three of the five records have been in early spring, February–March. The pattern of records up to 1968 was discussed in *Brit. Birds,* 64: 385.

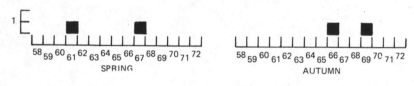

Escapes from wildfowl collections are now more likely than in the 1950s, when the first occurred.

Three of the four records in our period (and also the only previous one) were in the west, which perhaps points towards natural vagrancy rather than an escape source.

1 ●

SPRING

AUTUMN

49

Blue-winged Teal
Anas discors

Breeds North America.

Like large Teal *A. crecca* with pale blue forewing (brighter than blue-grey forewing of Garganey *A. querquedula*). Male has blue-grey head and large white face crescent; black undertail coverts, cut off by white patch. Females and immatures need to be carefully distinguished from corresponding plumages of Cinnamon Teal *A. cyanoptera. Scot. Birds,* 6: 28.

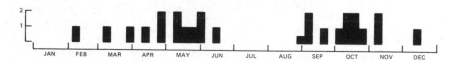

The records, distributed in February–June and September–December, show marked peaks in April–May and September–October. The pattern of European records up to 1968 was discussed in *Brit. Birds,* 64: 385.

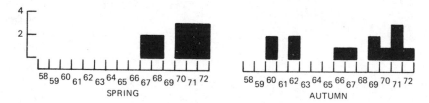

There has been a marked recent increase in records. At least 20 were recorded prior to 1958, four in the next eight years and then 22 in the seven years 1966–72. None had been recorded between April and September prior to 1970, but the three years since then have brought six in May and one in June. The species was rare in captivity and the escape likelihood low prior to 1970, but the situation has now changed, with unpinioned birds resulting from captive breeding providing a higher escape risk.

50

The spring records are mostly in England, with only two out of 13 in the west. This might suggest that they were birds which had crossed the Atlantic during a previous autumn and were on spring passage, or were not wild birds. One of the eastern birds (Suffolk, shot, 9th October 1971) had been ringed in New Brunswick, Canada (on 7th June 1971). The autumn records have a distinct westerly bias, with half of them in Ireland, strongly suggesting recent transatlantic crossings.

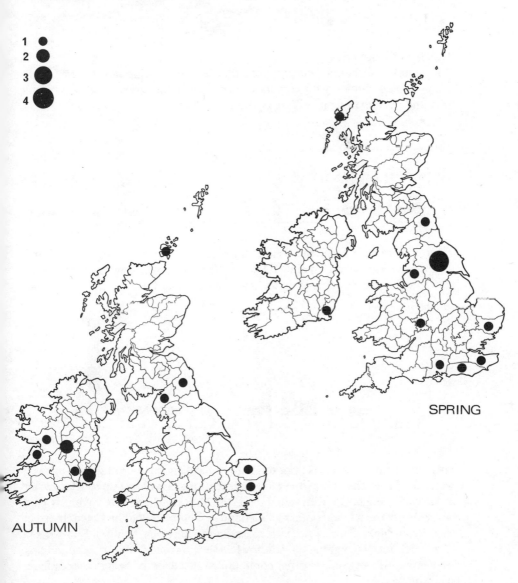

1
2
3
4

SPRING

AUTUMN

51

American Wigeon

Anas americana

Breeds North America.

Resembles Wigeon *A. penelope* but axillaries are white instead of dusky; male mainly pinkish-brown with creamy crown; female has greyer and less rufous head and neck than female Wigeon. *Scot. Birds,* 5: 23.

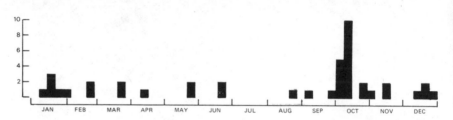

Though there have been records in every month except July, the peak is clearly in autumn and winter (mainly October–January), with few in spring. The pattern of European records up to 1968 was discussed in *Brit. Birds,* 64: 385.

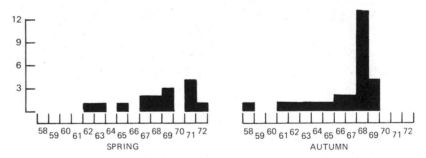

There were only 17 records prior to 1958, so the 42 in our period show a marked recent increase. The influx in 1968 was exceptional, involving up to 13 together at Akeragh Lough, Co. Kerry, on 6th–12th October. These were obviously wild birds. One of them (and another in Shetland in October 1966) had been ringed in New Brunswick, Canada (in both cases, in the previous August). Full-winged birds are not uncommon in wildfowl collections and, despite the ringing recoveries, British records often come under suspicion of being escapes from such sources.

52

Apart from the Kerry concentrations, there is no westerly bias to the records, which would have lent support to them being mainly transatlantic vagrants.

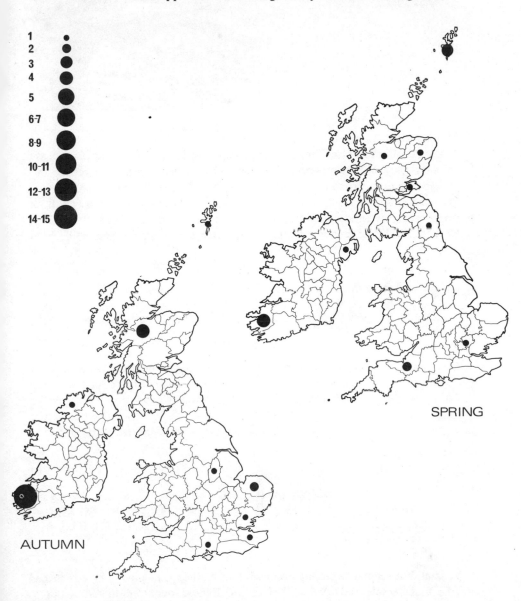

SPRING

AUTUMN

Ring-necked Duck

Aythya collaris

Breeds North America.

Male similar to Tufted Duck *A. fuligula* but flanks grey with white fore-peak; bill dark grey with two very striking white rings; head with flat forehead but peaked at back, and no crest. Female resembles female Tufted but has distinctive head-shape and bill, and whitish eyering and streak back from eye. Both sexes have grey (not white) wing-stripes; tail may be held cocked. *Brit. Birds,* 52: 427; 54: 72; *Irish Bird Rep.,* 22: 27; *London Bird Rep.,* 36: 86.

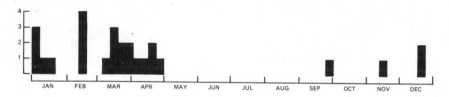

Considering that the only European record prior to our period was one in 1955 (Gloucestershire), the 35 shown here appear at first sight to be an avalanche. They probably concern at most 13 individuals, however. Many have stayed for long periods, but it is noteworthy that less than a quarter have appeared before January. The pattern of European records was discussed in *Brit. Birds,* 64: 385.

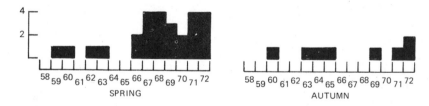

A small but regular wintering population of males seems now to be established (the first female recorded in Britain or Ireland occurred in Co. Cork in February–March 1974).

54

Apart from the series of records in Armagh, where one and then two birds stayed for long periods in eight winters from March 1960 to May 1970, most occurred on lakes and flooded gravel-pits in southern England. Here, too, individuals returned to the same localities in successive years (e.g. Dorchester gravel-pits in Berkshire/Oxford, near Reedham in Norfolk, Slapton Ley in Devon and Marlow gravel-pits in Buckingham).

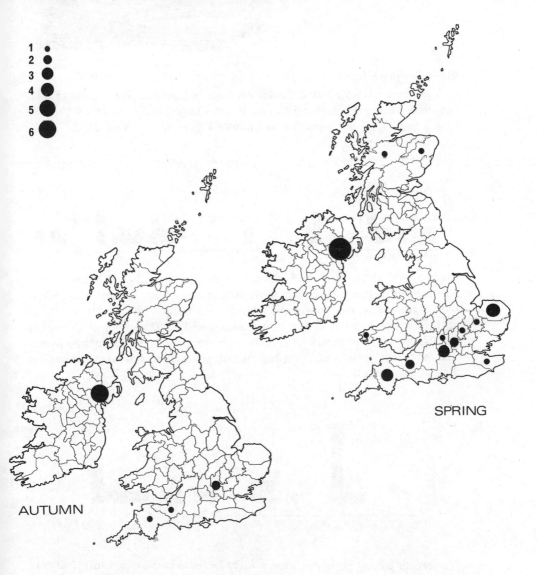

Bufflehead *Bucephala albeola*, see page 59.

Surf Scoter
Melanitta perspicillata

Breeds northern North America.

Both sexes resemble Velvet Scoter *M. fusca* but have no white in wing; male has white patches on forehead and nape and a large yellow, red and white bill; female has whitish head-patches like female Velvet Scoter. *Scot. Birds*, 7: 51; *Irish Bird Report*, 15: 21.

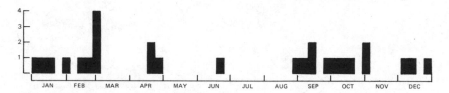

Most arrival dates were in September–February, but the 27 records were scattered through the year, with birds seen in every month except May. There were several cases of overwintering (the longest being 27th December 1965 to 27th February 1966 in Kirkcudbrightshire, and 15th December 1968 to May 1969 in Devon) and others remained for shorter periods (including into March and July). The pattern of European records up to 1968 has been analysed in *Brit. Birds*, 64: 385.

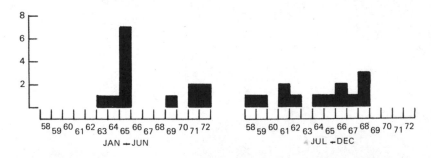

The recent pattern perhaps shows a slight increase in the mid-1960s, but compared with about 75 records prior to 1958 (some early ones poorly documented, however) the trend may be towards decreasing numbers.

56

Apart from a run of records (up to four together) in Kirkcudbrightshire from January 1964 to February 1966, occurrences have been widespread. The tendency for autumn and early winter records to be in the east and late winter and spring ones in the west is the opposite of what might be expected.

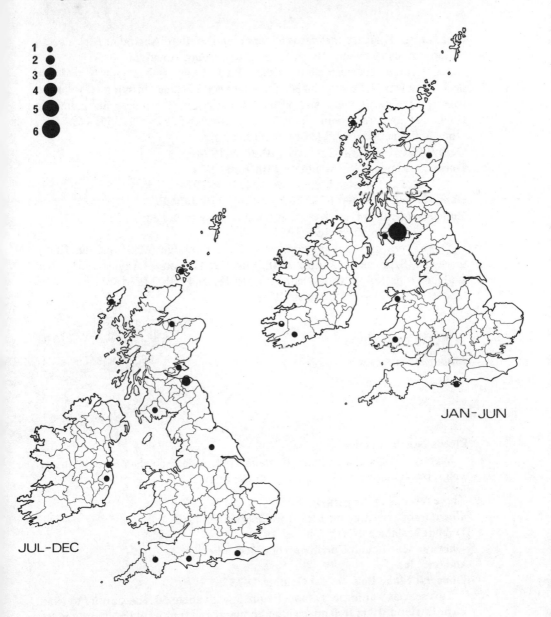

JAN–JUN

JUL–DEC

Great White Egret

Egretta alba

Breeds from Hungary eastwards to Japan and south to Australia; Africa south of Sahara; also southern North, Central and South America.

Much larger and also slimmer than Little Egret, with angularly-held thin neck; long legs black and pinkish; feet blackish; bill black in summer, yellow in winter, often partly black and partly yellow; no crest, but scapular plumes in summer; long narrow wings in flight. *Brit. Birds,* 45: 278, 291; 55: 475.

None in the period, but at least two birds since:

Derby: Clay Mills gravel-pits on 19th May 1974
Dorset: Lodmoor, Weymouth on 11th June 1974
 Brownsea Island, Poole, on 12th June 1974
Hampshire: Christchurch Harbour on 12th–13th June 1974
Yorkshire: Scaling Dam Reservoir on 28th May to 6th June 1974
 Spurn on 1st June 1974

There were only ten previous records: Cambridge (May or June 1849), Cornwall (September–October 1948, May 1951), Dorset (August 1951), East Lothian (June 1840), Nottingham (prior to 1838), Perth (May 1881), Yorkshire (about 1825, 1834 and summer 1868).

American Bittern

Botaurus lentiginosus

Breeds North America.

Slightly smaller than Bittern *B. stellaris*, and distinguished by dark tips to wings, brown crown and long black streak on neck.

Three records in the period:

Caernarvon: Bardsey on 12th–15th September 1962
Dublin: Malahide on 4th October 1970
Galway: near Lough Corrib on 16th December 1964
and one since:
Donegal: Malin Beg on 21st October 1973

This species was formerly more frequent, with about 50 records prior to 1958: 20 in England, 18 in Ireland, eight in Scotland and four in Wales, mostly in late autumn and prior to 1914.

Bufflehead

Bucephala albeola

Breeds North America.

Like a small Goldeneye *B. clangula* but with large white patch on head (male) or small white cheek patch behind eye (female); takes off directly from water, not pattering like other diving duck.

One record in the period:

Buckingham: Foscote Reservoir, near Maids' Moreton, on 28th February to 8th March 1961.

The only previous records were four in England and one in Scotland during 1830–1932 (one January, one February, one June, one 'winter' and one un-dated). The pattern of European records has been analysed in *Brit. Birds,* 64: 385.

Harlequin Duck

Histrionicus histrionicus

Breeds Iceland, Greenland, Canada, Siberia and from Alaska south to California.

Small and dark (male slaty-blue, female brown), swimming buoyantly. Male has chestnut flanks and conspicuous white streaks on head, neck, breast and back; female has white spots on head and can resemble Long-tailed Duck *Clangula hyemalis,* but has darker belly. *Brit. Birds,* 50: 445.

One or two records in the period:

Caithness: a pair near Wick on 18th April to 1st May 1965 were likely to have been the same as those seen a couple of months earlier in Shetland.

Shetland: a pair at Fair Isle on 16th January to 2nd February 1965.

There were five previous records, involving seven birds, all in autumn or winter, from Lancashire and Yorkshire northwards, in 1862–1954.

Steller's Eider
Polysticta stelleri

Breeds Arctic Russia, Alaska and northwest Canada.

Black and white male, with rufous or pale cinnamon underparts, black spot on side of breast and white head with green spot on nape, is unmistakable. Female distinguished from female Eider *Somateria mollissima* by much smaller size and lack of flat forehead. *Scot. Birds,* 1: 234; 7: 202.

A fifth record, in 1972 (Outer Hebrides), is not shown since the arrival date is not known beyond 'May'. In fact, only four individuals are concerned: two seen on single dates (September 1959 in Sutherland and November 1970 in Aberdeen) and two staying for long periods (9th May–13th June 1971 in Shetland and May to August and from 22nd November 1972 throughout 1973, 1974 and 1975 in Outer Hebrides).

With only five previous records (Norfolk in February 1830, Yorkshire in August 1845, two in Orkney in January 1947 and one there in November 1949), the three in the last three years of our period are noteworthy.

All four individuals in 1958–72 occurred in northern Scotland, as have all but two of the British total of nine, and the two non-Scottish records were on the North Sea coast (Norfolk and Yorkshire): a pattern one would expect of a vagrant from Arctic Russia.

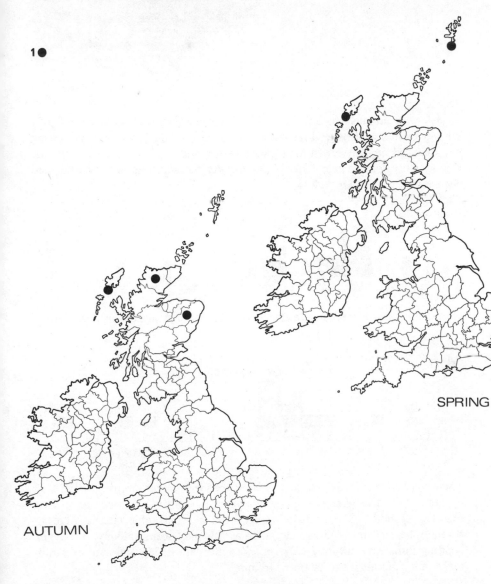

1●

SPRING

AUTUMN

King Eider
Somateria spectabilis

Breeds Arctic coasts.

Male with uniquely pale front one-third and black rear two-thirds; in flight: black back and white forewing; at close range: orange shield on forehead (giving blunt-headed appearance in flight), grey crown and nape and greenish cheeks; female like rufous female Eider *S. mollissima* but with less flat forehead and shorter bill. *Scot. Birds*, 6: 274.

Half of the records were in March–April, and another quarter in May–June.

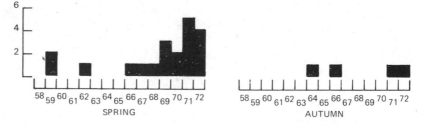

There were 24 records in our period, compared with about 60 prior to 1958. 17 of these 24 records were in the last five years (and a further dozen or so were reported in both 1973 and 1974), showing a remarkable recent increase. Breeding here of an Arctic species such as this may seem unlikely, but the increasing numbers, and long stays of some into late spring and summer, must make this a possibility to be borne in mind.

With 63% of the records in Shetland, it is strange that none was seen in Orkney.

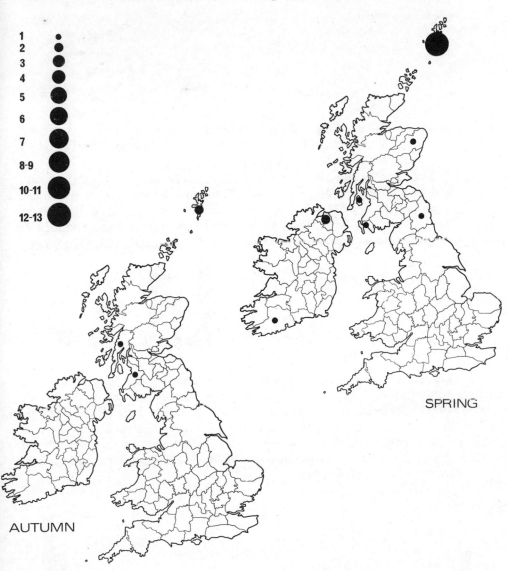

1
2
3
4
5
6
7
8-9
10-11
12-13

SPRING

AUTUMN

63

Ruddy Shelduck

Tadorna ferruginea

Breeds northwest Africa (still common) and southern Iberia (rare); also from extreme southeast Europe (Greece, Bulgaria and Rumania) eastwards to Manchuria and south to Israel and Iran.

Shape like Shelduck *T. tadorna* but slightly larger and mainly pale chestnut, with white wing coverts (conspicuous in flight); male has black collar, female has whitish head; wing-tips, tail, bill and legs black; greenish speculum. Needs to be carefully distinguished from other ornamental shelducks—Cape Shelduck *T. cana* with greyish head and Paradise Shelduck *T. variegata* with white head.

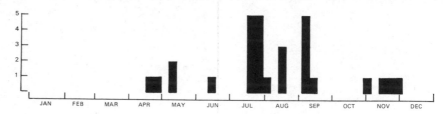

Though scattered from mid-April to November, most records were in July–September, including parties of five in Norfolk (immatures, September 1971), Cornwall and Yorkshire (July 1972). Unfortunately, however, the species is so commonly kept in captivity that observers often do not bother to report sightings. While some of those included here were not considered by the *British Birds* Rarities Committee, the picture is still incomplete, and the true pattern could be very different.

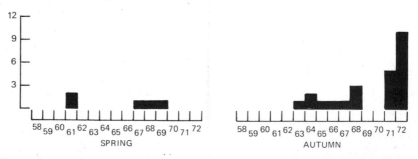

There were genuine invasions of wild birds on several occasions last century, particularly parties of up to six together in June–July 1886 and flocks of up to 20 in June–September 1892. Since then, however, most occurrences have been at-

64

tributed to escapes from captivity. The five in 1971 and ten in 1972 relate to parties of five birds (see above).

The reported records were all in the southern half of Britain. This pattern accords equally with escape from wildfowl collections and genuine vagrancy. The
incompleteness of the data makes assessment of the true situation impossible.

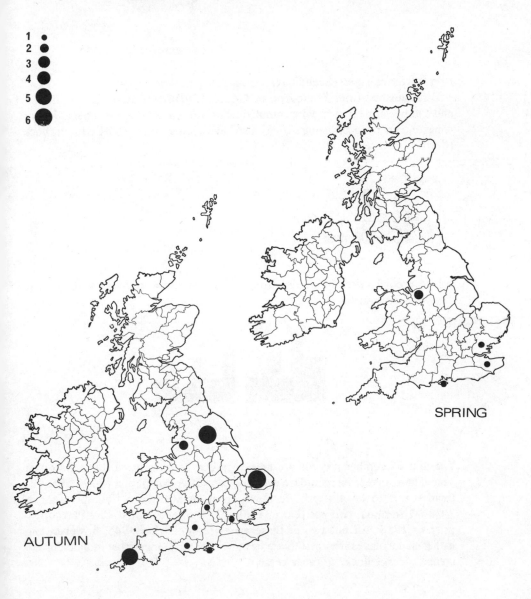

Lesser White-fronted Goose

Anser erythropus

Breeds from northern Scandinavia to northeast Siberia.

Distinguished from White-fronted Goose *A. albifrons* at all ages by darker and daintier appearance, with rounded head, very small bill, short neck, longer wings and yellow orbital ring. Adults also have white at base of bill extending back to crown. *Brit. Birds*, 49: 216; 68: 57.

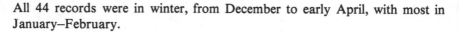

All 44 records were in winter, from December to early April, with most in January–February.

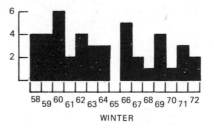

WINTER

The four December records are here regarded as referring to the subsequent year. There have been records in every recent winter except that of 1964/65. The trend seems to be a steady decrease, from an average of four per year in 1958–62 to about two per year in 1968–72. A total of about 45 was recorded prior to 1958. All but two of these were recorded after 1945, however, and earlier occurrences may well have been overlooked, since most individuals accompany large flocks of other geese.

66

Most occurrences have been in the Yare valley (Norfolk) with flocks of Bean Geese *A. fabalis* or at Slimbridge (Gloucestershire) with flocks of White-fronted Geese *A. albifrons*.

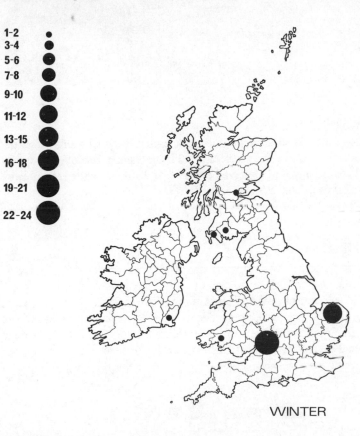

1-2
3-4
5-6
7-8
9-10
11-12
13-15
16-18
19-21
22-24

WINTER

Red-breasted Goose

Branta ruficollis

Breeds Arctic Siberia.

Small dark goose with small head and neck and striking white flank-stripe; chestnut earcoverts, neck and breast, separated from black of rest of plumage by white borders; white rump and undertail coverts. At distance, white stripes more evident than red areas. *Brit. Birds,* 51: 192.

Most records have referred to single birds, so that five together in Berwickshire on 21st March 1966 are generally regarded as likely to have been escapes from captivity and are not included here. All of the eight records in 1958–72 were in winter, between 31st December and 12th March.

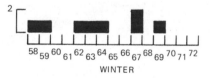

There were 14 records prior to 1958, compared with the eight since. This attractive species is not uncommon in wildfowl collections and some occurrences have been traced to escapes from such sources (e.g. one in August–September 1960 had almost certainly escaped from Bristol zoo one or two days before it was seen in Dorset). The 31st December record (1963) is here treated as referring to the next year (1964).

Most individuals have been with flocks of White-fronted Geese *Anser albifrons* and all have been in southern England, with five of the eight at Slimbridge in Gloucestershire. The two Hampshire birds were almost certainly the same individuals as two of the Slimbridge ones (immature in 1967 and adult in 1969) and are treated as such in the histograms.

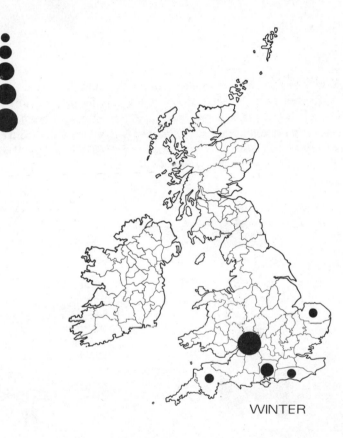

WINTER

Black Kite
Milvus migrans

ıw

Breeds most of Europe (except northwest), Asia, Africa and Australia.

Compared with Red Kite *M. milvus*, tail much less forked, the fork disappearing when tail spread; dark brown plumage, but immature brighter and more rufous; less rufous and more thick-set; arched wings distinguish from dark Marsh Harrier *Circus aeruginosus*, which holds wings raised in shallow V. *Brit. Birds,* 49: 140.

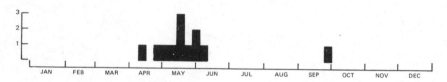

Though the 12 records may refer to only eight individuals, there is a most marked concentration in spring, with all but one in April to mid-June. The five records prior to 1958 were in the same periods (one in April, three in May and one in September).

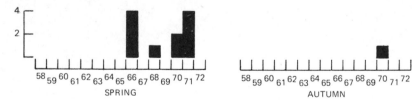

The spate of records from 1966 onwards is in striking contrast to the meagre scatter of records prior to 1958, five between 1866 and 1947.

Even though a single individual may have been concerned in Norfolk, Orkney and Shetland in 1966 and only two individuals in four records in Suffolk, Norfolk and Essex in 1971, there is a distinct concentration (at least three out of seven, perhaps five out of 11) in East Anglia in spring.

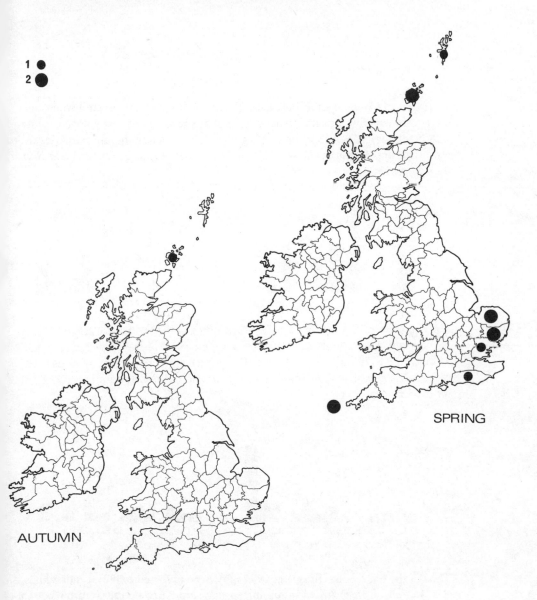

1 ●
2 ●

SPRING

AUTUMN

White-tailed Eagle *Haliaeetus albicilla*, see page 79.

Gyrfalcon
Falco rusticolus

Breeds Arctic.

Larger and heavier than Peregrine *F. peregrinus* with longer and wider tail, more rounded wing-tips and usually paler plumage (at palest, may appear white with black wing-tips); dark underwing coverts contrast with pale primaries; at rest, wing-tips do not reach end of tail. *Brit. Birds*, 49: 310; *Lundy Field Soc. Ann. Rep.*, 23: 26.

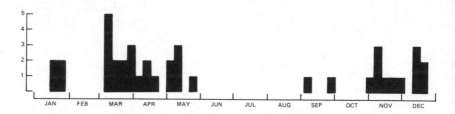

Most past records were in October–December and March–April, and during our period the pattern was similar, with most in November–January and March–May. Though there is always the spectre of the possibility of birds being escapes from captivity, the pattern of records points clearly to a natural origin for the vast majority.

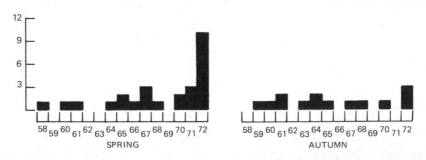

Though the ten records in spring 1972 may have involved only five individuals, this was an unprecedented influx in recent years—a welcome return, though perhaps only temporarily, to the bird's former status, when it was an irregular visitor rather than a vagrant.

72

Most that occur here are of the white *candicans* form which predominates in Greenland and Arctic Canada, and the geographical pattern (only one out of 40 records in an east coast county of Britain south of the Northern Isles) accords with an origin in the west.

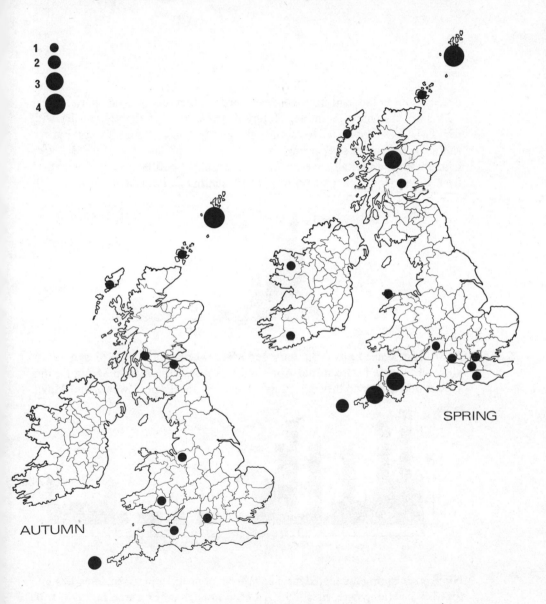

Red-footed Falcon

Falco vespertinus

Breeds from Poland and Rumania eastwards to Siberia and Manchuria.

In size and shape resembles Hobby *F. subbuteo*, but slightly smaller with wings slightly broader at base and tail slightly longer; often hovers, but for shorter spells and at steeper angle than Kestrel *F. tinnunculus*. Male dark grey with chestnut undertail coverts; female unstreaked buff below; juvenile differs from young Hobby by pale brown crown. *Lundy Field Soc. Ann. Rep.,* 23: 30.

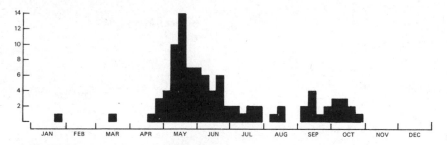

Apart from single birds in January and March (Lancashire in 1963 and 1959), all records were between mid-April and October, with 77% in spring (in this species taken as up to the end of July). The very marked peak was in mid-May.

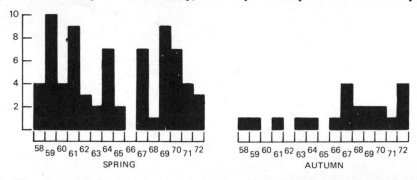

Numbers in spring fluctuated markedly, from none in 1966 to ten, including five together in Hampshire, in 1959. (An even greater influx came in 1973, with about 37 individuals in spring.) Autumn occurrences were few prior to 1967 (13%), since when they have become more regular (33%). On average there

74

seemed to be a steady decrease through the 15 years, taking into account the increase in the number of observers, but then in 1973 there were about 42 individuals, all but five of them in spring. The 94 records in 1958–72 compare with over 100 prior to 1958.

Most spring records were on the English south and east coasts, especially from Dorset to Lincolnshire. In autumn there was a higher proportion on the east coast (57%, compared with 37% in spring). Casual breeding records well beyond the normal breeding range are commoner in this species than in any other falcon. Though there are no published records, the possibility of Red-footed Falcons breeding in Britain bears consideration, especially after any abnormally large spring influx.

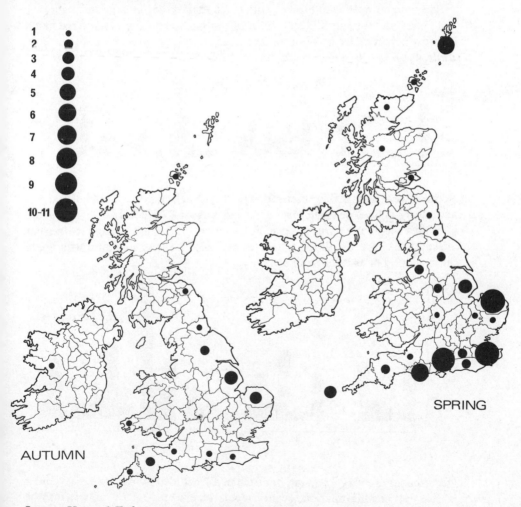

AUTUMN

SPRING

Lesser Kestrel *Falco naumanni*, see page 79.

75

Crane
Grus grus

Breeds from Scandinavia and Germany eastwards across Siberia, and small pockets southwards to Turkey.

Body grey (tinged with brown), with black, curved secondaries, giving bushy 'tail'; head and fore-neck black, with white stripe down from eye and red patch on crown; parties fly in V-formation; head and neck extended in flight. *Brit. Birds,* 49: 435; 56: 375.

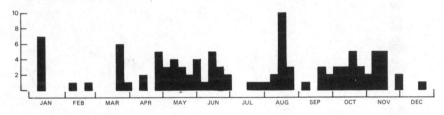

Records were remarkably scattered, with individuals in every month of the year and poorly-defined peaks in May–June and August–November. The peak of ten in August includes a party of seven in Devon in 1971. (This histogram does not include 1963 records.) Importations from Asia are increasing and, with them, the likelihood of escapes from captivity.

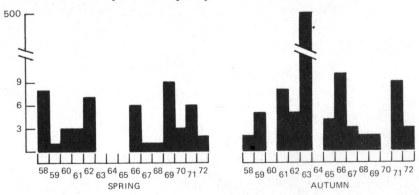

Occurrences are very irregular, but each peak included at least one party and it is clear that genuine migrants occur irregularly, even though the pattern may be partially clouded by escapes from captivity. Although Cranes bred in East Anglia until about 1600 and perhaps in Ireland until the 14th century and were rare visitors prior to the 1930s, they then became exceedingly rare here and the records in our period represent a recent upsurge. The unprecedented influx in 1963 is described in more detail overleaf.

Though both spring and autumn records are very scattered, there is a marked deficiency of records on the English south coast in spring, pointing to westwards displacement.

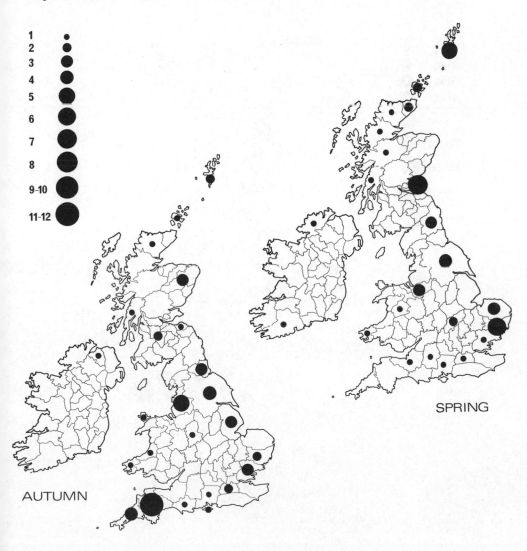

AUTUMN

SPRING

(Crane *continued*)

An influx of at least 500 Cranes occurred on 29th–30th October 1963—an incursion unprecedented in modern times. Most left on 3rd November. This influx was attributed to westward displacement in southeast winds with overcast, fog, mist and rain. Large flocks were seen and, because these moved considerable distances, splitting up and then rejoining, it proved very difficult to assess total numbers. There may have been well in excess of 500 individuals. Taking the minimum totals, the distribution during this exceptional week is mapped separately here. The influx is documented in detail in *Brit. Birds,* 57: 502–508.

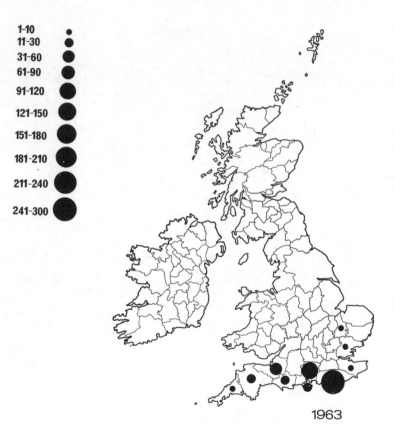

1963

Sora Rail *Porzana carolina*, see page 84.

White-tailed Eagle
Haliaeetus albicilla

Breeds Iceland and from Scandinavia, Germany and the Balkans eastwards into Siberia and north and east Asia; also southwest Greenland. Formerly also Britain and Ireland, becoming extinct as breeding species about 1916.

This large heavy eagle has very broad wings, with nearly parallel edges (like 'a flying barn door'), and the large head and short wedge-shaped tail project equally. *Brit. Birds,* 57: 458.

Two or three records in the period:
Norfolk: Blakeney and Holme on 6th, 15th and 24th December 1961
           Scolt Head on 7th January and 7th, 19th and 20th February 1962: perhaps the same bird as in late 1961
Sussex: Selsey Bill on 30th July 1961
and two others since:
Cornwall: Nare Head and Fal River area in last two weeks of December 1973
Fermanagh: Garrison on 11th January 1973

Since extinction as a breeding species here and reduction in numbers in Scandinavia and Iceland, records have become steadily fewer. The most recent before the ones listed above was one in Norfolk (and probably the same bird in Suffolk) during the winter of 1957/58.

Lesser Kestrel
Falco naumanni

Breeds Iberia, northwest Africa and southern Europe eastwards into Asia.

Similar to Kestrel *F. tinnunculus,* but more slender with more pointed wings and slightly wedge-shaped tail; underparts and underwing paler. In close views, unspotted upperparts of male and white claws are diagnostic. *Brit. Birds,* 47: 80.

Three records in the period:
Cornwall: St. Ives on 31st May 1968
           Porthgwarra on 11th October 1969

Scilly: St. Agnes on 28th October 1971
and four more since:
Essex: Rainham Marsh on 31st July to 3rd August 1974
Glamorgan: Vale of Neath on 7th November 1973
Stafford: Cannock Chase Reservoir on 4th November 1973
Sussex: Steyning on 4th November 1973

The 11 previous records included seven in February–May and three in October–November, the most recent being in 1926; they were scattered from Kent and Aberdeen in the east to Scilly and Dublin in the west.

Baillon's Crake

Porzana pusilla

Breeds from Iberia and France discontinuously eastwards through Asia to Japan and Australasia; also southern Africa.

Even smaller than Little Crake, with more rufous tinge to upperparts, which are distinctly streaked with white; flanks boldly barred black and white; bill lacks Little's red base and legs are brownish rather than green. *Brit. Birds,* 53: 518.

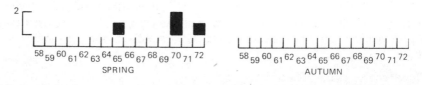

The four records were all in spring. Previous records were mostly concentrated in March–May and September–November.

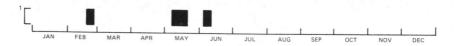

Three of the four records were in the last three years of our period. Sporadic breeding occurred in East Anglia in the 19th century and this species was

80

formerly much commoner here than the Little Crake. Recently, however, the position has reversed, and there were only two records (1953 and 1965) in the 21 years from 1949 to 1969.

Both Baillon's and Little Crakes are skulking species, difficult to observe. Probably only a tiny proportion of those occurring are ever seen by ornithologists. The Berkshire record was in February and the Yorkshire and Leicestershire ones were in May–June.

SPRING

Little Crake

Porzana parva

Breeds from Germany eastwards to Kazakhstan and southwards to north Iran; also north Italy and spasmodically elsewhere (e.g. France).

Males distinguished from Baillon's Crake by pale olive-brown upperparts with indistinct pale flecks, more pointed wing-tips and lack of barring on flanks; females have buff underparts. Both sexes have green legs and green bill with red base. *Brit. Birds*, 53: 518; *Scot. Birds*, 6: 277.

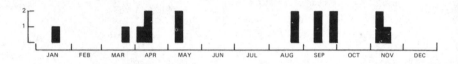

Apart from one in January (Glamorgan 1967), the records were almost equally divided between March–May and August–November (there was one undated April record, in Shetland).

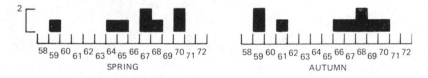

The 17 records in our period compare with about 68 records prior to 1958. There was no obvious trend during 1958–72.

With the exception of two in Shetland, all spring records were in the extreme south of Britain and Ireland. Autumn records were more scattered. The records in Co. Cork were all in one small area on Cape Clear Island, where there were also three other records of small crakes, either this species or Baillon's, in March 1961, September 1966 and October 1967. Thus, there may have been as many as seven in this one area (including a male and a female or juvenile together in August–September 1968) in the eight years 1961–68. It may be that breeding in Ireland should be considered as a possibility worthy of investigation if a similar series of records recurs.

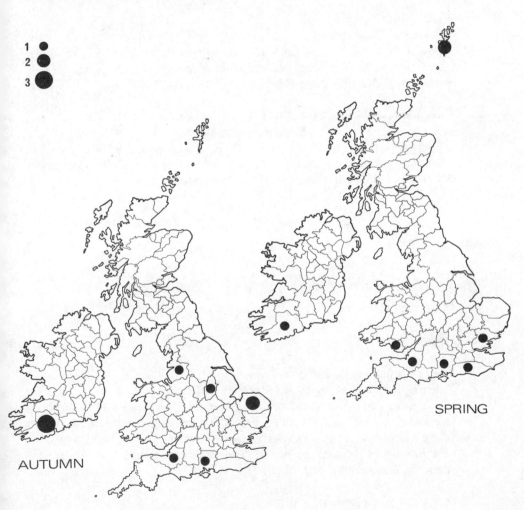

1
2
3

SPRING

AUTUMN

Sora Rail
Porzana carolina

Breeds North America.

Similar to Spotted Crake *P. porzana* but triangular yellow bill has no green tinge and lacks red at base, and neck and upper breast lack white spotting; adults have black face-patch and stripe down breast; immatures can be very pale and buff-coloured. *Isles of Scilly Bird Rep.* (1973): 19.

There were no records in the period, but one since:

Scilly: St. Agnes on 26th September to 9th October 1973

There are only five previous records, the most recent being in Galway in April 1920. The others were Argyll (October 1901), Berkshire (October 1864), Glamorgan (1888) and Outer Hebrides (November 1913).

American Purple Gallinule
Porphyrula martinica

Breeds North, Central and South America.

Size and shape like long-legged Moorhen *Gallinula chloropus* but adults have purple head and underparts, metallic-green upperparts, pale blue shield on forehead and whole of undertail coverts white; immatures are rather more like young Moorhens but are sandy-coloured with glossy bronze back, and share with the adults the diagnostic lack of Moorhen's dark centre to white undertail and white flank-stripes. *Brit. Birds,* 53: 145.

One record in the period:

Scilly: Hugh Town, St. Mary's, exhausted immature picked up on 7th November 1958, died on 9th.

This is the only record for Britain and Ireland.

Great Bustard

Otis tarda

IW

Breeds Iberia, Germany, Austria, Poland and southeast Europe discontinuously eastwards through Asia; formerly Britain.

Males are heavier and have longer wings than a Mute Swan *Cygnus olor* and even the females look about the size of a Greylag Goose *Anser anser* in flight; both show a broad white band across the upper primaries and secondaries and black trailing edges to the wings in flight. On the ground, these stately turkey-like birds are unmistakable. *Brit. Birds,* 58: 43; 59: 22, 491; *Scot. Birds,* 6: 171.

Three records in the period:
Kent: two near St. Mary's Bay on 11th January 1970
Norfolk: South Creake on 28th March 1963
Shetland: Fair Isle on 11th January 1970 (note coincidence of date with the two in Kent)
and one since:
Yorkshire: Goathland Moor on 18th August 1973

At one time bred in parts of England but became extinct as a breeding species here in the first half of the 19th century and there were only five vagrant records (eight birds) between 1910 and 1963. An attempt is now being made to reintroduce Great Bustards to Salisbury Plain, Wiltshire.

Houbara Bustard

Chlamydotis undulata

Breeds from Egypt, Israel and east Turkey eastwards to Mongolia; also northern Africa.

Males are almost as large as female Great Bustards but primaries and secondaries are largely black and there is a prominent white patch on the forewing. In flight, which is low and with slow wing-beats, the wings are kinked, rather like a Stone Curlew *Burhinus oedicnemus*. On the ground, looks mainly sandy, with a black and white ruff down either side of the neck. *Brit. Birds,* 57: 247; 58: 43.

One record in the period:
Suffolk: Westleton on 21st November to 29th December 1962

The four previous records were all in October, all last century and all in eastern Britain (Aberdeen 1898, Lincoln 1847 and Yorkshire 1892 and 1896).

Little Bustard

Otis tetrax

Breeds France, Iberia and northwest Africa eastwards through southern Europe to Kazakhstan.

Looks size of Mallard *Anas platyrhynchos* in flight, when wings (largely white) are decurved and action, including gliding with occasional wing-flicks, resembles Red Grouse *Lagopus lagopus*. Female and winter male are largely sandy-brown marked with black; breeding male has grey head and striking black and white neck pattern. *Brit. Birds,* 58: 43; 60: 80.

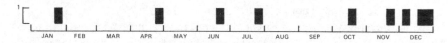

Though there were records in seven months of the year, two-thirds were during October–January, the period when most previous birds had occurred.

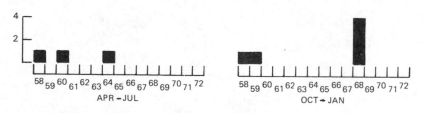

Four of the nine birds in our period occurred during 23rd November 1968 to 28th January 1969 (latter bird shown in 1968 here). The average of less than one per year compares with a total of probably over 90 prior to 1958.

86

Taking all the records, 56% were in East Anglia and the patterns clearly point to arrival from the east rather than the south. Indeed, most are thought to originate from eastern populations and all but a handful of the specimens have shown the characteristics of birds from there rather than those breeding in western Europe.

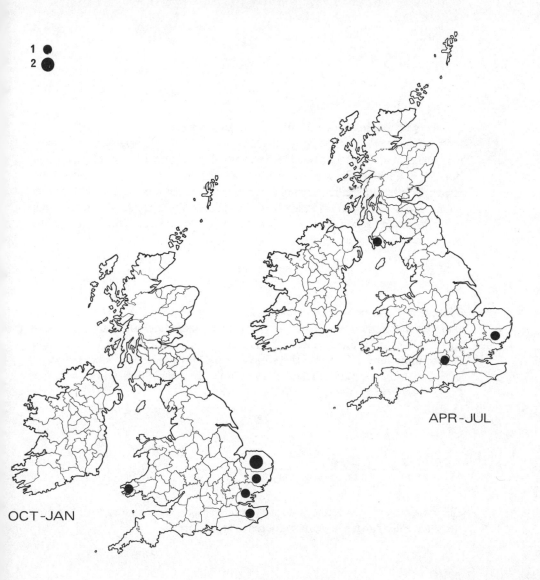

Houbara Bustard *Chlamydotis undulata*, see page 85.

Sociable Plover
Vanellus gregarius

Breeds from Volga eastwards through Kazakhstan.

Stands taller than Lapwing *V. vanellus* but can look plumper and, with dark belly patch, can vaguely resemble Partridge *Perdix perdix*; flight like Lapwing but rounded wings are narrower; largely pinkish brown, with black crown and striking white supercilia meeting on nape; tail white with black subterminal band; upper-wing pattern resembles Sabine's Gull *Larus sabini*, with black primaries, white secondaries and dusky coverts. *Brit. Birds,* 45: 295; 55: 233.

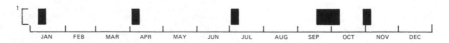

The five records prior to 1958 (1860–1951) were all during August–December, and with five of the seven in our period being in September–January, 83% have been in autumn and winter. Those in April (Dorset 1961) and July (Northumberland 1971) were therefore unusual. Two stayed for long periods—23rd September to 12th November 1963 in Devon and 28th September to 18th November 1968 in Kent.

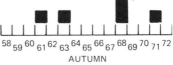

This is a distinctive species and seven in our 15 years, compared with five prior to 1958, may suggest a genuine increase in vagrancy.

Though scattered from Devon to Orkney, there is an easterly bias to the records, as would be expected (though it should be noted that two of the previous five were in Ireland).

White-tailed Plover *Vanellus leucurus*, see page 118.

Killdeer

Charadrius vociferus

Breeds North America, West Indies and Peru.

Suggests large Ringed Plover *C. hiaticula,* but has long wedge-shaped rufous tail with black subterminal and white terminal bands, brilliant golden-rufous rump and double breast band (immature has only one); strong white wing-stripe; very vociferous in flight.

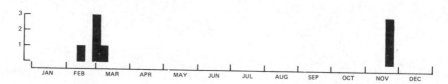

Winter occurrences are typical and all (nine prior to 1958 and eight in our period), except for one undated, were in November–April. The timing suggests that arrival is due to late autumn and winter storms, which sometimes result in northward movements on the American Atlantic coast (*Brit. Birds,* 52: 205). It is a strange coincidence that six out of eight individuals should be first seen within periods totalling only six days of the year—26th–29th February and 19th–20th November. Two overwintered in the Isles of Scilly in 1963/64, staying from 19th November to at least 16th January.

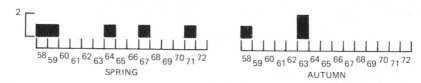

There is no sign of the increase shown by most other Nearctic wader records, perhaps partly because this obvious and distinctive bird is unlikely to have been overlooked in the past. The pattern of records is also discussed in *Scarce Migrant Birds in Britain and Ireland.*

Six of the eight records were in the west, as were all but one (Aberdeen) of the previous nine—a pattern typical of Nearctic vagrants.

1 ●
2 ●

SPRING

AUTUMN

Lesser Golden Plover

Pluvialis dominica

Breeds northern Siberia, Alaska and Canada.

Resembles chunky but long-legged Golden Plover *P. apricaria*, with shorter neck and dusky underwings and axillaries; upperparts spangled regularly with small, fine dots, more uniform than Golden's; dark crown; at distance, autumn birds' upperparts appear greyish and underparts buffish; in summer, black of belly more extensive than Golden Plover's. *Irish Bird Rep.,* 14: 29.

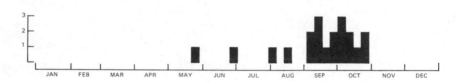

82% of the 22 records were in September–October and two August records were probably associated with these, leaving singles in May and June. The six records prior to 1958 were all in August–November.

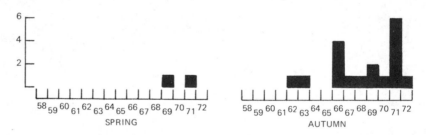

With only eight records prior to 1966, 18 in the seven years 1966–72 represent a most remarkable change in status. The 1966 records (all in Ireland) may well have drawn observers' attention to the possibility of occurrences, so that migrant golden plovers subsequently received more than just a casual glance. It is very likely that earlier occurrences were overlooked to some extent.

All records were in the west, suggesting that the vast majority were of the American race *P. d. dominica* (though two in Cornwall during 23rd–29th October 1971 were considered to be of the Asiatic race *P. d. fulva*). The six records prior to 1958 included three Asiatic (Surrey, Orkney and Essex) and two American (Mayo and Meath).

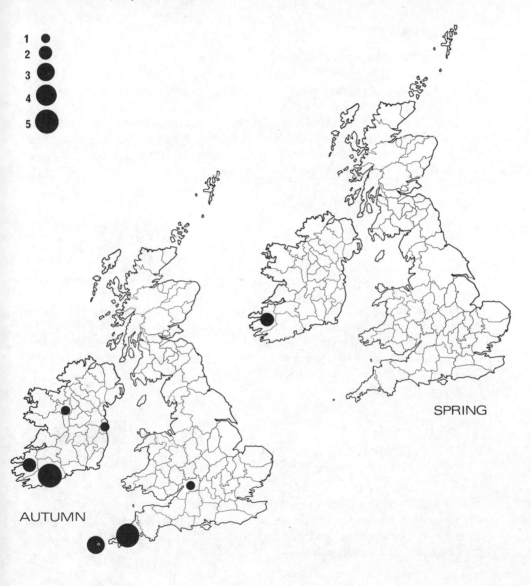

Short-billed Dowitcher *Limnodromus griseus*, see page 96.

Long-billed Dowitcher

Limnodromus scolopaceus

Breeds northeast Siberia and northwest Alaska.

Dowitchers resemble Snipe *Gallinago gallinago* but have white tail and rump, with white wedge extending up back; trailing edge of wing white; they feed by rapid 'sewing-machine' action of long bill in mud. Specific identification of Long-billed and Short-billed Dowitchers in the field demands very careful observation: best single feature is width of tail-barring, the dark bars being wider than the white ones in Long-billed. Call note 'keek' is probably diagnostic. *Brit. Birds,* 54: 343; 61: 366; 65: 305.

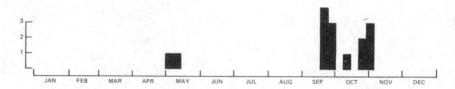

Out of 81 dowitchers during 1958–72, 15 were identified as Long-billed and two as Short-billed. The difficulties involved in identification make analysis of the few records open to error. Nevertheless, occurrences are clearly mainly in late autumn, from late September to early November. The ten records prior to 1958 were all in September or October.

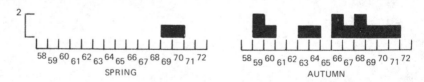

Though dowitcher numbers increased through our period (see p. 97), the proportion identified has not increased as a result of recent identification papers. Out of 112 records of dowitchers up to 1972, 25 have been identified as Long-billed and six as Short-billed.

With 79% of the dowitchers recorded in Britain and Ireland remaining unidentified as to species, the pattern of the 15 definite Long-billed does not necessarily
reflect the true distribution of occurrences—merely the distribution of those individuals which provided the opportunity for detailed study (e.g. one which
stayed at Hayle, Cornwall, from 30th October 1966 to 22nd April 1967 and
eventually assumed breeding plumage). Of the ten records prior to 1958, six
were in the west of Britain or Ireland and four in the east of Britain (Fife to
Sussex).

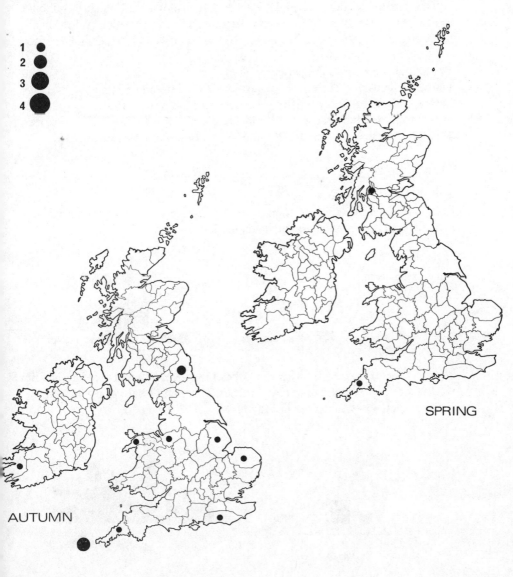

SPRING

AUTUMN

95

Short-billed Dowitcher

Limnodromus griseus

Breeds northern North America.

Very similar to Long-billed Dowitcher but distinguished by dark tail-bars being narrower than the white bars inbetween. Field identification of dowitchers requires great care and detailed notes. *Brit. Birds,* 54: 343; 61: 366; 65: 305.

Two certain records in the period:
Lincoln/Norfolk: Wisbech sewage-farm on 28th September 1963
Sussex: Sidlesham Ferry on 14th February to 15th March 1965

The four previous records were in Hampshire (September 1872; October 1902), Middlesex (autumn 1862) and Norfolk (October–November 1957).

Dowitchers

Limnodromus sp.

Since only 21% of the dowitchers recorded during 1958–72 were specifically identified, all the records are amalgamated here.

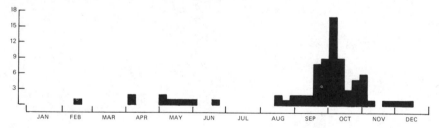

Though there were records in nine months of the year, 53% occurred in the four weeks from mid-September to mid-October. There was a subsidiary peak in late October, and six occurrences in May.

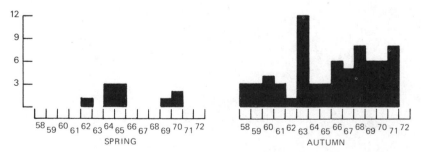

96

The 81 records in our period compare with only 31 prior to 1958. The unusual influx of 12 in autumn 1963 included four and later five at Rahasane, Co. Galway during 2nd–10th October, and six of the other seven occurred between 1st and 13th October. The complete absence of records in 1972 is very striking in contrast to the regularity of occurrences which had almost become taken for granted.

The autumn records show the western bias one would expect of vagrants from America, with 37% in Ireland alone. The few spring records show no such bias, from which one may tentatively infer that they concern birds which had crossed the Atlantic during a previous autumn. The vagrancy pattern of Nearctic waders is also discussed in *Scarce Migrant Birds in Britain and Ireland*.

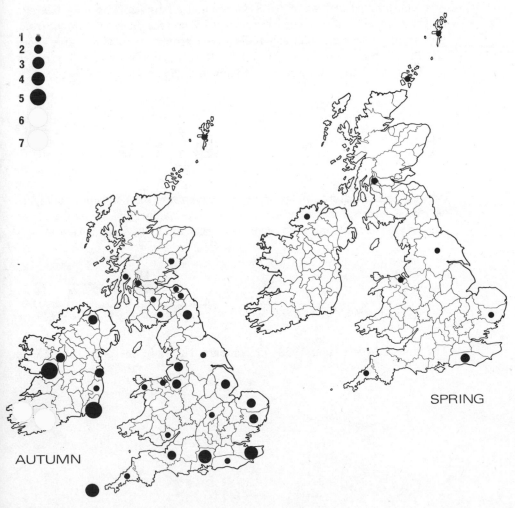

AUTUMN

SPRING

Stilt Sandpiper

Micropalama himantopus

Breeds northern North America.

A tall, long-necked wader with exceptionally long legs and long bill with decurved tip, in flight recalling a long-winged Wood Sandpiper *Tringa glareola*, with unpatterned wings; pale supercilia always prominent; in winter, grey above and whitish below, recalling Greenshank *T. nebularia*; in summer has rufous earcoverts and barred underparts and rump. *Brit. Birds*, 48: 18; 56: 64; 57: 125, 126.

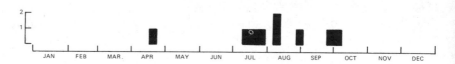

Whereas most Nearctic waders occur in September–October, Stilt Sandpipers have been recorded much earlier in the autumn, mainly July–September. (The only previous British and Irish record—Yorkshire 1954—was in August.)

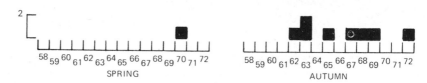

SPRING   AUTUMN

The nine records during 1958–72 compare with only one prior to 1958 (in 1954).

Though few records are involved, the pattern of autumn occurrences—mostly in eastern England—is strange for a transatlantic vagrant. Together with the early timing, this suggests the possibility that the records include individuals—perhaps fewer than nine—which have crossed the Atlantic in previous years.

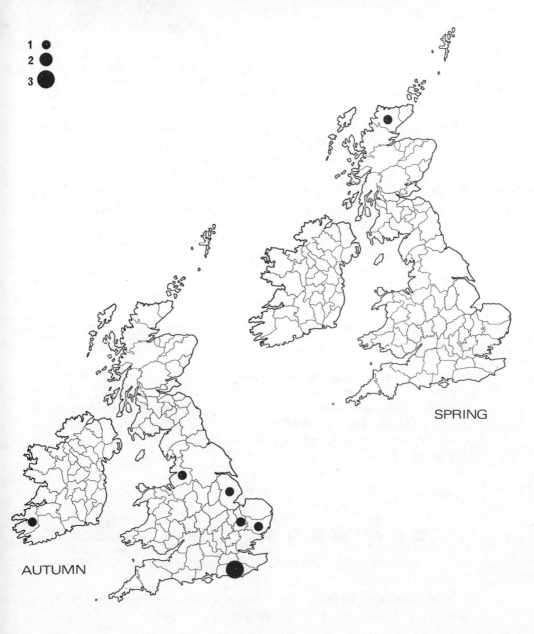

1

2

3

SPRING

AUTUMN

Great Snipe
Gallinago media

Breeds Scandinavia and from Poland and Finland eastwards to west Siberia.

Larger than Snipe *G. gallinago*, with shorter, stouter bill and heavier, unswerving flight, recalling Woodcock *Scolopax rusticola*, with bill held more horizontally; black speculum bordered by white tips to wing coverts and secondaries; adults have smaller area of belly unbarred and extensive white on outer edges of tail; when flushed, usually rises silently (but may utter short grunting croak) and flies only short distance; often in drier habitats than Snipe. Observers should beware of confusion with large, sluggish, silent Snipe, particularly *G. g. faeroeensis. Brit. Birds,* 58: 504; *Scot. Birds,* 8: 31.

The remarkable scatter of records, in every month from August to May, superficially suggests that there is a tiny wintering population here. 81% (perhaps 85%) were seen on only a single date, however, and a further 12% stayed for less than a week. This makes the eight-week stay of one on watercress-beds in Buckingham (December 1962 to February 1963) particularly noteworthy.

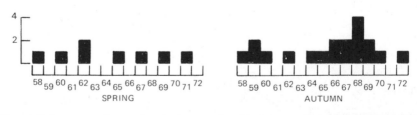

Great Snipe were formerly almost regular in autumn (especially September), with over 180 records prior to 1958, compared with 27 in our period. The records in 1958–72 suggest a continuing decline (as well as the change in timing of occurrences). Though the accepted records indicate the general pattern, this species is difficult to identify positively in the field and it has one of the highest rates of rejection of any species, with less than half of the claimed British occurrences during 1958–72 being accepted by the Rarities Committee.

There are marked concentrations in Shetland and eastern England south of the Humber, as would be expected with a vagrant from the north and east; and also in observer-saturated Scilly.

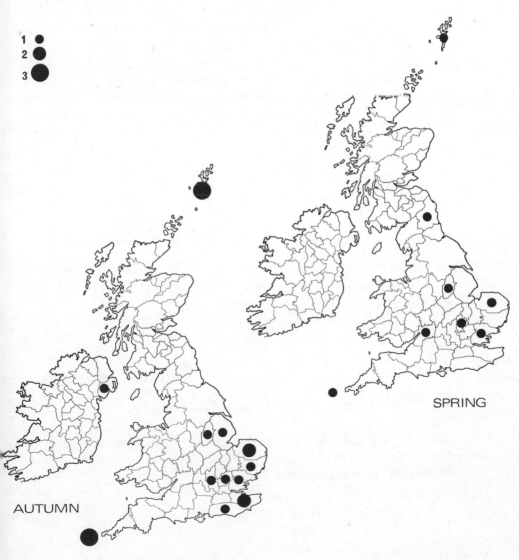

Upland Sandpiper

Bartramia longicauda

Breeds North America.

Strange shape, with small head, long neck, long wings and long wedge-shaped tail; size of Ruff *Philomachus pugnax*; plumage brown and buff, rather like Curlew *Numenius arquata* but with prominent supercilia; legs and bill yellowish; flight may recall Common Sandpiper *Tringa hypoleucos*; runs plover-like in short bursts; call distinctive 'quip-ip-ip-ip'. *Scot. Birds,* 6: 445; *Irish Bird Report,* 15: 28; 19: 35.

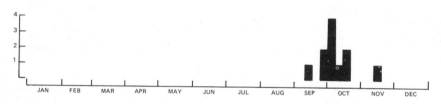

All records were in September–November, with 82% in less than four weeks from 24th September to 19th October. The records prior to 1958 were also all in late autumn/winter, September–December.

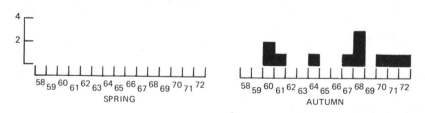

The 11 records in our period compare with 15 prior to 1958. This species and Greater Yellowlegs were the only Nearctic waders recorded in smaller numbers during 1958–72 than previously.

Nine of the 11 records in our period, and 12 of the 15 prior to 1958, were in the west—a typical pattern for a Nearctic vagrant.

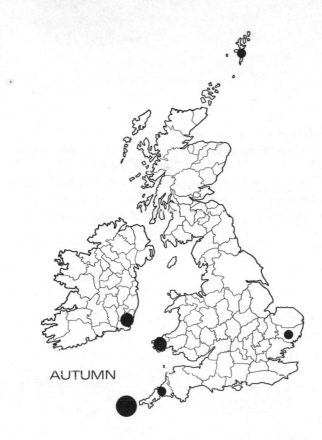

Slender-billed Curlew *Numenius tenuirostris*, see page 118.

Solitary Sandpiper
Tringa solitaria

Breeds northern North America.

Recalls Wood Sandpiper *T. glareola* but lacks white rump: the central portion of tail dark brown and outer barred brown and white; conspicuous orbital ring; wings extend beyond tail; paler than Green Sandpiper *T. ochropus* but upper- and underwing same colour; commonest call a thin 'pwik', single or double, with similar but longer double or treble note in flight. *Brit. Birds*, 56: 63; 58: 191; 61: 265; *Irish Bird Rep.*, 19: 36; 22: 33.

All records were in August–September. The dated records prior to 1958 were between mid-July and October.

The six records in our period match the six prior to 1958.

This species tends to have a less westerly bias than most other Nearctic waders. Only two of the six in our period were in the west, and a similar pattern is shown by the records prior to 1958 (two in Norfolk, and singles in Cornwall, Kent, Lanark and Scilly).

1●

AUTUMN

Spotted Sandpiper
Tringa macularia

Breeds North America.

Similarity to Common Sandpiper *T. hypoleucos* demonstrated by the fact that it was for a time considered conspecific. Quite distinct in breeding plumage, with boldly spotted underparts and yellow bill with black tip. Great care needed to distinguish birds out of breeding plumage but Spotted has wing-coverts barred with blackish and greyish-white; call is quieter, 'teep-teep' (and variants), rather than a ringing 'tsee-wee' or 'tsee-wee-wee'; legs are often brighter and yellower. *Brit. Birds*, 63: 168; 64: 124, 318; 65: 305.

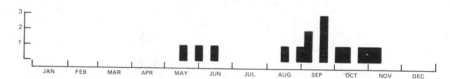

There were clear concentrations in May–June and mid-August to mid-November, with 80% in the autumn period. The autumn birds remained for long periods. Only three were seen on single dates and the average length of stay was 17 days. The two May birds were seen for one and four days, but the June bird (Wisbech sewage-farm in 1971) was also seen at the end of July and the end of August. This species nested in the Highland region of Scotland in 1975—the first known instance of a Nearctic species breeding in Europe.

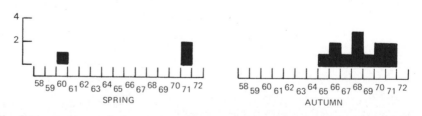

The low numbers prior to 1958 (only seven records: three in spring, three in autumn and one in winter) may be partly explained by the lack of knowledge of the characters separating Spotted from Common Sandpipers in winter and juvenile plumages.

106

Three-quarters of the autumn birds were concentrated in Scilly and Cornwall. The spring records had no such westerly bias, suggesting that they were birds which had crossed the Atlantic in a previous autumn.

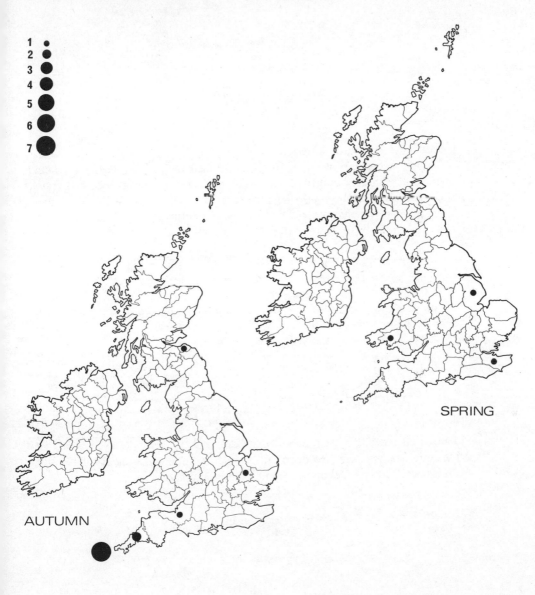

SPRING

AUTUMN

Greater Yellowlegs

Tringa melanoleuca

Breeds northern North America.

Slightly larger and more angular than Greenshank *T. nebularia*, with long, even stouter, slightly upturned bill; white tail and rump patch not extending up back in wedge; bright yellow legs (beware of Greenshanks with yellow legs); larger and heavier than Lesser Yellowlegs. *Irish Bird Rep.*, 19: 38.

Six of the seven records were in autumn, July–November, and the other in April. 58% of the records prior to 1958 were in July–October.

The seven records in our period compare with 12 prior to 1958. Only two Nearctic waders were recorded in smaller numbers during 1958–72 than previously: Greater Yellowlegs and Upland Sandpiper.

108

A typical westerly pattern for a Nearctic wader, with four of the six autumn records in Ireland. Seven of the previous 12 were also in the west: Ireland, Scilly, Cornwall and Devon.

1●

SPRING

AUTUMN

Lesser Yellowlegs
Tringa flavipes

Breeds northern North America.

About size of Redshank *T. totanus,* but much more graceful and slender, with long neck, fine bill and very long yellow legs extending beyond tail in flight; upperparts spangled with whitish dots; tail (apart from dark bars at tip) and rump white. *Irish Bird Rep.,* 13: 26; 17: 37; 18: 31.

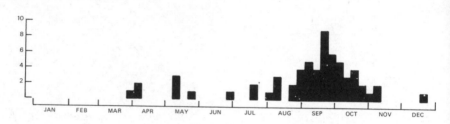

While there were records in every month from March to December, 71% occurred in the ten weeks from 20th August to 28th October, with the peak in the last fortnight of September. At least one overwintered, in Northamptonshire from 26th September 1971 to 3rd May 1972 (and perhaps another, in Cork harbour in December–April 1969/70).

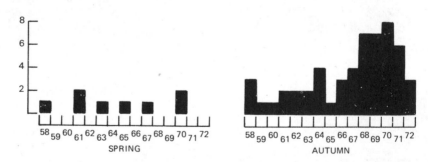

The 62 records in our period compare with about 35 prior to 1958. While the spring records show no trend, autumn numbers rose markedly during 1968–71.

While there was the usual westerly bias typical of Nearctic species, it is also very noticeable that there were no autumn records north of Dublin–Lancashire–Lincolnshire (in fact, none north of 54°08′N).

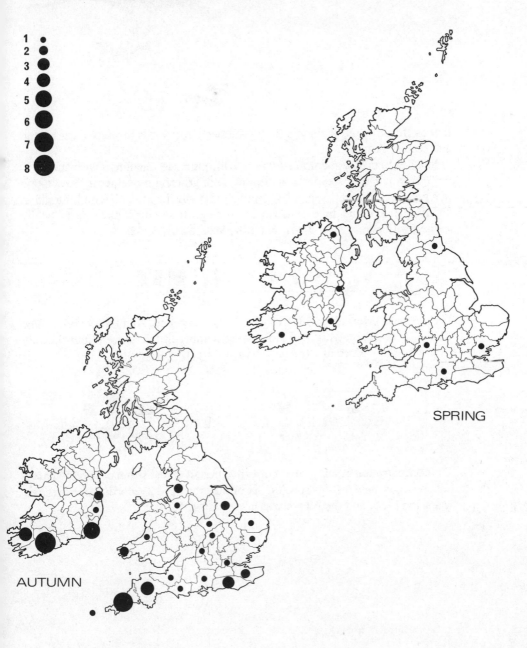

111

Marsh Sandpiper
Tringa stagnatilis

Breeds Bulgaria and Rumania discontinuously eastwards through Kazakhstan and eastern Asia.

Smaller than Redshank *T. totanus* with plumage recalling Greenshank *T. nebularia*, but very slender and elegant, with graceful movements, needle-thin straight black bill and very long greenish legs which extend beyond the tail in flight; forehead and face conspicuously pale; in summer, upperparts boldly spotted with black. *Brit. Birds,* 48: 138; *Scot. Birds,* 6: 42.

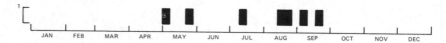

The records prior to 1958 were in April–May and August–October. The 1958–72 records in May and August–September fit this pattern, but the July record, in Lancashire in 1968, was unusually early (or late).

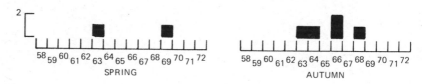

The concentration of all seven records in a period of just seven of our 15 years is not unprecedented for this species. Six of the previous 12 records came in the six years 1951–56, and then there was none until 1963.

Apart from the aberrant July record (Lancashire), all were in the east of Britain, as were 11 of the 12 records prior to 1958. (The Kent bird (1963) crossed the River Thames into Essex during its stay, but is shown here only in Kent.)

1 ●

SPRING

AUTUMN

Terek Sandpiper
Xenus cinereus

Breeds from Finland eastwards through Russia to eastern Siberia.

Size and build somewhat resemble Common Sandpiper *Tringa hypoleucos,* with similar tail-bobbing, flicking wing-action and rather short legs, but paler, with long, slender, upturned bill; legs yellow/orange; dark brown streaks on scapulars; flight pattern resembles Redshank *T. totanus,* but with much less contrast; very dashing gait. *Brit. Birds,* 45: 36; 52: 85; 66: 377.

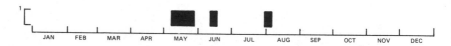

The records in our period, and also the three previous ones (30th May 1951 in Sussex, 2nd–6th June 1951 in Suffolk, and 27th–28th September 1952 in Durham), have all been in May–June or August–September.

The eight records up to 1972 occurred during 1951–52, 1961–63 and 1969–72. These little spates of records suggest that periodic high population levels are being reflected by increased vagrancy (unless a small number of individuals successfully assume a more westerly route than the majority of the population and recur regularly for a few years—a pattern shown by some Temminck's Stints *C. temminckii: Scarce Migrant Birds in Britain and Ireland*).

114

Though there are so few records, those in spring suggest arrival from the south, while that in autumn (and the 1952 record) arrival from the northeast.

1●

SPRING

AUTUMN

Least Sandpiper
Calidris minutilla

Breeds northern North America.

Small, exceedingly active, dark brown stint, with small, square head, short wings, very thin bill and short legs (frequently flexed); leg colour varies from yellowish-green to dark brown/black, but is usually pale; call typically high, drawn-out 'kreet'. *Brit. Birds,* 57: 124; 58: 16; 67: 1; *Irish Bird Rep.,* 14: 32.

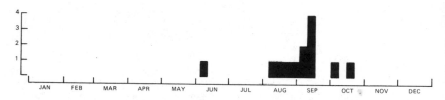

Twelve of the 13 records in our period (and all those prior to 1958) were in August–October. Three of the four during 10th–16th September were in 1966, when four occurred during the seven days from 8th to 14th September.

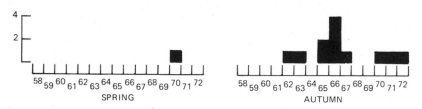

The 13 records in our period compare with six prior to 1958 (only two of which were this century, in 1955 and 1957).

There is the usual pattern of records in the west which one associates with Nearctic birds. The previous six records were similarly distributed, with three in Devon, two in Cornwall and one in Shetland.

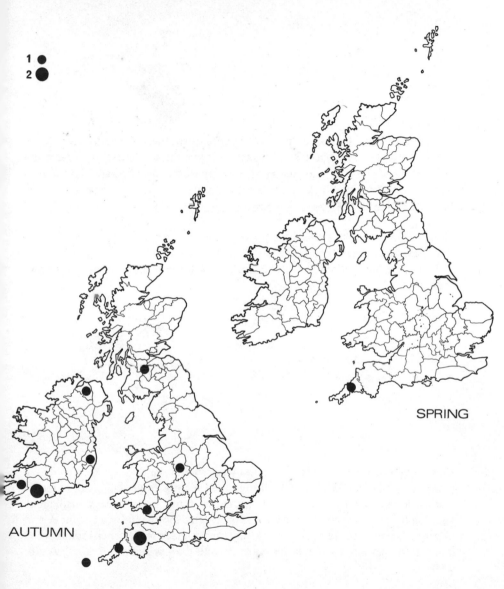

1 ●
2 ●

SPRING

AUTUMN

White-tailed Plover

Vanellus leucurus

Breeds Iraq, Iran, Turkestan and northwards to southern Kazakhstan.

Smaller and more elegant than Lapwing *V. vanellus*, with strikingly long bright yellow legs, white tail, pale vinous-brown upperparts and breast, white underparts and contrasting black-and-white wing pattern in flight; black bill and eyes contrast with generally pale plumage.

None in the period, but one since:
Warwickshire: Little Packington on 12th–18th July 1975

This is the only record; it is still under review for admission to the British and Irish list.

Slender-billed Curlew

Numenius tenuirostris

Breeds eastwards from Kazakhstan and western Siberia.

Size of Whimbrel *N. phaeopus* (though with slightly longer bill), with plumage like Curlew *N. arquata* except underparts and rump purer white, conspicuous heart-shaped spots on breast and flanks (spots often look round at a distance), and upperparts paler and more uniform: altogether brighter and cleaner-looking than Curlew; in flight, pale secondaries contrast with dark primaries. *Brit. Birds,* 56: 294.

None in the period, but one since:
Sussex: Shoreham on 23rd November 1975

This is the only record; it is still under review for admission to the British and Irish list.

118

Red-necked Stint
Calidris ruficollis

Breeds north and northeast Siberia and, marginally, Alaska.

Closely resembles Little Stint *C. minuta* and Semipalmated Sandpiper, but blackish-brown upperparts show no (or only a faint) pale V; underparts, especially chest, whiter; bill rather stubby; long wings with well-defined wing bar. Detailed observations are essential for identification of all small *Calidris* species. *Brit. Birds,* 67: 1.

No records in the period, but three birds claimed in eastern Britain in September 1973, 1974 and 1975. These, and at least one earlier bird, are still under review for admission to the British and Irish list.

Sharp-tailed Sandpiper
Calidris acuminata

Breeds northeast Siberia.

Similar in shape to Pectoral Sandpiper but is stockier, with shorter legs and neck; lacks clearly defined gorget and has dark or rufous crown, clearly defined by prominent supercilia. *Brit. Birds,* 58: 18; 67: 351; *Irish Bird Rep.,* 21: 16.

Three records in the period:
Bedford: Bedford sewage-farm on 4th–11th September 1961
Durham: Cowpen Marsh on 21st–24th August 1963
Middlesex: Staines reservoir on 28th September 1966
and five since:
Berkshire: Manor Farm, Reading on 15th–22nd August 1975
Cork: Ballycotton on 30th August 1973
Flint: Shotton on 14th–24th October 1973
Merioneth: Morfa Harlech on 14th–15th October 1973
Scilly: St. Mary's on 20th–29th September 1974

The five previous records were in Norfolk (September 1848, September 1865, January 1868 and August 1892) and Lanark (October 1956).

Baird's Sandpiper
Calidris bairdii

Breeds from northeast Siberia eastwards across northern North America to northwest Greenland.

Size of large stint or small Dunlin *C. alpina*, with very long wings extending beyond tail; usually buffish, with round-tipped scaling on back; buff breast patches or band; horizontal stance; legs sometimes held flexed; call a liquid, musical 'pre-e-e-e' or 'krreep'. *Irish Bird Rep.*, 14: 34; 16: 28; 18: 33.

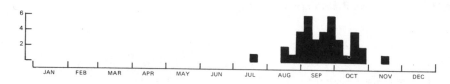

89% of the records were between mid-August and October, with singles in July and November. Records peaked in September both in the west (Ireland, Scilly, Cornwall and Pembroke) and on the English east coast (60% and 47%, respectively), but 37% of those in the west were in October, compared with only 10% of those on the east coast. Four of the five records prior to 1958 were in September, with the other in May.

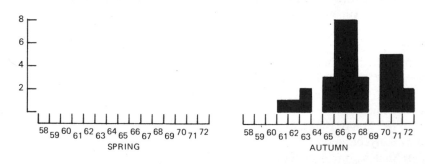

There were 38 records in our period, compared with only five (1903, 1911, 1950, 1952 and 1955) prior to 1958. There were nearly four times as many during the eight years 1965–72 as the grand total up to then. Of the small American waders, this is one of the easiest to identify, but that fact was not appreciated on

120

this side of the Atlantic until the mid-1960s. The increase in records may, therefore, partly reflect observers' increasing competence and confidence.

Like other Nearctic waders, there is a distinct westerly bias, with 50% in Ireland, Scilly, Cornwall and Pembroke. 26% were on the English east coast, however, compared with 21% of the Pectoral Sandpipers *C. melanotos* (which, like Baird's, also breeds in Siberia) and 22% of the White-rumped Sandpipers, but only 12% of all the other Nearctic waders together. Why are these three species conspicuously different? Are they more successful at overwintering on this side of the Atlantic? If so, why? Do a proportion of the Siberian Baird's and Pectorals reach eastern Britain from the east? But what of the White-rumped, which does not breed in Siberia?: is there perhaps an undiscovered breeding population now in northern Europe? We can only conjecture, and the solution is still a puzzle.

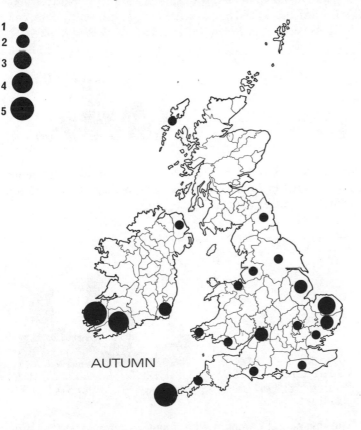

AUTMN

121

White-rumped Sandpiper
Calidris fuscicollis

Breeds northern North America.

More slender than Dunlin *C. alpina*, with shorter dark legs; short, straight, black bill; long wings extend beyond tail; obscure wing-stripe; white rump; call a thin, squeaky 'peet' or 'jeet'. *Brit. Birds*, 46: 260, 261; *Irish Bird Rep.*, 5: 12.

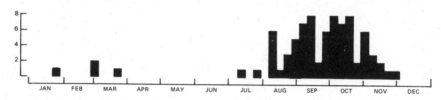

95% of the records were in autumn, July–November, mostly September–October. The four records in January–March might perhaps be regarded as overwintering individuals rather than spring migrants.

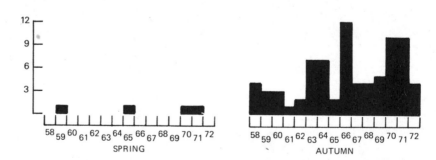

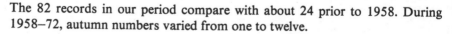

The 82 records in our period compare with about 24 prior to 1958. During 1958–72, autumn numbers varied from one to twelve.

There was the usual westerly bias typical of Nearctic birds, with 56% in Ireland, Scilly, Cornwall and Devon, but there were also 22% on the English east coast. In the west, 47% were in October and 16% in August, whereas on the east coast only 18% were in October but 47% in August. This very marked difference in timing suggests that the majority of the early autumn ones on the east coast had crossed the Atlantic in a previous autumn and successfully overwintered and summered on this side. One wonders whether this species, the third commonest Nearctic wader here, has yet bred in northern Europe.

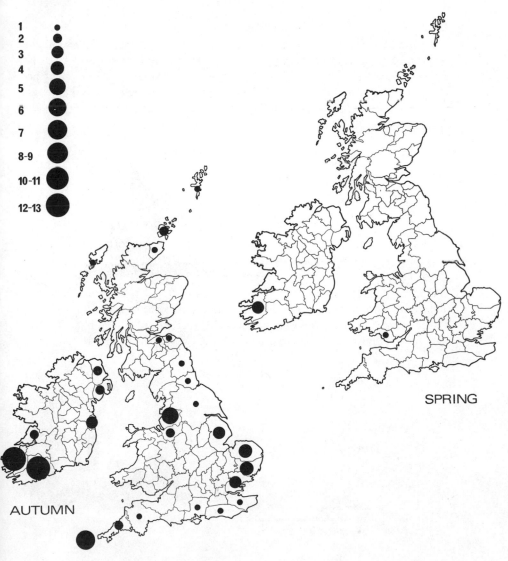

1
2
3
4
5
6
7
8-9
10-11
12-13

SPRING

AUTUMN

Pectoral Sandpiper

Calidris melanotos

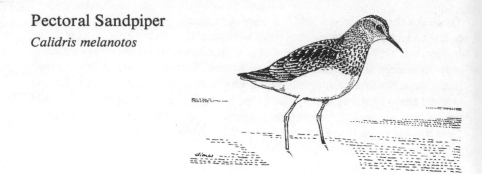

Breeds northeast Siberia and northern North America.

Larger than Dunlin *C. alpina* with stance often resembling Ruff *Philomachus pugnax*; upperparts rich brown and black, with pale stripes down back like Snipe *Gallinago gallinago*; throat and upper breast finely streaked, giving pectoral band sharply demarcated from white lower breast and belly; legs greenish/yellow; call 'quilp', 'chirrup', 'treep'; fast swerving flight. *Irish Bird Rep.,* 6: 14; 9: 13.

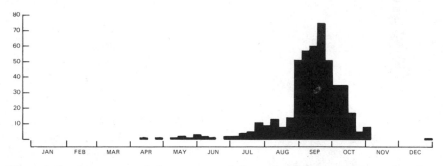

Though there were records in every month from April to December, no less than 75% occurred in just seven weeks, from 27th August to 14th October. The July and early August records were mostly on the English east coast.

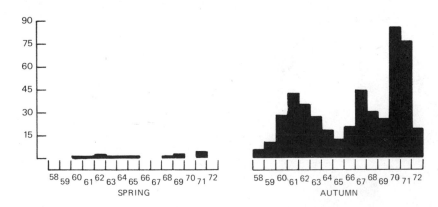

SPRING   AUTUMN

Pectoral Sandpipers are the commonest Nearctic waders in Europe. The 488 in our period compare with about 150 prior to 1958. After autumn peaks of over 40 in 1961 and 1967, there were unprecedented numbers in 1970 (85) and 1971 (76). In the latter year, the records included congregations of 11 at Akeragh Lough (Kerry) on 13th October and six at Ballycotton (Cork) on 11th September.

Records were mostly in the west, both in spring (86%) and autumn (52%), suggesting that the birds had recently crossed the Atlantic. In autumn, 21% were on the English east coast, compared with only 12% of all the other Nearctic waders, excepting Baird's and White-rumped Sandpipers (26% and 22%). This discrepancy is discussed at length in *Scarce Migrant Birds in Britain and Ireland*.

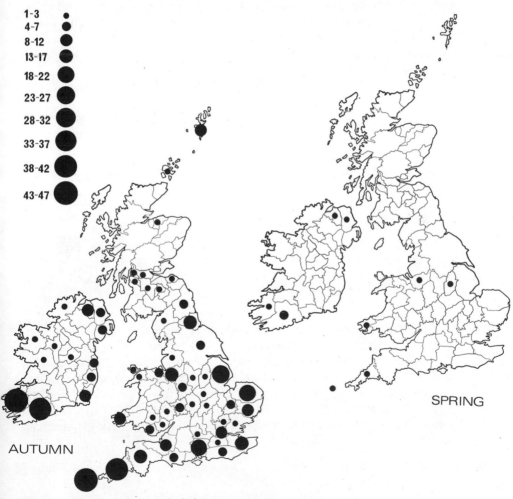

1-3
4-7
8-12
13-17
18-22
23-27
28-32
33-37
38-42
43-47

AUTUMN

SPRING

Sharp-tailed Sandpiper *Calidris acuminata*, see page 119.

Semipalmated Sandpiper
Calidris pusilla

Breeds northern North America.

Resembles Little Stint *C. minuta* but slightly larger and bulkier; back paler and duller recalling Dunlin *C. alpina* and with only faint stripes; pale collar; bill stubbier and blunt-ended; feet semi-palmated; usual call 'chrrup', 'chep'. *Brit. Birds,* 67: 1; *Irish Bird Rep.,* 14: 36.

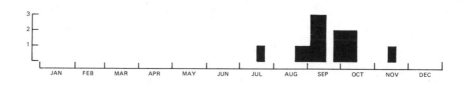

All records were in autumn: July–November, mostly September–October.

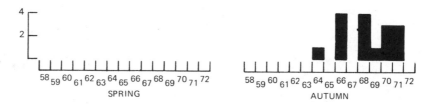

The difficulty of separating some individuals of this species from Little Stint, Western Sandpiper and Red-necked Stint *C. ruficollis* may necessitate a thorough review of British and Irish records. Four British records accepted in the past are omitted here, pending this review. Other recent records are still under consideration. There were only one or two records prior to 1958 (the first was in 1953), compared with the 16 or more during 1964–71. This marked increase may merely represent observers' increasing awareness of American waders.

All but two of the records were in the southwest, especially Kerry and Cork: a pattern typical of many Nearctic waders. Neither the addition of the few extra records not included here, nor the possible eventual deletion of a few others, is likely to alter the pattern significantly.

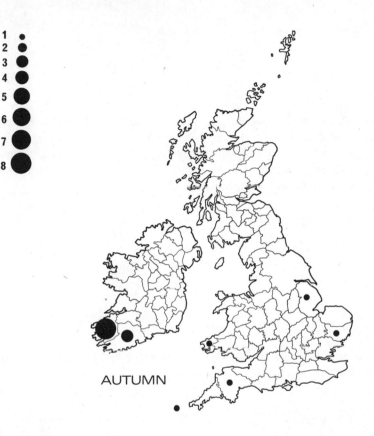

AUTUMN

Western Sandpiper *Calidris mauri*, see page 144.

Buff-breasted Sandpiper

Tryngites subruficollis

Breeds Alaska and northwest Canada.

Resembles small Ruff *Philomachus pugnax* but has buff underparts (sometimes whitish in centre of belly), short bill, small rounded head, long neck, distinctive black-and-white patterned underwing, plain wings and rump, yellowish legs and high-stepping gait. *Brit. Birds,* 51: 193; *Cape Clear Bird Obs. Rep.,* 9: 69; *Lundy Field Soc. Ann. Rep.,* 24: 21.

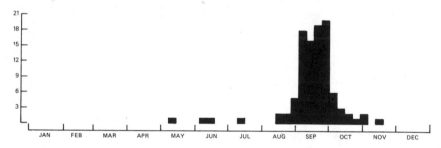

There were records in every month May–November, but 72% were concentrated in just four weeks, from 3rd–30th September.

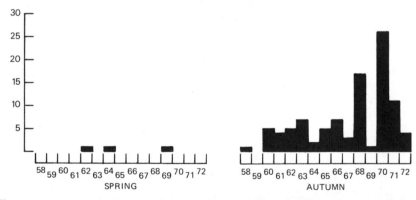

The autumn records show striking peaks in 1968 and 1970. Those in 1970 included up to seven together on St. Mary's (Isles of Scilly). The 101 records in our period compare with about 30 prior to 1958.

128

The three records in May–June were scattered, geographically and chronologically. The only July record (1971), perhaps better regarded as spring/summer than as autumn (since it is five weeks earlier than the first of the bulk of autumn records), however, was at the same locality (Annagh, Co. Mayo) as one in June 1969. The odds must surely favour it being the same individual. In autumn, 72% were in the west (Ireland, Scilly and Cornwall). The very small number on the English east coast (only 7%) shows, not only that few penetrate that far after crossing the Atlantic, but that either they do not successfully overwinter and summer in the Old World, or that the return autumn passage after doing so does not pass through eastern England (*cf.* Pectoral, White-rumped and Baird's Sandpipers, with 21%, 22% and 26% on the English east coast).

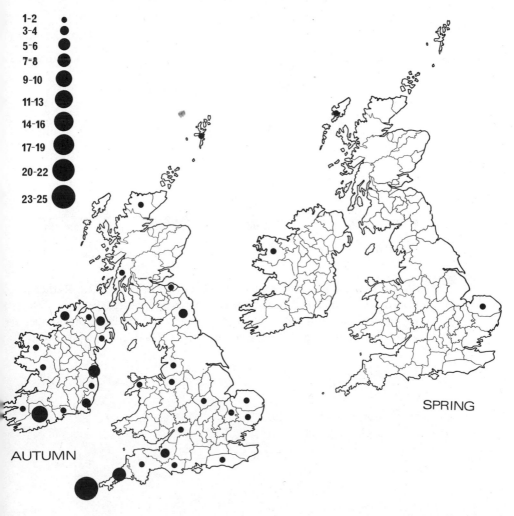

Broad-billed Sandpiper

Limicola falcinellus

Breeds Norway, Sweden and northern Finland, and probably northern Siberia.

Smaller than Dunlin *Calidris alpina*, with shorter legs, striking double supercilia and long bill, strongly kinked at tip; call a low, dry trill. *Brit. Birds,* 51: 194; 54: 320; 66: 378.

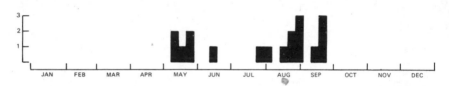

Two-thirds of the records were between late July and September, and the others in May–June. Previous records were also mostly in autumn, August–September.

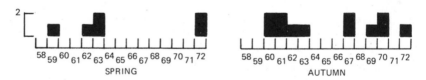

The 18 records in our period compare with about 23 prior to 1958. Rather a high proportion (over 47%) of the submitted records are rejected, because of the possibility of confusion with small, lethargic Dunlins. Nevertheless, the number reported has not kept pace with the increasing number and competence of observers.

130

The pattern in spring suggests westerly displacement, whereas the autumn pattern suggests the possibility of a regular (though tiny) passage through Britain. The two Northern Ireland records in spring were both in 1963.

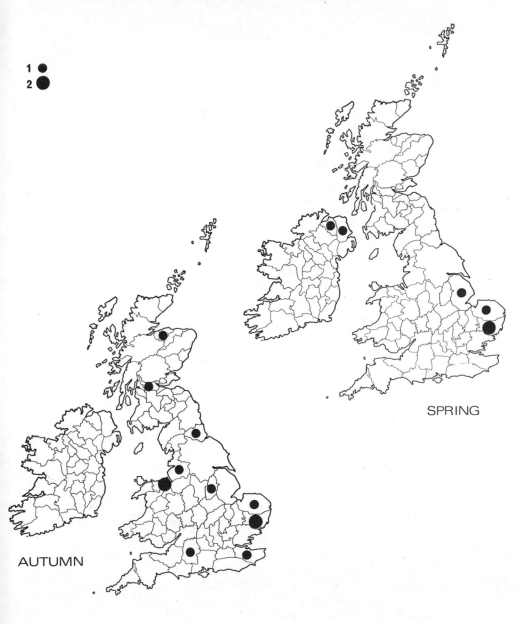

1 ●
2 ●

SPRING

AUTUMN

Black-winged Stilt
Himantopus himantopus

Breeds southern Eurasia, Australia, Africa and the Americas.

Completely unmistakable, with enormously long pink legs which trail beyond tail in flight; long, straight, black bill; black back and wings; otherwise white, though male has black on head and hind neck in summer; wings long and pointed, with black under- as well as upper-surfaces.

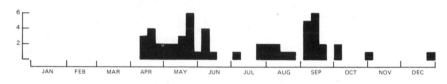

Recorded from April to November, but mostly April–June and August–September. There were approximately equal numbers in spring and autumn (28 and 26). One overwintered, staying in Lincolnshire from 25th December 1968 to 6th February 1969.

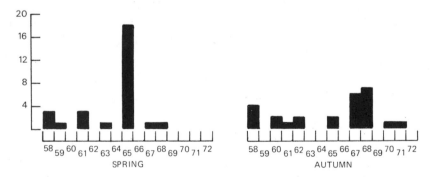

Occurrences have been very sporadic, but the only marked influx was in spring 1965, when up to 18 (three singles, six records of two and one of three together) were seen in April–May. Parties of five in Devon and Essex in September 1967 and 1968 each made up a large proportion of the totals in those years. The 54 in our period compare with about 100 prior to 1958.

132

The spring records suggest arrival from the southeast but in autumn there is a more southerly element to the pattern, with only two north of Essex on the east coast (compared with ten of those in spring).

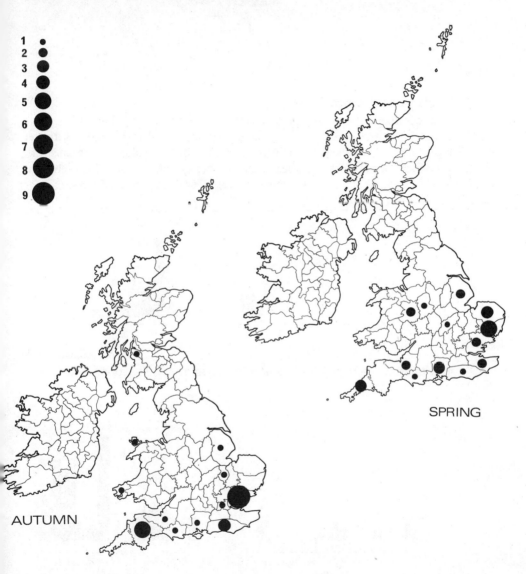

SPRING

AUTUMN

Wilson's Phalarope

Phalaropus tricolor

Breeds North America.

Larger than Grey Phalarope *P. fulicarius* or Red-necked Phalarope *P. lobatus*, and swims rather less often; very pale, grey above and white below, with thin black bill and long legs, usually pale, often yellowish (black in summer); no wing-bars, but distinct white rump; in summer has black and reddish-chestnut patterning on neck and back (paler in male). *Brit. Birds*, 48: 15; 52: 385; 53: 29; 55: 183; 60: 516.

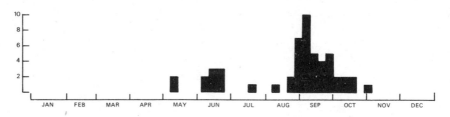

There were records from May to November, but 81% were in autumn, with 60% in just five weeks, from 27th August to 30th September. The spring records were mostly in June.

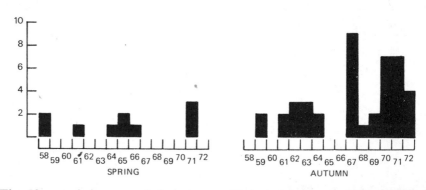

The 52 records in our period compare with just one prior to 1958 (in Fife in September–October 1954), making those in 1967—nine records in just 36 days, from 27th August to 1st October, after none in the two previous autumns—a most striking influx.

134

Though there was a westerly bias (40%) in autumn, there were also a number inland and in eastern Britain. Interestingly, those in the east were not earlier than those in the west (the usual pattern with Nearctic waders), 53% of those in Ireland, Scilly and Cornwall being during 27th August–9th September and 42% of those in eastern Britain being during 3rd–16th September. The spring records were mostly in eastern Britain, suggesting that they were not new transatlantic arrivals, but had wintered in the Old World (or crossed the South Atlantic in spring). The records of one at Scaling Dam Reservoir (Yorkshire) on 20th–21st June 1965 and one, dead for about a week, at the same place on 22nd June 1966 suggest the possibility of the same bird recurring in successive years.

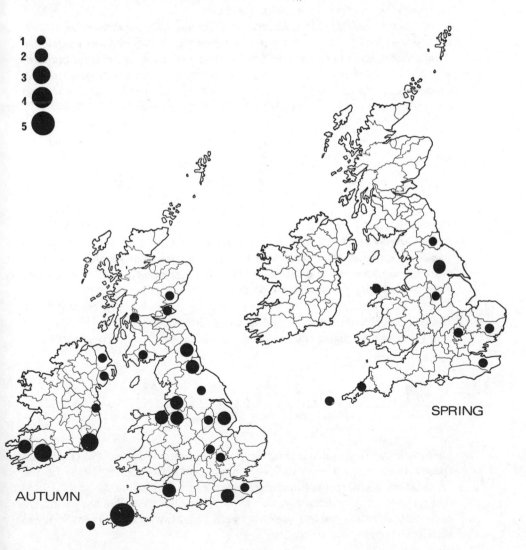

135

Collared Pratincole
Glareola pratincola

Breeds from Iberia and northwest Africa eastwards to Kazakhstan and south to Iran and Iraq; also Africa south of Sahara.

Tern-like in general shape, forked tail, flight and call; upperparts brown and tail black with white base—in flight may momentarily suggest Green Sandpiper *Tringa ochropus*; underparts buff, with white belly; throat creamy, bordered with black; axillaries rufous, but can look merely dark. Best distinguished from Black-winged Pratincole by strongly contrasting wing-pattern with pale inner primaries and secondaries, which have white trailing edge. *Brit. Birds,* 49: 312.

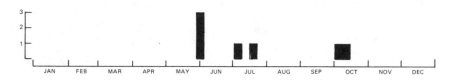

The records were between late May and July (5), and in October (2). July records are here regarded as referring to the spring. Since this species and Black-winged Pratincole are often difficult to separate, and some records (especially old ones) cannot be assigned to one or the other, one must look at the combined pattern. Including indeterminate birds in October 1962 (Kent), May 1971 (Kent) and September 1971 (Surrey), the 39 dated records of pratincoles *Glareola sp.* in Britain and Ireland up to 1972 were in February (1), May (11), June (3), July (3), August (8), September (5), October (4) and November (4).

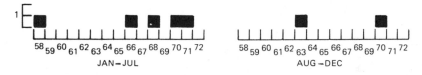

Even if the indeterminate birds (spring 1971; autumn 1962 and 1971) were this species, there was not more than two in any one season during 1958–72. The seven (at most ten) records in our period compare with about 31 prior to 1958 (but perhaps some of those were *G. nordmanni*). After the end of our period, the occurrence of five in just five weeks, between 14th May and 17th June 1973, was therefore probably unprecedented.

136

Both the spring and autumn records were widely scattered.

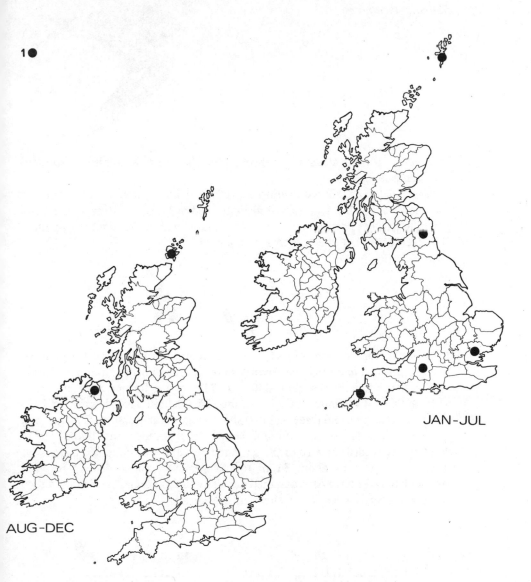

1●

JAN-JUL

AUG-DEC

Black-winged Pratincole
Glareola nordmanni

Breeds from Rumania eastwards through the Ukraine to Kazakhstan, south to the Caucasus.

Very similar to Collared Pratincole; rufous axillaries of Collared Pratincole may look black in the field, so best distinguished by lack of contrast in wing and generally darker upperparts, which contrast more with white rump, giving more of a black-and-white effect. *Brit. Birds,* 49: 312.

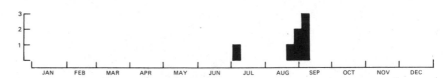

The records were in early July (1) and late August/early September (6). Thus, while *G. pratincola* and *G. nordmanni* were recorded in equal numbers during 1958–72, the timing was quite different: 71% of the former were in spring, whereas 86% of the latter were in autumn. The definite records prior to 1958 (one May, one June and three August) show a comparable pattern. Through not justified with so few data, one could conjecture from them that five of the 18 dated spring records and 18 of the 21 dated autumn ones up to 1972 were this species, and perhaps about 31 of the 53 pratincoles recorded up to 1972 (although only 12 have been assigned definitely to this species). An examination of the old records is needed to check on this surmise.

There was not more than two in any one season (even if indeterminate birds in spring 1971 and autumn 1962 and 1971 were *G. nordmanni*). The seven records in our period compare with five prior to 1958 (but many earlier records referred to *G. pratincola* may have been this species).

138

All records were in the southern half of England. The definite records prior to 1958 were in Shetland (May 1927), Somerset (June 1957), Yorkshire (August 1909), Mayo (August 1935) and Sussex (August 1955), but it may well be that up to about a score of other pratincole records in fact referred to this species.

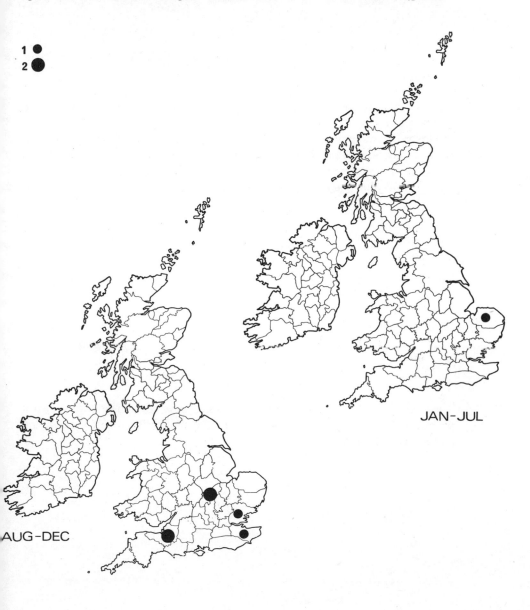

1 ●
2 ●

JAN-JUL

AUG-DEC

Cream-coloured Courser

Cursorius cursor

Breeds desert regions of north and east Africa, and southwest Asia east to Afghanistan.

Plover-like wader the size of a Starling *Sturnus vulgaris* with sandy-coloured plumage and long white legs; a white stripe from eye to nape is bordered with black (stripes obscure in immature plumage); bill curved; underwing and distal half of upperwing black. *Brit. Birds,* 65: 120.

The four records were all in October. All previous records were in September–December, mostly October.

There were about 26 records prior to 1958, compared with only four in our period, a discrepancy which suggests that the species is genuinely becoming scarcer as a vagrant.

140

The records were scattered, but most of the 30 or so up to 1972 were in England (mostly southeast), with three in Wales, two in Scotland and one in Ireland.

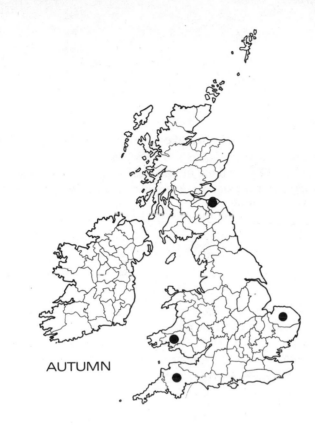

1●

AUTUMN

Ivory Gull
Pagophila eburnea

Breeds Arctic.

Horizontal stance, rounded dove-like head and heavy chest, long tapering body and long wings; dark eye and short dark legs; adult wholly white, but immatures have dark subterminal bar on tail and variable amount of sooty-brown blotching and spots on head and wings; buoyant flight. *Brit. Birds,* 44: 354; 52: 124; 55: 442; *Scot. Birds,* 6: 173.

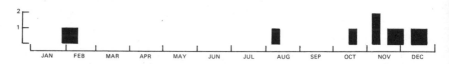

Apart from one in August (Galway, 1971), all records were in October–February. Six were seen on a single date, three on three to 12 days and just one stayed for a longer period, 18th December 1970 to 23rd February 1971 (Durham/Northumberland). Previous records were in all months except July, but mostly December–February.

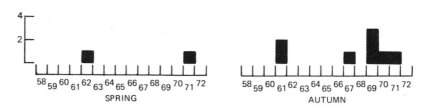

SPRING   AUTUMN

There were only ten records in our period, compared with about 76 prior to 1958, but three of the recent ten were in October–November 1969 (Shetland, Argyll and Cork).

142

Though recorded south to the English Channel and west to Ireland, most past records were in Scotland (mainly Orkney and Shetland). There was the same scatter in our period, with three of the ten in Shetland, but records south to Cork and Sussex.

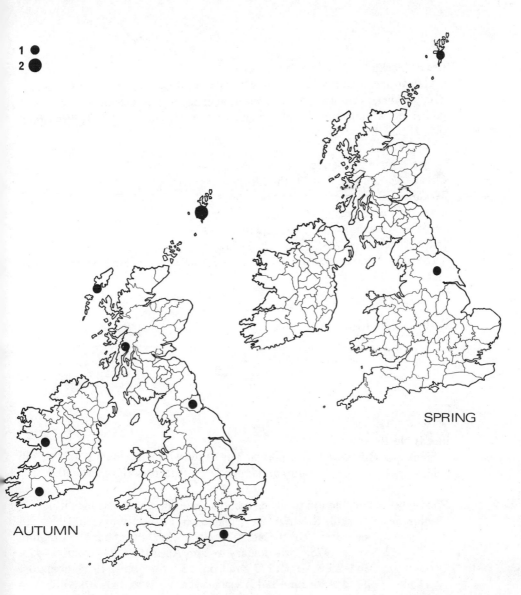

1 ●
2 ●

SPRING

AUTUMN

Western Sandpiper

Calidris mauri

Breeds Alaska and northeastern Siberia.

Almost size of Dunlin *C. alpina* with bill almost as long, drooping from deep base; pale head with white facial appearance; upperparts a mixture of grey and rufous; feet semipalmated; call 'cheet'. *Brit. Birds,* 56: 55; 67: 1; *Irish Bird Rep.,* 12: 22.

Two records in the period:
Kerry: Akeragh Lough on 17th–23rd September 1961
Wicklow: Kilcoole on 14th October 1960
and two others since:
Devon: Axmouth on 9th–12th September 1973
Essex: Rainham on 21st–23rd July 1973

The only previous record was on Fair Isle (Shetland) on 28th May to 3rd June 1956.

Ring-billed Gull

Larus delawarensis

Breeds North America.

Similar to Common Gull *L. canus* but larger with paler mantle, thicker bill (which has black ring near tip) and longer legs. *Brit. Birds,* 66: 115, 509, 513.

None in the period, but five to eleven records since (all at the same locality):
Glamorgan: Blackpill, Swansea Bay, adults on 14th–31st March 1973, 5th December 1973 to 2nd April 1974, 28th November 1974 to 30th March 1975, 24th January to 24th April 1975, 21st March 1975, 22nd–25th April 1975 and from 17th November 1975; immature on 3rd–14th June 1973; second-year birds on 3rd–7th April 1974 and 27th April to 6th May 1974; first-summer on 23rd June to 22nd July 1975.

These are the only records.

Slender-billed Gull

Larus genei

Breeds southern Spain, eastern Mediterranean and very discontinuously in central and southern Asia.

Despite name, bill is not slender, but has decurved upper mandible and is longer, deeper and heavier than that of Black-headed Gull *L. ridibundus*. This, combined with a flat forehead, small head and long neck, gives the bird a rather prehistoric appearance. Wing pattern resembles Black-headed Gull's, but head is wholly white and tail wedge-shaped; in flight head and neck droop below body. *Brit. Birds,* 55: 169; 57: 242.

Three records in the period:

Kent: Dungeness, with occasional absences, from 21st July to 12th September 1971

Suffolk: Minsmere on 15th August 1971—almost certainly the Kent bird

Sussex: Langney Point, with gaps, from 19th June to 10th July 1960

      Rye Harbour on 28th April 1963

    These are the only records.

Great Black-headed Gull

Larus ichthyaetus

Breeds south Russia and west and central Asia.

Large size and black hood of adults in breeding plumage is distinctive. Subadults and immatures not easy to distinguish from young Herring Gulls *L. argentatus*, though bill longer, tipped darker and with heavier gonys; and larger size and dark tail-band obvious in flight. *Brit. Birds*, 66: 378.

Two records in the period:

Isle of Man: Calf of Man on 21st May 1966

Yorkshire: near Knaresborough on 31st March to 14th April 1967

    The five previous records were all in southern England: Devon (May or June 1859), Hampshire (November–December 1924), Norfolk (March 1932) and Sussex (January 1910 and August 1932).

Laughing Gull
Larus atricilla

Breeds North America and Caribbean.

Slightly larger than Black-headed Gull *L. ridibundus* with black (not brown) head in summer and slate-grey mantle blending into black wing tips, large bill and legs deep red; in flight, white trailing edge to wing; in winter, head smudgy and legs and bill black; immature has wide black terminal band to tail, white rear edge to wing and dark blotched breast and axillaries. *Brit. Birds,* 60: 157, 159; 61: 415; 65: 79; 68: 158.

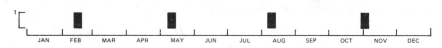

The records were spread out through the year; and the previous two records, in July and December, create an even wider scatter. The lack of pattern suggests individuals wandering after arrival. Three of the four were seen on only a single date but one in Dorset stayed from 17th February to 6th October 1969.

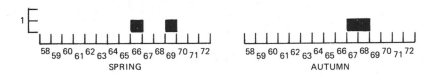

The six records up to 1972 were in 1923, 1957 and annually during 1966–69.

The two autumn records were in the west and the spring ones on the English Channel coast. While perhaps only coincidence, this is the pattern one would expect from autumn crossings of the Atlantic followed by wandering, perhaps with other gulls. The previous records were in Sussex (July 1923) and Essex (December 1957).

SPRING

AUTUMN

Franklin's Gull *Larus pipixcan*, see page 162.

Bonaparte's Gull
Larus philadelphia

Breeds northern North America.

Like small Black-headed Gull *L. ridibundus* (beware runts), but primaries have white undersides, bill is more slender and black, legs are orange and flight is very tern-like. Hood is slate-grey in summer. *Scot. Birds,* 5: 175; 7: 258.

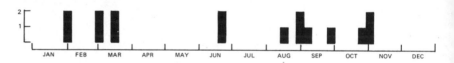

The records were mostly in late January to March and August to early November, with two in June (Sussex 1961 and Yorkshire 1969). Previous records were mostly in January–February (4) and October–November (4), but with one in March–April and another two in June–July. With one in June 1973 (Sutherland), no less than 17% of the records up to 1973 have been in mid-summer.

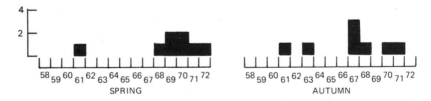

Records of an adult at St. Ives (Cornwall) in March–April 1968, March–April 1969, February–April 1970 and late January 1971 may have concerned only one individual. The 16 records (perhaps only 13 individuals) in our period compare with 11 prior to 1958.

148

The four 'spring' (late January to April) records in Cornwall may relate to only one individual. The scatter of other records suggests that wandering birds in coastal waters are identified where gulls congregate and observers take the trouble to scrutinise them closely. It seems strange that there was none in Ireland, and indeed only one ever there (near Belfast in February 1848). The other records prior to 1958 were in Cornwall (3), Dunbarton, Hampshire, Northumberland, Sussex (3) and Yorkshire.

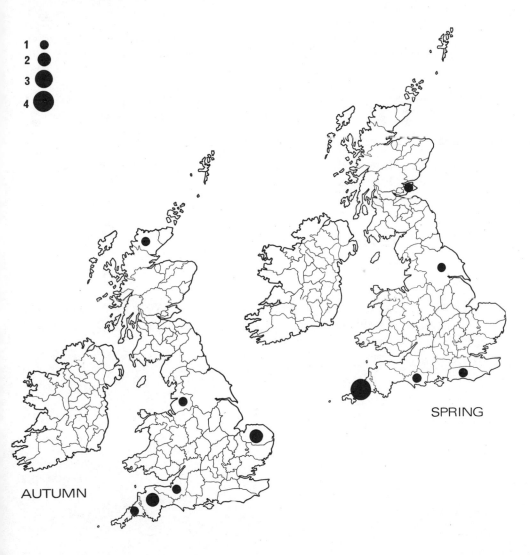

AUTUMN

SPRING

Ross's Gull

Rhodostethia rosea

Breeds northeast Siberia.

Small tern-like gull with wedge-shaped tail, long wings virtually lacking black, small delicate black bill and narrow black necklace. *Brit. Birds*, 52:422; 55:480.

The records were scattered through the year and, as yet, no clear pattern is emerging. The two previous records were in 'winter' and April.

The eight records in our period compare with two prior to 1958 (1846–47 and 1936). With six of the ten records up to 1972 in the six years 1967–72, a genuine increase in vagrancy may be occurring.

150

The previous records were in Yorkshire and Shetland, so eight of the ten up to 1972 were in counties bordering the northern North Sea (Shetland, Northumberland, Durham and Yorkshire).

1 ●
2 ●

SPRING

AUTUMN

White-winged Black Tern
Chlidonias leucopterus

Breeds from Hungary and Bulgaria eastwards through Asia.

Unmistakable in summer, with black body and underwing coverts, and white rump, tail and upperwing coverts. In winter, requires careful separation from winter-plumaged Black Tern *C. niger* by lack of dark patches at sides of breast, black ear-coverts separated from black crown, shorter bill, etc. Juveniles have distinctive dark brown mantle, giving saddle effect in contrast with white collar and rump. *Brit. Birds,* 53: 243; 61: 405.

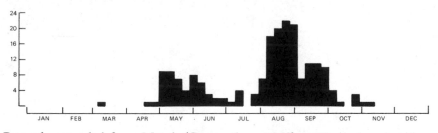

Records extended from March (Carmarthen, 1958) to November, but there were clear peaks in May to early June and August–September. Four of the five early July records were in Scotland or Northern Ireland, suggesting that they were not new autumn arrivals. Taking the division at 15th/16th July, therefore, 29% were in spring and 71% in autumn.

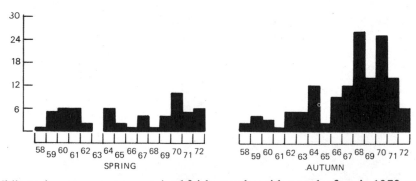

While spring occurrences remained fairly steady, with a peak of ten in 1970 and an average of four per year, autumn records varied from one (1961) to 26 (1968). Though the difficulty of separating birds in winter plumage from Black

152

Terns and Whiskered Terns (generally thought to be impossible until about 1960) makes it difficult to compare past and present records, there were only about 50 prior to 1958 compared with about 199 during our period, suggesting a marked increase. The increase in the number of observers during 1958–72 would account for most of the apparent increase in records of White-winged Black Terns, though the decline to only six in autumn 1972 suggests that there may have been a genuine upsurge during 1968–71.

There was no concentration in spring, with most (only 10%) in Sussex and a very wide scatter, north to Shetland, and 12% in Scotland. The autumn records were more concentrated, with 19% in Kent (46% in the six coastal counties from Lincolnshire to Sussex) and none in Scotland. The records of this species are discussed at length in *Scarce Migrant Birds in Britain and Ireland*.

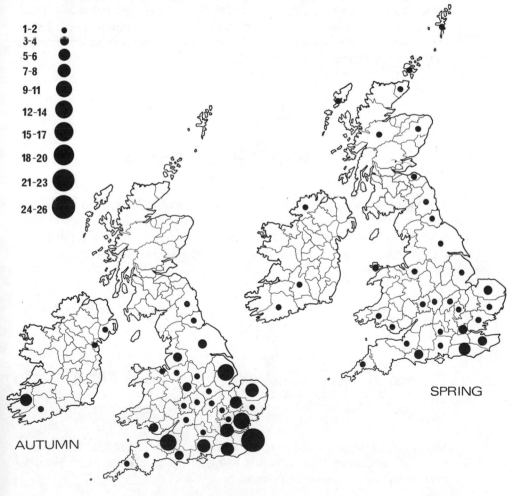

1-2	
3-4	
5-6	
7-8	
9-11	
12-14	
15-17	
18-20	
21-23	
24-26	

SPRING

AUTUMN

153

Whiskered Tern
Chlidonias hybrida

Breeds from southwest Europe (Iberia and France) discontinuously eastwards to Manchuria, and south to southern Africa, Australia and New Zealand.

Easily distinguished from other marsh terns in summer by white cheeks separating black crown from dusky underparts. Out of breeding season, lacks shoulder patches of Black Tern *C. niger* and has grey nape and rump. Bill deeper than Black or White-winged Black Tern, and actions resemble *Sterna* terns, as does winter plumage. *Brit. Birds,* 53: 243.

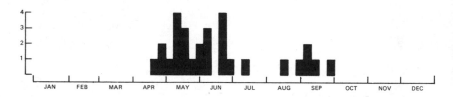

The records were all from mid-April to mid-July and mid-August to September, with 79% in the spring period (taken as prior to 16th July). Though birds in autumn plumage are more difficult to identify than those in spring, this is also true of White-winged Black Terns, which showed the opposite pattern, with most in autumn.

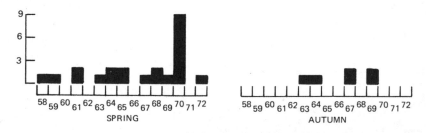

The 29 records in our period compare with about 20 prior to 1958. The influx in 1970—nine between 19th April and 28th June, four of them in the five days 10th–14th May—was unprecedented.

154

With 43% in Ireland and southwest England, spring records show a distinctly more westerly bias than White-winged Black Terns (15% in the west), giving a clear indication that they derive from overshooting by the west European population and not from the east. The autumn records, on the other hand, were all in the eastern half of England, so perhaps came from eastern Europe, where the ranges of the two species overlap, or were wandering birds.

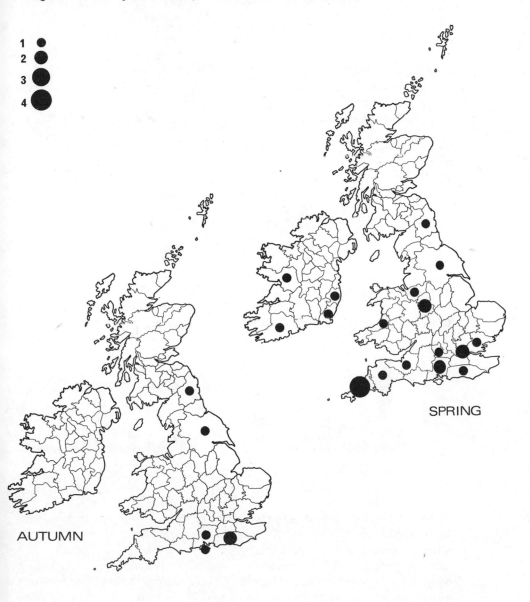

1

2

3

4

SPRING

AUTUMN

Gull-billed Tern
Gelochelidon nilotica

Breeds from Denmark, southern France and Iberia discontinuously eastwards to eastern Kazakhstan and south to northwest Africa, Pakistan, southeast China and Australia; also North, Central and South America.

Distinguished from Sandwich Tern *Sterna sandvicensis* by wholly black, stubby, 'swollen' bill, shallowly-forked grey tail, stockier and broader-winged appearance and heavier flight. *Brit. Birds,* 45: 357.

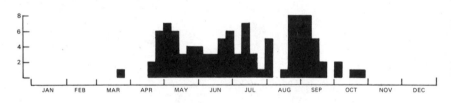

The records extended from March (East Lothian, 1968) to October, but most were from late April to mid-July and mid-August to mid-September. Records up to 5th August are here treated together as spring/summer.

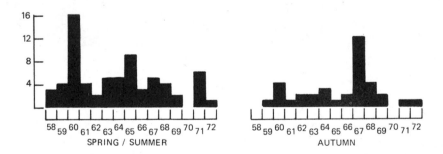

SPRING / SUMMER   AUTUMN

The exceptional number of spring/summer records in 1960 (six in Sussex in April–May, five in Kent in mid-June, four in Sussex in July and one in Flintshire in early August) may have included some duplication of individuals. The autumn influx of 1967, however, involved 12 individuals in eight counties between 15th August and 25th October. The 105 records in our period compare with about 50 prior to 1958, but the increase in sea-watching, especially from places like Selsey Bill (Sussex) in the 1960s, must account in part for this increase.

The spring/summer records included singles west to Galway and north to Shetland, but 77% were in Sussex, Kent and Hampshire. The scatter of records right through the summer and the concentration in the counties at the eastern end of the English Channel suggest that most are birds from the north European colonies. Autumn records were almost as widespread as those in spring/summer (14 counties at both seasons) but 33% were in Kent (and only another 11% in Sussex and Hampshire). Again, an origin in northern Europe is indicated. The patterns are discussed in more detail in *Scarce Migrant Birds in Britain and Ireland.*

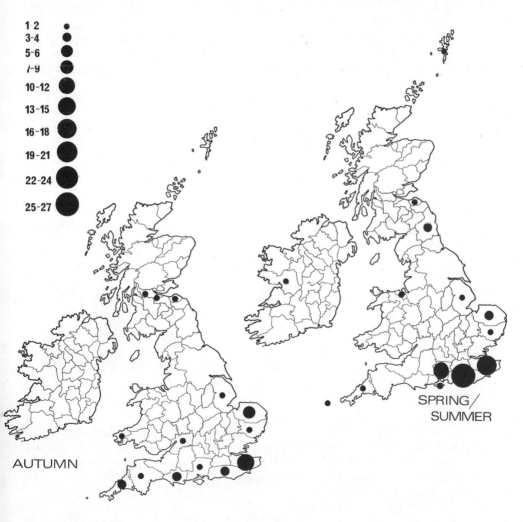

Caspian Tern

Hydroprogne caspia

Breeds Baltic and Black Sea coasts, Tunisia and very discontinuously eastwards to Manchuria and south to southern Africa, Australia and New Zealand; also North America.

Almost the size of a Herring Gull *Larus argentatus* with huge orange-red bill; dark undersides to primaries; crown wholly black in summer and wholly mottled in winter, without white forehead. *Brit Birds,* 47: 393; 64: 314.

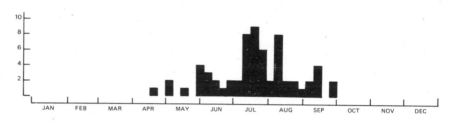

The records show a strange pattern, with more in July than April–June or August–September. Those prior to 1958 were mostly in May–June.

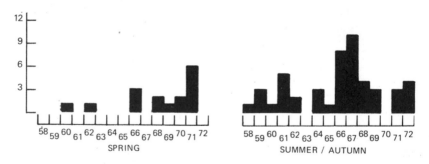

There were about 30 prior to 1958, compared with 64 in our period. Records have included two together on three occasions (Minsmere, Suffolk, in July and August 1967, East Lothian in July 1971) and the possibility of a breeding attempt at some time in the future should be borne in mind.

158

A ringed American bird (Lake Michigan, July 1927) has reached Britain (Yorkshire, August 1939), but the distributions, with most in the southern North Sea and eastern English Channel counties, clearly suggest that the majority come from the east, probably the Baltic population (in Finland, for instance, 200 pairs in 1938 had increased to 700 pairs by 1958).

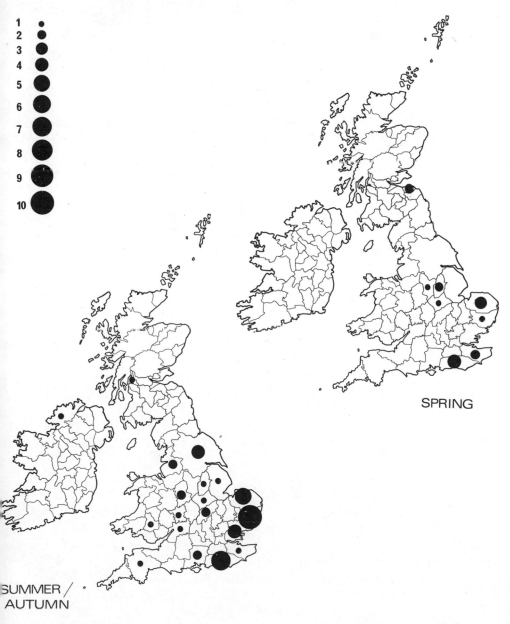

Sooty Tern
Sterna fuscata

Breeds on tropical and subtropical islands in all oceans, and Red Sea.

Slightly smaller than Sandwich Tern *S. sandvicensis*, largely black above and white below, with very deeply forked tail; white forehead extends back only to eye. *Brit. Birds*, 50: 385; *Sea Swallow*, 23: 18.

The arrival dates of the six records (perhaps only four birds) were strangely concentrated into only three weeks of the year. Three in 1966 (Suffolk, 11th June; Norfolk, 14th–19th June and 11th July; and Northumberland, 21st June) may have involved just one individual. The Norfolk 1966 bird was the only one to be seen on more than a single date.

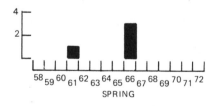
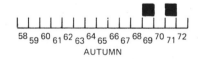

The four to six in our period compare with 16 prior to 1958. One in our period (Hampshire, August 1969) and most of those prior to 1958 were found dead or dying.

160

The three on the English east coast were all in 1966 and may have concerned only one individual. The 22 records up to 1972 have been scattered in 17 counties north to Orkney, but there has yet to be a record in Ireland.

1●

SPRING

AUTUMN

Franklin's Gull

Larus pipixcan

Breeds North America.

Similar to Laughing Gull but distinguished by size (smaller than Black-headed Gull *L. ridibundus*), shorter bill and legs, adults' pale grey centre to white tail, and the black wing tips being separated from the dark grey of rest of wing by a white band, which also extends along trailing edge. *Brit. Birds,* 64: 310; 65: 81.

Two records in the period:

Hampshire: Langstone Harbour and Farlington Marshes on 21st February to 16th May 1970

Sussex: Arlington Reservoir on 4th July 1970. Considered to be a different individual to that in Hampshire, as the earlier bird had a damaged bill.

These are the only records.

Bridled Tern

Sterna anaethetus

Breeds Caribbean, northwest Africa, Red Sea, Persian Gulf, Indian and Pacific Oceans.

Distinguished from Sooty Tern by smaller size, whitish band round nape, narrower white stripe which extends behind eye, and browner back and wings. *Brit. Birds,* 51: 303; *Sea Swallow,* 23: 18.

One record in the period:

Somerset: near Weston-super-Mare on 17th October 1958

The three previous records, like that in 1958, refer to birds found dead: Dublin (November 1953), Glamorgan (September 1954) and Kent (November 1931).

162

Royal Tern
Sterna maxima

Breeds North America, Caribbean and northwest Africa.

Similar to Caspian Tern but smaller, bill more slender, paler and oranger, tail longer and more deeply forked, primaries paler and forehead usually white. *Brit. Birds,* 48: 118; 61: 559.

Two records in the period:
Cornwall: St Ives on 2nd September 1971
Kent: Sandwich Bay on 28th–29th July 1965
and one since:
Cheshire and Flint: Hilbre Island and Point of Air on 8th and 22nd September 1974

The only previous record was one (long dead) at North Bull, Dublin, on 24th March 1954.

Brünnich's Guillemot
Uria lomvia

Breeds on Arctic coasts and islands.

Similar to Guillemot *U. aalge* but bill shorter and thicker, with pale lateral lines. *Scot. Birds,* 5: 285.

Three records (all of dead birds) in the period:
Argyll: Loch Caolisport on 11th October 1969
Lancashire: near Morecambe on 15th April 1960
Shetland: Norwick, Unst, on 20th March 1968

The three previous records were in Dublin (October 1945), East Lothian (December 1908) and Wicklow (September 1938).

Pallas's Sandgrouse
Syrrhaptes paradoxus

Breeds from Kirgiz and Aral-Caspian steppes eastwards to Manchuria.

Sandgrouse shape, in flight resembling Golden Plover *Pluvialis apricaria* and on ground resembling ridiculously short-legged Partridge *Perdix perdix* with dove-like head; long pointed tail; small black belly patch. *Brit. Birds*, 60: 416; *Scot. Birds*, 6: 204.

The records were scattered, in May, September and December. Past records have mostly been in May.

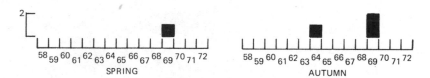

The four British records were all matched by others in western Europe at the same times. Apart from two unidentified sandgrouse (either this species or Black-bellied *Pterocles orientalis*) in Wexford in May 1954, the record in Kent in December 1964 was the first here since 1909. Large invasions occurred in May 1863 and May 1888, and some were recorded in ten other years during 1859–1909. Some even bred here, two clutches of eggs being found in Yorkshire in 1888, and young being reared in Morayshire in 1888 and 1889. These invasions occurred after heavy snowfall or a hard snow crust had prevented feeding in the breeding area (*Brit. Birds*, 62: 452).

All the records happened to be in eastern Britain. In the invasions between 1859 and 1909, birds were recorded in many counties, west to Cork, Clare, Galway, Mayo and the Outer Hebrides.

1 ●
2 ●

SPRING

AUTUMN

Rufous Turtle Dove *Streptopelia orientalis*, see page 170.

Great Spotted Cuckoo
Clamator glandarius

Breeds from Iberia and southern France discontinuously east to southwest Iran and south to South Africa.

Larger than Cuckoo *Cuculus canorus*, with white-spotted brown upperparts, creamy underparts and a crest; rounded wings and long graduated tail make flight silhouette resemble Magpie *Pica pica*. *Brit. Birds*, 53: 358.

The records were all between mid-March and mid-May, and in August. Past records were in March–April and July–October, and there have now been almost equal numbers at the two seasons. One in Cornwall stayed from 23rd April to the end of June in 1968.

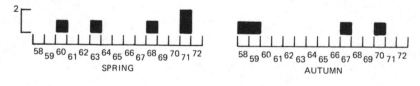

The nine records in our period compare with six prior to 1958.

The spring and autumn patterns are very distinct. Taking all 15 records up to 1972, 88% in spring were in the west (from Scilly and Kerry north to Isle of Man and Galway), whereas 100% of those in autumn were in the east (Sussex to Orkney).

1 ●

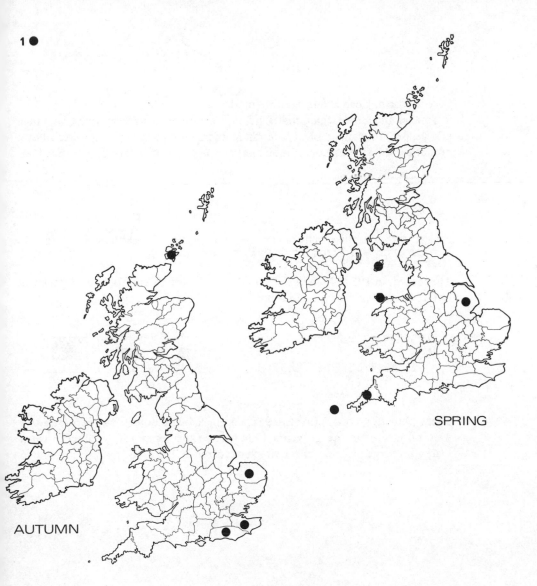

SPRING

AUTUMN

Yellow-billed Cuckoo

Coccyzus americanus

Breeds North, Central and South America.

Smaller and more elegant than Cuckoo *Cuculus canorus,* with long graduated tail, yellow lower mandible, black tail feathers with large white tips and rufous primaries, showing as conspicuous patches in flight. *Brit. Birds,* 47: 164, 172, 173.

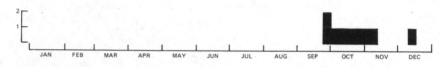

The records in 1958–72, and also all those previously, were from late September to December, with most in October.

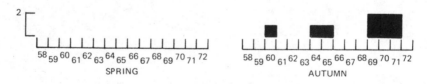

There were 22 records prior to 1958, compared with nine in our period. There were only three in the 15 years 1954–68, so the six in 1969–71 represent a marked resurgence, akin to six which occurred in 1952–53.

Five of the nine in our period, and many of the previous ones, were dead or dying when discovered. Of the 31 records up to 1972, four were in Ireland, three in Wales, 14 from Scilly to Sussex and eight in Scotland, but only two on the English east coast: the pattern one would expect of a gale-blown transatlantic vagrant.

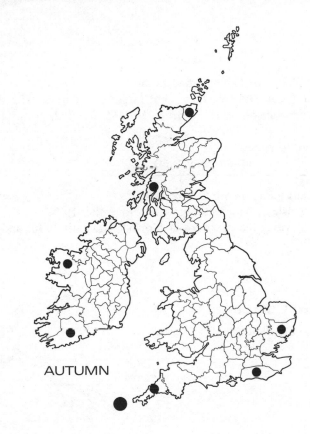

1 ●
2 ●

AUTUMN

Rufous Turtle Dove

Streptopelia orientalis

Breeds from Urals east to China and Japan.

Similar to Turtle Dove *S. turtur* but larger and darker, with duller wing coverts and no white on tail. *Brit. Birds,* 53: 445; 67: 352.

One record in the period:
Scilly: St. Agnes on 2nd–6th May 1960
and two since:
Cornwall: Land's End on 5th October 1973
Shetland: Fair Isle on 31st October to 1st November 1974

The two previous records were in Norfolk (January 1946) and Yorkshire (October 1889).

Black-billed Cuckoo

Coccyzus erythropthalmus

Breeds North America.

Similar to Yellow-billed Cuckoo but lacks rufous in wings, has far less white in tail, and bill is black. *Brit. Birds,* 47: 164.

Two records (both of dying birds) in the period:
Cornwall: Gweek on 30th October 1965
Devon: Lundy on 19th October 1967
and one since:
Yorkshire: Redcar on 23rd–24th September 1975

The four previous records were also all in late autumn: Antrim (September 1871), Argyll (November 1950), Scilly (October 1932) and Shetland (October 1953).

Hawk Owl
Surnia ulula

Breeds from Scandinavia eastwards to northeast Siberia, Alaska and Canada.

Truly a very hawk-like owl, in flight resembling a Kestrel *Falco tinnunculus*, with short, rather pointed, wings and long tail. Often perches in conspicuous position and is fearless of Man. Underparts are barred and has flat-topped head and striking black border to face. *Brit. Birds,* 46: 398; 53: 446.

Two records in the period:

Cornwall: Gurnard's Head on 14th August 1966

Lancashire: near Chipping on 13th September 1959

There are eight previous records, two (marked †) of the Eurasian race *S. u. ulula* and three (marked *) of the American race *S. u. caparoch*: Aberdeen (November 1898†), Cornwall (March 1830*), Lanark (December 1863*), Northampton (November 1903), Renfrew (November 1868), Shetland (winter 1860/61), Somerset (August 1847*) and Wiltshire (prior to 1876†).

Tengmalm's Owl
Aegolius funereus

Breeds in central and southeast Europe and from Scandinavia eastwards to northeast Siberia, Alaska and Canada.

Comparable in size to Little Owl *Athene noctua* but with large rounded head and wide, deep facial discs bordered with black, spotted crown and general reddish-chocolate colouration; does not have Little Owl's bounding flight and is exclusively nocturnal. *Brit. Birds,* 46: 15; 52: 12.

Two records in the period:

Orkney: Cruan Firth on 26th December 1959 to 1st January 1960

Stromness on 1st May 1961

Formerly much commoner vagrant, with nearly 50 records, mostly in Scotland and eastern England in October to February prior to 1918.

Scops Owl
Otus scops

Breeds from France, Iberia and northwest Africa east to Japan and Indonesia.

Smaller and slimmer than Little Owl *Athene noctua* but with typical wavering flight of other owls, lacking Little's undulations, and is far more strictly nocturnal; head smaller and flatter than Little Owl's, but has ear-tufts which, when raised, give Scops the appearance of miniature Long-eared Owl *Asio otus*; song monotonous low whistle, repeated regularly. *Brit. Birds,* 45: 401; 51: 149; *Scot. Birds,* 7: 55.

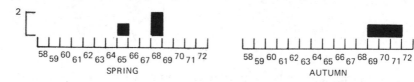

The records were equally divided between April–June and September–November. Previous records were all in April–September (mostly spring), so that the two most recent (November 1970 in Orkney and October 1971 in Kent) were also the latest ever.

There were 64 records prior to 1958 compared with the six in our period—a very marked decrease. There were only six in the 17 years 1951–67, so the five in the four years 1968–71 may represent the start of a resurgence.

The scattered pattern in our period is also found in those prior to 1958 (40 England, 13 Scotland, nine Ireland and two Wales).

1●

SPRING

AUTUMN

Snowy Owl
Nyctea scandiaca

Breeds Arctic from Iceland and Scandinavia east to Siberia, Alaska, Canada and Greenland.

Huge white owl, females flecked and barred with brown. Combination of colour, size and yellow eyes diagnostic, but Barn Owls *Tyto alba* are still occasionally misidentified as Snowy Owls by tyros. In flight, broad rounded wings give similarity to Buzzard *Buteo buteo. Brit. Birds,* 47: 432.

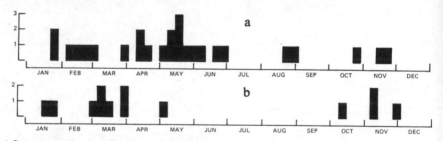

After records in Shetland in the summers of 1963 and 1964, and then throughout the year in 1965 and 1966, the first recorded breeding in Britain and Ireland occurred on Fetlar in each year since 1967, with a total of 14 young fledging as a result of successful nesting in 1967–71 (see *Brit. Birds,* 61: 119; 62: 33; *Scot. Birds,* 5: 244). With up to nine individuals there at one time, Shetland records are omitted from the histograms. The Scottish records (outside

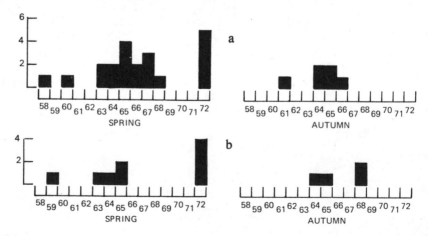

174

Shetland) (a) and those elsewhere (b) are here treated separately, as the patterns are different. Some Scottish birds stayed for long periods and the pattern suggests a small wandering 'resident' population rather than migrants. The records outside Scotland, on the other hand, clearly relate to wintering birds, from October to May.

The records outside Shetland (Scotland, and elsewhere) suggest that incursions occurred in 1963–65 and 1972.

The eastern bias to the spring records in mainland Scotland suggests a Scandinavian (rather than Icelandic or Nearctic) orgin. The small dot in the Outer Hebrides in fact represents a pair which remained throughout 1972 (and 1973). Those in southern England and Wales have been suspected of having a captive origin, but this seems highly unlikely as they occurred in the same years as most Scottish records.

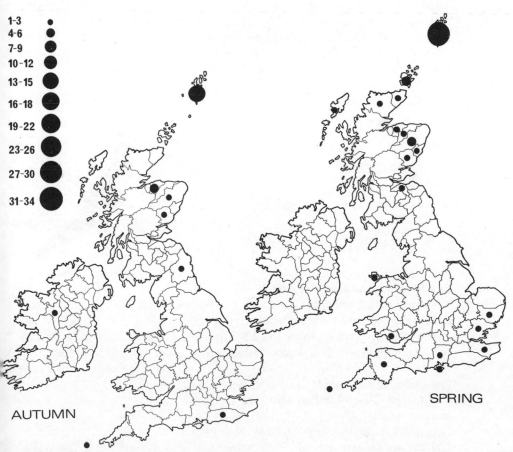

AUTUMN

SPRING

Hawk Owl *Surnia ulula*, see page 171.
Tengmalm's Owl *Aegolius funereus*, see page 171.

175

Nighthawk
Chordeiles minor

Breeds North America.

Slightly smaller than Nightjar *Caprimulgus europaeus*; long, pointed wings, slightly forked and barred tail and large white oval patch on each wing apparent in flight. Brit. Birds, 65: 301, 302.

Two records in the period:
Nottingham: Bulcote on 18th–21st October 1971
Scilly: St Agnes on 12th–13th October 1971

The two previous records were both in Scilly: one on 17th September 1927 and two on 28th September 1955 (one staying until 5th October).

Little Swift
Apus affinis

Breeds Africa and southern Asia.

Smaller than Swift *Apus apus* with less pointed shorter wings and square-ended tail; prominent square white rump patch, broader than that of White-rumped Swift *A. caffer* (which—like Horus Swift *A. horus*—has deeply forked tail), white throat patch and pale forehead. *Brit. Birds,* 60: 286; 61: 160.

One record in the period:
Cork: Cape Clear Island on 12th June 1967
and one since:
Denbigh: Llanrwst on 6th–7th November 1973

These are the only records.

176

Pallid Swift
Apus pallidus

Breeds northwest Africa and eastwards from Iberia through the Mediterranean Basin to south Iran.

Same size as Swift *A. apus*, but with broader head; paler with more conspicuous white throat and pale forehead, and secondaries slightly paler than rest of wing; slower wing-beats. Warning: differences are slight even when both species are seen together in ideal conditions.

None in the period, but one since:
Lincoln: North Coates and Saltfleetby on 5th–6th November 1975

This is the only record; it is still under review for admission to the British and Irish list.

Needle-tailed Swift
Hirundapus caudacutus

Breeds eastern Siberia to Japan.

Much larger than Swift *Apus apus,* though smaller than Alpine Swift; white forehead, chin and upper breast; white U-shaped patch under tail; conspicuous pale greyish triangular patch on back; tail square-ended (needle-like projections seldom, if ever, visible in the field). *Brit. Birds,* 53: 431; 59: 109.

One record in the period:
Cork: Cape Clear Island on 20th June 1964

The two previous records were both in mid-summer last century: Essex (July 1846) and Hampshire (July 1879).

Alpine Swift

Apus melba

IW

Breeds from Iberia and northwest Africa, through southern Europe (north to the Alps) eastwards to India, and eastern and southern Africa.

Large size, brown colour and white belly are diagnostic. White throat, separated by brown breast-band from white belly, not easy to see except at close range. *Brit. Birds,* 52: 221; *Scot. Birds,* 6: 209.

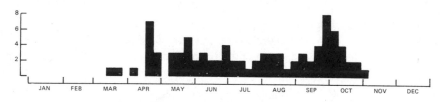

The records, between 15th March and 30th October, show a surprising lack of pattern, except for a marked peak in the last week of September and first of October.

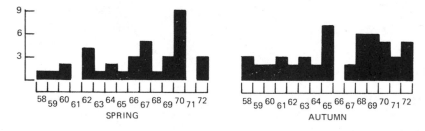

The 87 records in our period compare with about 50 records of single birds prior to 1958, but there were also some records of parties, including about 100 flying northwest over Kingsdown (Kent) on 15th July 1915 (and five on 22nd July and five on 3rd August in the same year). The influx of nine in spring 1970 included five during the four days 16th–19th April, while the influx of seven in autumn 1965 included five during the nine days 26th September–4th October.

178

Both spring and autumn records were mostly in coastal counties. There was a noticeably greater number in the west in July–October (41% west from Devon) than in April–June (14%). A September bird in Scilly (1969) had been ringed as a nestling in Switzerland two months previously.

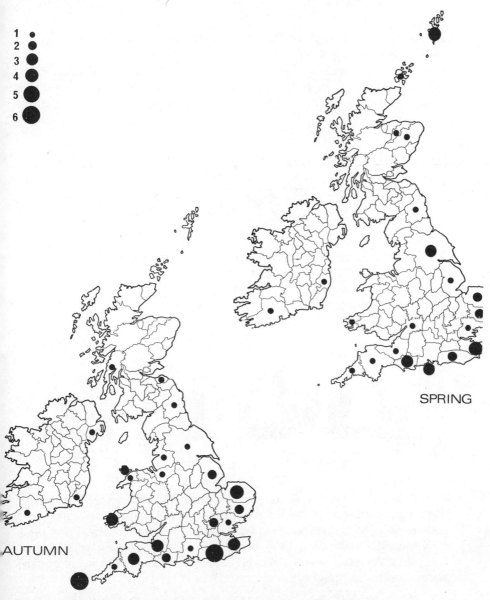

SPRING

AUTUMN

Needle-tailed Swift *Hirundapus caudacutus*, see page 177.

Bee-eater

Merops apiaster

Breeds from Iberia, southern France and northwest Africa east to Kashmir and eastern Kazakhstan; also South Africa.

Brilliantly-coloured with turquoise underparts, tail and primaries, bright yellow throat, chestnut crown, head and nape and yellow scapular patches; projecting central tail feathers, long curved bill, graceful flight and liquid call-note. *Scot. Birds,* 6: 46.

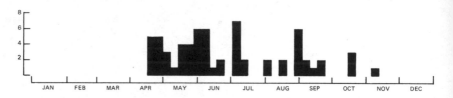

Records were scattered from mid-April to early November (this last bird staying in Cornwall from 10th November to 3rd December 1963, then found dead), but most were in spring (71% up to 22nd July). There were 41 records of single birds, six of two together and four of three together.

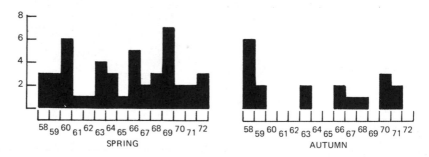

The 65 records in our period compare with over 150 prior to 1958. It is likely that a steady decrease has occurred during 1958–72, since annual totals have not kept pace with the increase in observers. The apparent peaks (in spring 1960, 1966 and 1969, and autumn 1958) are all due to the occurrence of small parties. One pair of Bee-eaters attempted to breed in Midlothian in 1920 and three pairs nested (two successfully) in Sussex in 1955.

Most at both seasons were scattered in southern Britain, but the spring records in the Northern Isles are clearly part of a genuine pattern, for small parties occurred there in four of the 15 years.

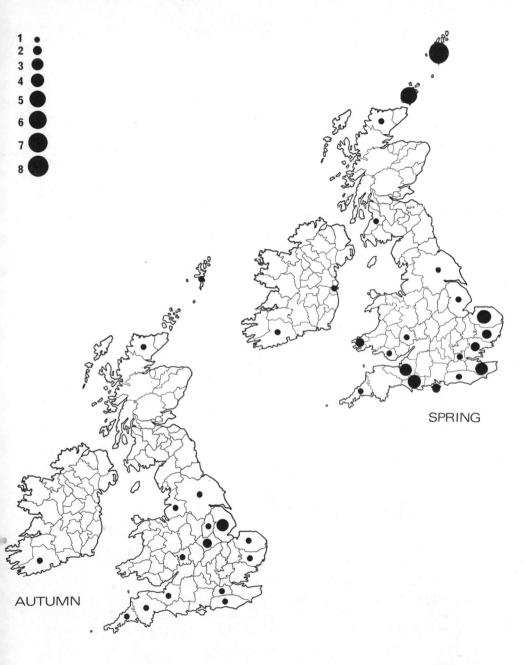

Roller

Coracias garrulus

IW

Breeds Iberia, southern France and northwest Africa, and from Germany and Italy north to Estonia and east to Kashmir and southwest Siberia.

Habits rather like a huge shrike, often sitting on prominent perch (especially telegraph wires) and dropping to ground to take prey; shape and flight resemble Jackdaw *Corvus monedula* or Jay *Garrulus glandarius*; brilliantly-coloured, mostly pale turquoise and blue, with chestnut back. *Brit. Birds,* 56: 58; *Scot. Birds,* 7: 55.

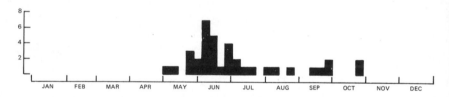

Records extended from May to October, but 76% were in spring (up to 22nd July), with a clear peak in early June. Most previous records were also in May–July. Apart from those found dead, or which died, long stays were the rule rather than the exception: only seven were seen on a single date and the average length of stay in one place was ten days.

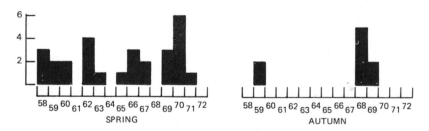

The 37 records in our period compare with about 135 prior to 1958. Appearances are very erratic. Even in years when unusual numbers occur, records are not concentrated: the six in spring 1970 were spread over a period of seven weeks and the five in autumn 1968 over a period of at least 11 weeks.

182

Records were very scattered at both seasons, though half of the spring ones were in southeast England, East Anglia and the Northern Isles.

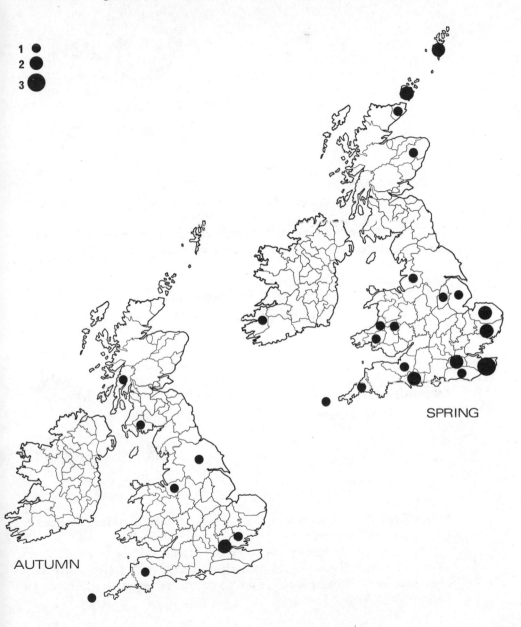

SPRING

AUTUMN

Yellow-bellied Sapsucker

Sphyrapicus varius

Breeds North America.

Small woodpecker, between Great Spotted *Dendrocopos major* and Lesser Spotted *D. minor* in size, with black and white mottled back, black wings with narrow white stripe, and red crown; throat red in male, white in female; sooty-brown immature also has diagnostic white wing-stripe.

None in the period, but one since:
Scilly: Tresco on 26th September to 6th October 1975
  This is the only record; it is still under review for admission to the British and Irish list.

Calandra Lark

Melanocorypha calandra

Breeds from Iberia and Morocco eastwards through the Mediterranean to Kazakhstan and Afghanistan.

Large lark with the bulk of a Song Thrush *Turdus philomelos*, but with very short tail; broad rounded wings; underparts whitish with conspicuous black neck patches; underwing black with white trailing edges; white outer tail feathers. *Brit. Birds,* 55: 44.

One record in the period:
Dorset: Portland Bill on 2nd April 1961
  This is the only record.

Bimaculated Lark
Melanocorypha bimaculata

Breeds southwest Asia.

Resembles a rufous Calandra Lark, but smaller, lacks white in outer tail and on trailing edges of wing; whiter supercilium and white tips to tail feathers, forming a terminal band. *Brit. Birds*, 58: 309.

One record in the period:
Devon: Lundy on 7th–11th May 1962
and one since:
Scilly: St Mary's on 24th–27th October 1975
These are the only records.

Lesser Short-toed Lark
Calandrella rufescens

Breeds from Spain and north Africa eastwards to Manchuria.

Like Short-toed Lark but lacks dark patches on neck and usually has regular well-defined streaking on breast and usually on flanks; tertials shorter, not reaching tips of primaries; high-crowned, round-headed appearance; wings more uniform, lacking dark median coverts; typical call sharp, loud, protracted 'prrrrt'. *Brit. Birds,* 53: 241; 68: 238.

One record in the period:
Wexford: five on Great Saltee on 22nd March 1958, and up to four seen irregularly until 25th.

The three previous records were also all in Ireland, all in 1956: 30 at Tralee Bay, Kerry on 4th January, five at Great Saltee, Wexford on 30th–31st March, and two at Belmullet, Mayo on 21st May.

Short-toed Lark

Calandrella cinerea

Breeds from Iberia, southern France and northwest Africa east to Manchuria.

Small compact lark, reddish- or greyish-brown above and whitish below, with variably distinct dark patches at sides of upper breast; dark-centred median coverts form dark bar; long tertials almost reaching tips of primaries; usually has flat-crowned appearance; flight may recall small Lapland Bunting *Calcarius lapponicus*; colouring and bill may recall young Linnet *Acanthis cannabina*; typical calls are short, dry 'tchirrup' and plaintive 'wee-oo'. *Brit. Birds*, 48: 512; 68: 238; *Lundy Field Soc. Ann. Rep.*, 23: 28.

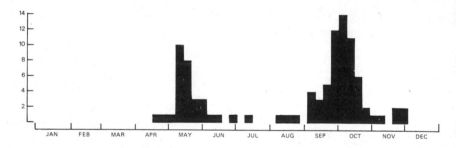

Though occurrences were noted from mid-April to late November (one staying into early December), the peaks were exceedingly well marked, with 58% of those up to 22nd July during the two weeks 7th–20th May and 56% of the autumn records in just three weeks from 24th September to 14th October.

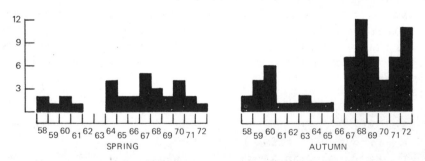

The 97 records in our period compare with about 40 prior to 1958. Autumn records, mostly involving greyish birds of the eastern races, have increased

186

dramatically since 1976. Spring records, which usually involve birds of the reddish southern races, have, on the other hand, remained fairly steady, at an average of about two per year.

The two archipelagos of Shetland (especially Fair Isle) and Scilly accounted for the lion's share of the records. Shetland had almost equal numbers at the two seasons, 61% of those in spring and 33% of those in autumn. Scilly, on the other hand, had only 6% of the spring records but 32% of those in autumn. During 1958–72, 25 of the 97 records were assigned to the greyish or reddish forms. The greyish eastern birds were in June, September (2), October (11) and November (3), whereas the reddish southern birds were in May (5), September (2) and October.

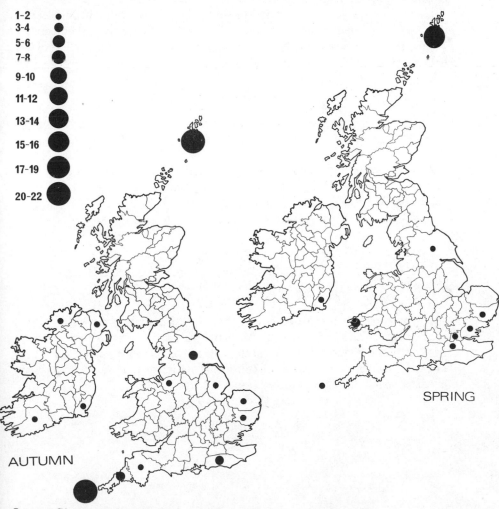

Lesser Short-toed Lark *Calandrella rufescens*, see page 185.

Crested Lark

Galerida cristata

Breeds throughout Continental Europe south of southern Sweden, east to Korea, Arabia and northern Africa, both north and south of Sahara.

Large, short-tailed lark with conspicuously large crest; tail has dark centre with buff sides; no white in tail or wing; bill longer and more pointed and underwing more warmly coloured than in very similar Thekla Lark *G. theklae*. *Brit. Birds*, 46: 210; 55: 37; 58: 337.

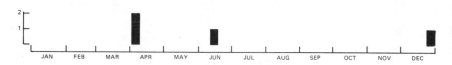

The December bird stayed for 13 days (Devon 1958/59), but the others were seen on single dates. Previous dated records were in March–April (3), June, September–October (5) and November–January (5).

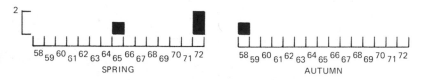

The four records in our period compare with 13 (including two together twice) prior to 1958. The increase in observer-activity in recent years has resulted in no increase in the frequency of this species, which breeds just the other side of the English Channel. Despite claims of more than one instance of breeding in Britain in recent years, this has yet to be established.

Apart from the one in Yorkshire (June 1972) and one in Shetland (November 1952), all 15 of the other records have been in southern English counties—Cornwall (6), Devon, Somerset, Sussex (4), London (2) and Kent. This largely sedentary species clearly does little more than stagger across the English Channel.

1●

SPRING

AUTUMN

Red-rumped Swallow

Hirundo daurica

RAR

Breeds Iberia, southern France and northwest Africa; Balkans east to Japan; central Africa.

Very distinct from Swallow *H. rustica* not only in plumage but also shape, with blunter wings, shorter and thicker, incurved, tail streamers; lacks Swallow's dark gorget and tail spots; pale rump (cream or buff and rufous) and orange-red supercilia, neck and nape. *Brit. Birds*, 46: 263, 264, 265; 56: 416.

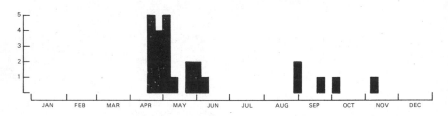

The records were in two distinct periods, mid-April to mid-June and late August to early November. 70% of those in spring were in just three weeks, from 16th April to 6th May.

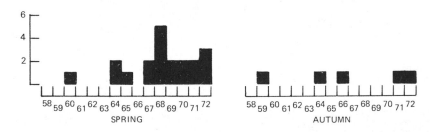

The 25 records in our period compare with only seven prior to 1958: three on Fair Isle (Shetland) on 2nd June 1906, one in Hertfordshire in June 1949 and singles in Norfolk, Devon and Wexford in March–April 1952. The increase in vagrancy here has occurred as the species has spread northwards from extreme southern Spain into France. The five in spring 1968 were in a 17-day period from 18th April to 4th May.

There is a distinct easterly bias to the records at both seasons, with only Sussex, Kent and Yorkshire recording more than one in spring or autumn in the 15 years.

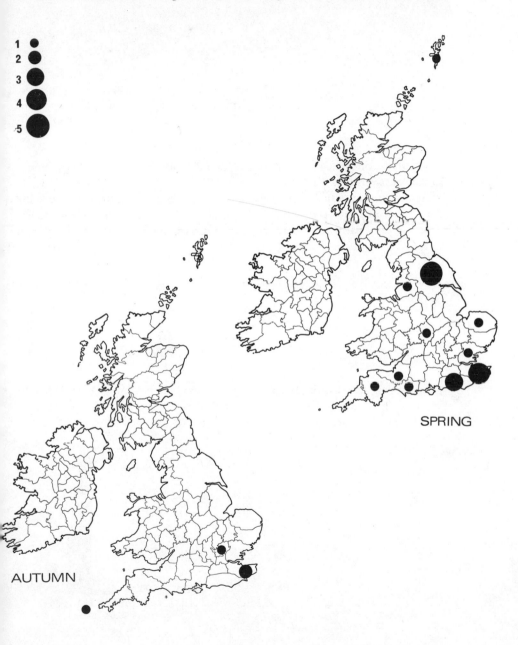

1
2
3
4
5

SPRING

AUTUMN

Nutcracker

Nucifraga caryocatactes

Breeds mountains of central and southeastern Europe and from southern Fenno-Scandia eastwards to Kamchatka.

Slightly smaller than Jay *Garrulus glandarius*, dark brown flecked with white spots, but most conspicuous features are white under tail coverts, white tip to underside of tail and habit of perching on the tips of conifers. *Brit. Birds,* 45: 60; 63: 353.

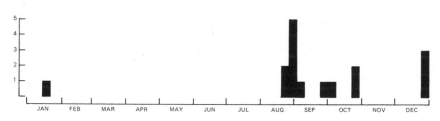

The normal pattern was a scattering of records in August–January, and prior to 1958 most had been in October–December. Records for 1968–69, when there was an unprecedented influx, are omitted from this histogram.

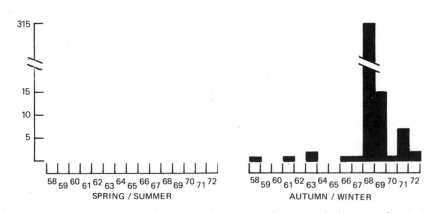

Nutcrackers averaged only just over one per year in our period, except for the invasion in 1968. In that year, at least 315 arrived, from 6th August to October,

192

with some staying through until autumn 1969. This irruption has been documented in great detail in *Brit. Birds*, 63: 353–373. The apparent small influx in 1971 was largely due to five in Peebleshire on 28th August. Prior to 1958 there were about 45 records in Britain (there has still been none in Ireland).

The four counties from Norfolk to Kent accounted for the majority of the records in 'normal' years, and also in the 1968 invasion. Only two British records have been referred to the thick-billed race *N. c. caryocatactes* (Cheshire 1860 and Sussex 1900), all others which have been identified being of the slender-billed eastern race *N. c. macrorhynchos*, which periodically irrupts when an abundant cone crop of its food the Arolla Pine *Pinus cembra* is followed by a poor crop in the following year, the high numbers of Nutcrackers, facing a food shortage, being forced into long-distance wandering.

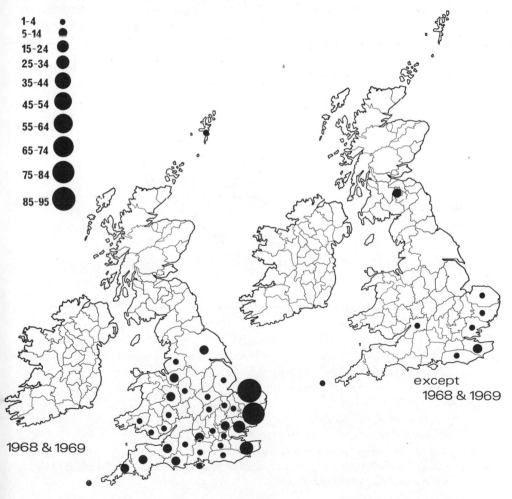

1-4
5-14
15-24
25-34
35-44
45-54
55-64
65-74
75-84
85-95

except
1968 & 1969

1968 & 1969

Penduline Tit

Remiz pendulinus

Breeds discontinuously from Spain, southern France, Italy, Germany and the Balkans eastwards to Manchuria.

Smaller than Blue Tit *Parus caeruleus,* with longer tail; plumage suggests a tiny pale male Red-backed Shrike *Lanius collurio,* with rufous upperparts, pale grey head and neck and black face patch; frequently utters distinctive thin plaintive call. *Brit. Birds,* 60: 517.

One record in the period:
Yorkshire: Spurn on 22nd–28th October 1966
This is the only record.

Wallcreeper

Tichodroma muraria

Breeds in mountains discontinuously from Pyrenees and Alps eastwards to China.

A blue riband bird. Unmistakable, with very broad rounded wings which are constantly flicked at rest and give a butterfly-like appearance to the bird in flight; plumage various shades of grey, with white spots on wing and tail feathers, and large brilliant crimson patches on wings. *Brit. Birds,* 63: 163.

One record in the period:
Dorset: Worth Maltravers on 19th November 1969 to 18th April 1970
The six previous records were in Dorset (April 1920), Lancashire (May 1872), Norfolk (October 1792), Somerset (September 1901) and Sussex (about 1886 and June 1938).

194

Short-toed Treecreeper
Certhia brachydactyla

Breeds Continental Europe (including the Channel Islands), northwest Africa and Asia Minor.

Exceedingly similar to Treecreeper *C. familiaris* but tends to have duller, greyer upperparts, duskier underparts with brownish flanks, a less rufous rump and shorter and less distinct supercilia; longer and more curved bill and shorter hind claws are difficult characters, even in the hand. Two of several call-notes, a shrill, piping, explosive, loud 'zeet', recalling Dunnock *Prunella modularis*, and a penetrating, quite loud 'chink', slightly recalling Chaffinch *Fringilla coelebs*, seem to be specific to *brachydactyla*. Very great care and detailed descriptions are needed to establish identity, even of trapped birds. *Brit. Birds*, 69: 117.

At least one record in the period:
Kent: Dungeness, trapped, 27th–30th September 1969
Several other records are still under review.

Eye-browed Thrush
Turdus obscurus

Breeds Siberia.
Smaller than Redwing *T. iliacus*; prominent white supercilia and unstreaked underparts with apricot-coloured flanks. *Brit. Birds*, 61: 218.

Three records in the period, all in 1964:
Northampton: Oundle on 5th October
Outer Hebrides: North Rona on 16th October
Scilly: St Agnes on 5th December
These are the only records.

Brown Thrasher *Toxostoma rufum*, see page 220.
Dusky Thrush *Turdus naumanni*, see page 200.
Black-throated Thrush *Turdus ruficollis*, see page 200.

195

American Robin

Turdus migratorius

Breeds North America.

Shape, behaviour and size resemble Blackbird *T. merula* but rufous breast and belly and white chin, throat, incomplete orbital ring, under tail coverts and tips to outer tail feathers. *Brit. Birds,* 46: 364, 368; 59: 41.

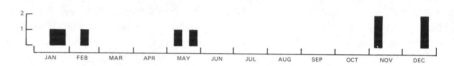

The records were mostly November–February, but there were also two in May. Four records in 1952–55, together with seven in 1876–1937 which are not always accepted as wild birds, formed a similar pattern: September, October (3), December (4), January, April or May and May.

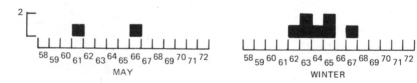

January–February records are shown in the previous year. The run of records—annually from 1961–67—is not unique, as past records included similar series in 1891–94 and 1952–55.

Though there is now a risk of escapes from captivity, the pattern of records, mostly in the west, suggests that transatlantic vagrants are involved in the majority of cases. Past records show a similar pattern, with seven out of 11 in the west (five in Ireland, two in Devon, two in Kent and singles in Leicestershire and Shropshire).

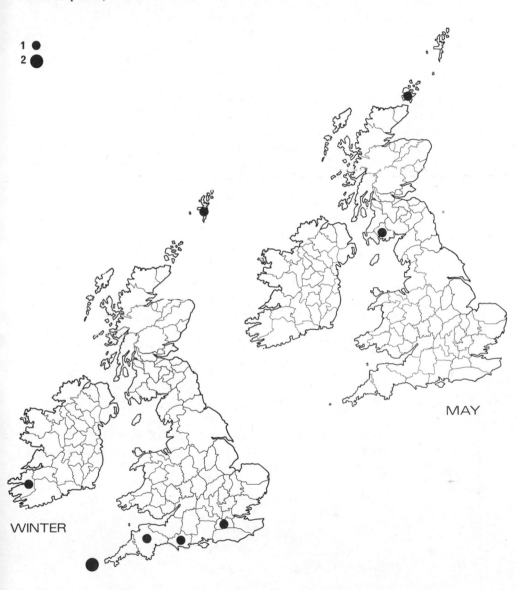

1 ●
2 ●

MAY

WINTER

White's Thrush
Zoothera dauma

Breeds from central Siberia east to Japan and south to Tasmania.

Stance resembles Mistle Thrush *T. viscivorus* but is even larger, with striking gold-and-black-and-white crescentic barring on upper- and underparts; underwing has bold black and white stripes; vaguely similar juvenile Mistle Thrushes easily distinguished by white underwing and lack of mottling on rump. *Brit. Birds,* 46: 455; *Scot. Birds,* 8: 33.

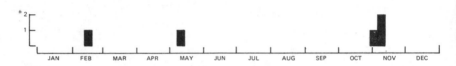

Most past records were in October–January, so the three in autumn (30th October–7th November) and February fit the pattern. The May bird (Cheshire 1964) was atypical, but there was one previous spring record (Longford 1867).

The five records in our period compare with about 28 prior to 1958, of which only four were since 1940. The February record (Shetland 1971) is here treated as autumn/winter 1970.

198

The records up to 1972 were scattered in 20 counties, south to Cornwall and west to Cork and Mayo, but 58% were on the British east coast from Shetland to Suffolk, with five in Shetland and five in Yorkshire.

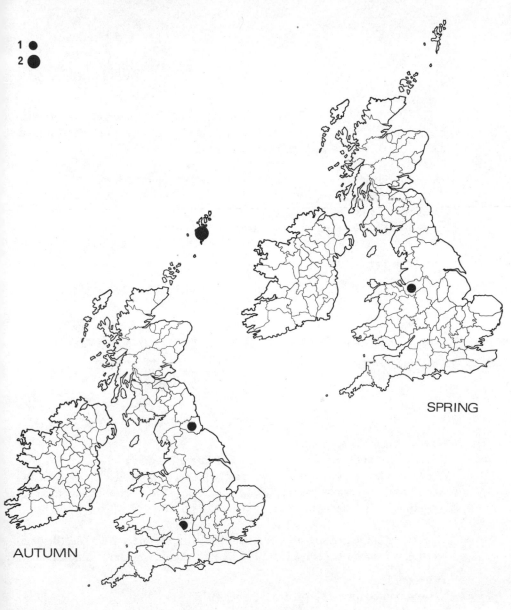

1 ●
2 ●

SPRING

AUTUMN

Dusky Thrush

Turdus naumanni

Breeds Siberia.

Size of Song Thrush *T. philomelos*, with whitish supercilia; two blackish breast bands (lower one incomplete); wings and rump with much chestnut; tail dark. *Brit. Birds*, 53: 275; *Scot. Birds*, 5: 392.

Three records in the period:
Durham: Hartlepool on 12th December 1959 to 24th February 1960
Shetland: Fair Isle on 18th–21st October 1961
　　　　　Whalsay on 24th September 1968
The only previous record was at Gunthorpe, Nottinghamshire on 13th October 1905.

Black-throated Thrush

Turdus ruficollis

Breeds central Asia.

Size and shape (including long tail) of Fieldfare *T. pilaris*, with upright stance recalling Wheatear *Oenanthe oenanthe*; uniform grey-brown upperparts and whitish lower breast and belly; male has black throat and upper breast; this area is whitish and spotted with black in female. *Brit. Birds*, 51: 195.

No records in the period; but this is splitting hairs, for one at Fair Isle, Shetland on 8th December 1957 stayed into 1958, being last seen on about 22nd January.

Two records since:
Norfolk: Holkham on 21st–24th October 1975
Shetland: Tolob on 5th–6th October 1974
The two previous records were also in winter: Perth (February 1879) and Sussex (December 1868).

200

Hermit Thrush
Hylocichla guttata

Breeds North America.
   Small thrush, resembling Veery in size and shape, but has olive-brown back and reddish or chestnut-brown tail, which is distinctively cocked at intervals.

None in the period, but one since:
Shetland: Fair Isle on 2nd June 1975
   This is the only record.

Olive-backed Thrush
Hylocichla ustulata

Breeds North America.
   Very similar to Grey-cheeked Thrush but distinguished by buff eye-ring, ear-coverts uniform with rest of head, buff chin and monosyllabic call. *Brit. Birds*, 66: 35.

Two records in the period:
Cork: Cape Clear Island on 14th–16th October 1968
Pembroke: Skokholm on 14th–19th October 1967
   The only previous record was one found dead at Blackrock Lighthouse, Mayo, on 26th May 1956.

Grey-cheeked Thrush

Hylocichla minima

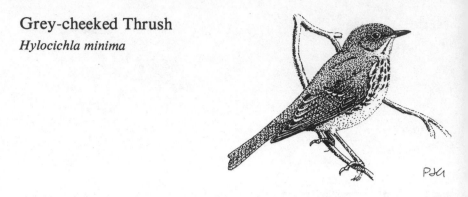

Breeds northern North America and northeastern Siberia.

Like tiny plump Song Thrush *Turdus philomelos*. Distinguished from other small thrushes by greyish ear-coverts, lack of rufous in plumage and absence of distinct eye-ring. *Brit. Birds,* 47: 266; 52: 316; 56: 192.

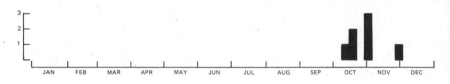

All records have been in late autumn, October–November. The only previous record was on 5th October (Shetland 1953).

All records have been since 1953, seven of the eight being in our period.

202

The records are distinctly more northerly than most Nearctic passerines, with none in Scilly and none in Ireland. Five of the seven were dead or dying when discovered, including two of the three on Bardsey (Caernarvonshire). The 1961 (Caernarvon) bird was referred to *C. m. bicknelli* (southern Quebec, Nova Scotia and northeast United States) and the November 1965 (Moray) bird to *C. m. minima* (central and west Canada and northeast Siberia).

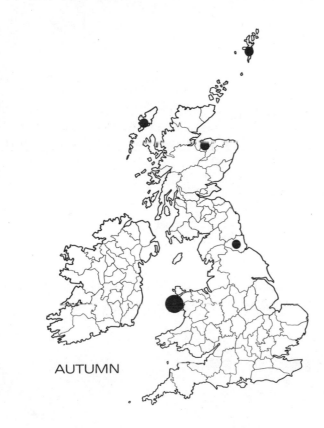

Veery *Hylocichla fuscescens*, see page 210.

Rock Thrush

Monticola saxatilis

PJ4

Breeds from Iberia and northwest Africa, through southern Europe (north to Switzerland) eastwards to Mongolia.

Habits and shape resemble large, plump, short-tailed Wheatear *Oenanthe oenanthe*, but has habit of quivering tail like Redstart *Phoenicurus phoenicurus*; both sexes and all ages have tail chestnut, with brown centre; female largely brownish, barred; male has bright blue head, throat and nape, chestnut breast and belly, blackish-brown wings and rump, and white patch on lower back. *Brit. Birds,* 49: 268; 56: 66; 62: 23; *Scot. Birds,* 6: 336.

All records in our period were in May–June. Those prior to 1958 were in May–June (4) and October–November (2).

The five in our period compare with six prior to 1958.

204

The records were scattered from Devon and Norfolk north to Outer Hebrides (St Kilda) and Shetland. The previous records were similarly scattered—Kent, Hertfordshire and Orkney in spring, and Shetland in autumn. Five of the 11 up to 1972 were in the Northern Isles.

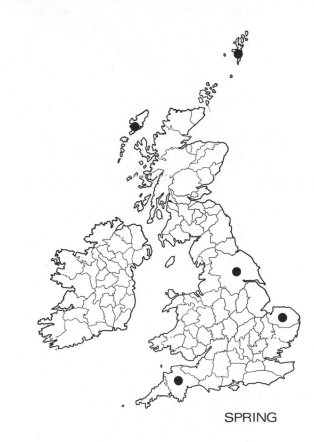

1●

SPRING

Desert Wheatear

Oenanthe deserti

Breeds north Africa from northern Sahara, Arabia and southern Caucasus east to Mongolia.

Slightly smaller and more slender than Wheatear *O. oenanthe* with at least the distal 50–60% of tail wholly black; buffish upper- and underparts; male has black throat like some Black-eared Wheatears. *Brit. Birds*, 50: 77; 51: 275; *Scot. Birds*, 6: 446.

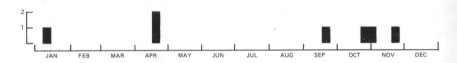

The records were scattered in September–January, and April. Previous records were all in August–December (mostly October–November), except for one in June (Orkney 1906).

The January record (Essex 1958) is omitted from this histogram, on the grounds that it is best regarded as a late 1957 record. The six (seven) in our period compare with 12 (11) prior to 1958.

206

The coastal distribution in eastern Britain is shown by almost all of the 18 records up to 1972. Apart from singles in Cornwall and Clackmannan, all were in eastern coastal counties from Hampshire to Shetland.

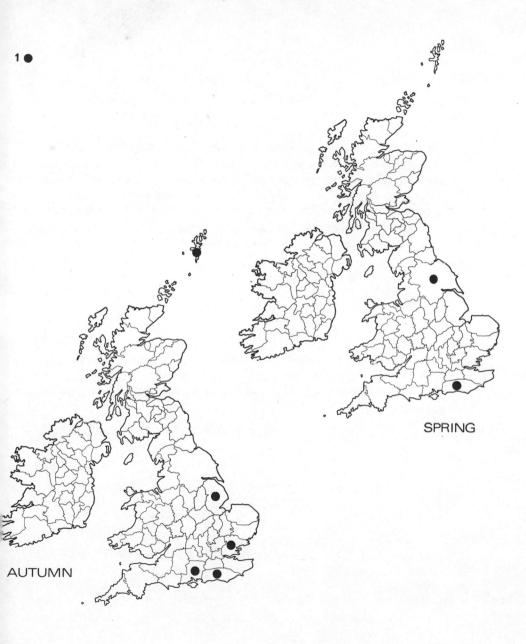

1 ●

SPRING

AUTUMN

Black-eared Wheatear
Oenanthe hispanica

Breeds from Iberia and northwest Africa through southern Europe east to Iran.

Slightly smaller and more slender than Wheatear *O. oenanthe*, and more prone to perch on trees, bushes, thistles, etc. Males have black mask, with throat either white or black; body pale buff; wings and scapulars black; distinguished from Desert Wheatear by white sides to tail, as Wheatear; female closely resembles Pied Wheatear, but lacks pale buff fringes to feathers of back and mantle; distinctive rasping call. *Scot. Birds,* 6: 214.

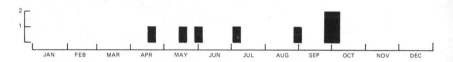

The records were in April–May and late August to early October, with one (Caithness 1969) in early July (regarded as associated with the spring records). Previous records were mostly in April–May (8) and September (4), with others in March, June and November.

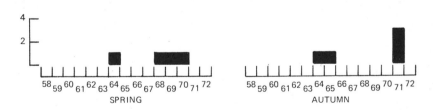

The nine records in our period compare with 15 prior to 1958. The three in 1971 were in Scilly on 24th September and Cornwall on 2nd October and 2nd–5th October.

208

Five of the nine in our period were in the west and this pattern is shown by all
records up to 1972, 13 being in the west (Scilly and Wexford to Outer Hebrides)
and nine in the east (Middlesex to Shetland).

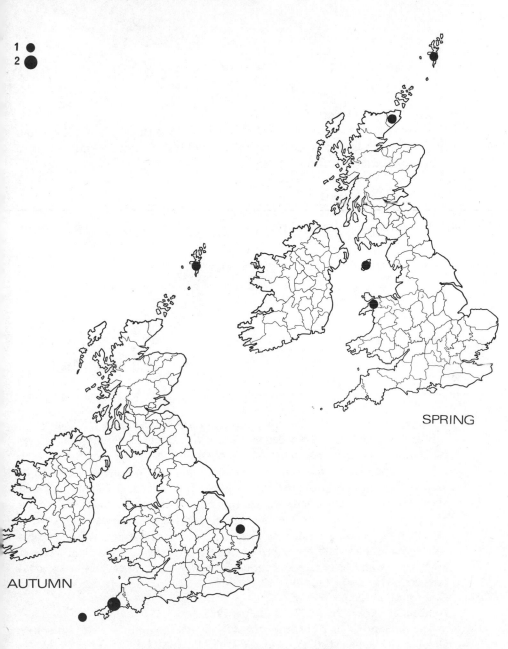

1 ●
2 ●

SPRING

AUTUMN

Veery

Hylocichla fuscescens

Breeds North America.

Resembles Grey-cheeked and Olive-backed Thrushes in size and shape, but has rich warm brown or rusty upperparts and less distinct and less extensive spots on breast. *Brit. Birds,* 65: 45.

One record in the period:
Cornwall: Porthgwarra on 6th October 1970
 This is the only record.

Pied Wheatear

Oenanthe pleschanka

Breeds extreme southeast Europe eastwards through south-central Asia.

Slightly smaller and more slender than Wheatear *O. oenanthe* with similar call and tail-pattern (but more black on outer feathers); like Black-eared Wheatear, perches more often on trees, etc. than does Wheatear; has habit of dropping shrike-like from perch on to prey; male has black back, wings and mask, with rest of underparts whitish (tinged buff except on undertail coverts) and crown and nape whitish; female very closely resembles female Black-eared Wheatear but feathers of back and mantle fringed distally with pale buff in fresh plumage, and dark buff upper breast more clearly demarcated from white of lower breast and belly. Identification of female/young wheatears needs great care. *Brit. Birds,* 48: 130; 49: 317.
One record in the period:
Pembroke: Skokholm on 27th October 1968

The three previous records were also all in late autumn: Dorset (17th–19th October 1954), Fife (19th October 1909) and Orkney (1st November 1916).

210

Isabelline Wheatear

Oenanthe isabellina

Breeds from southeast Russia, southern Greece and the Middle East eastwards to Mongolia.

Larger and longer-legged than Wheatear *O. oenanthe*, with heavy head and bill, stubby tail and upright stance; sexes similar, mainly pale sandy-coloured, lacking dark ear-coverts of Greenland *O. o. leucorrhoa*; whitish underwing. *Brit. Birds,* 67: pl. 12b.

One record in the period:
Scilly: St Mary's on 1st November 1971

The only previous record was one at Allonby, Cumberland, on 11th November 1887. The 1971 record is still under review.

Black Wheatear

Oenanthe leucura

Breeds Iberia, southern France/northwest Italy and northwest Africa.

Larger, and more thrush-like in shape, than any other European wheatear; tail pattern like Wheatear *O. oenanthe* and under tail coverts white; otherwise entirely black, except for tinge of brown in wings; female similar but browner; distinguished from female and immature White-crowned Wheatear *O. leucopyga* by black tips to outer tail feathers. *Brit. Birds,* 48: 132; 53: 553.

One record in the period:
Donegal: Portnoo on 10th June 1964 (*O. leucopyga* was not eliminated).

The four previous records were all in autumn: Cheshire (August 1943), Kent (October 1954) and Shetland (September 1912 and October 1953).

Red-flanked Bluetail *Tarsiger cyanurus*, see page 220.

Thrush Nightingale

Luscinia luscinia

Breeds from Denmark and southern Sweden east to south central Siberia.

Very closely resembles Nightingale *L. megarhynchos*, but has dusky-mottled throat and colder brown upperparts and rump, with less rufous tail. *Brit. Birds*, 51: 198, 356; *Scot. Birds*, 6: 283.

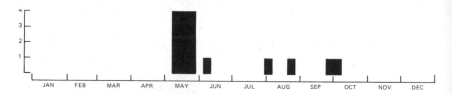

The records were in May–June and late July to early October, with 71% in just three weeks from 7th–27th May.

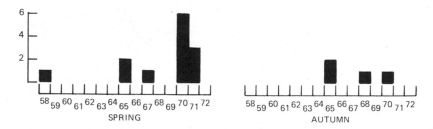

The 17 records in our period compare with just two prior to 1958 (both Shetland in May, 1911 and 1957). The six in spring 1970 were all on Fair Isle (Shetland) and Isle of May (Fife) during 8th–17th May.

212

All have been in the east of Britain, from Sandwich Bay (Kent) to Hillswick (Shetland), with all but one from Yorkshire northwards.

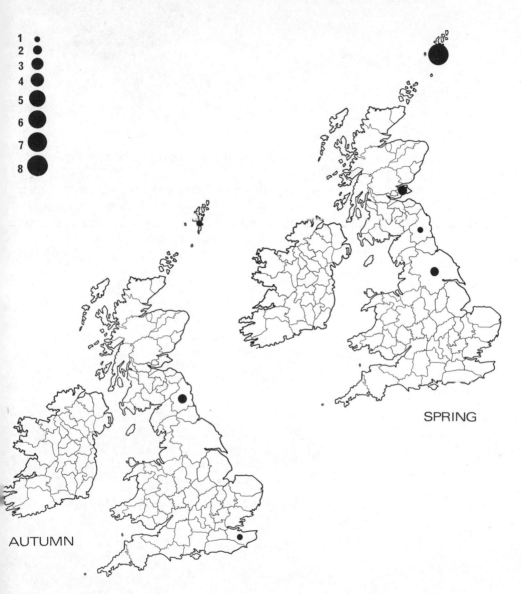

SPRING

AUTUMN

Siberian Rubythroat *Luscinia calliope*, see page 221.

Rufous Bush Robin

Cercotrichas galactotes

Breeds Iberia, north Africa (both north and south of Sahara) and east to Pakistan and eastern Kazakhstan.

Frequently cocks, wags and fans very striking long graduated tail, which is tipped black and white; upperparts rufous (western race) or greyish-brown (eastern races); long pale legs; perches conspicuously and hops rapidly on ground. *Brit. Birds*, 53: 122, 225, 265; 58: 221; 63: 294.

The autumn records in September–October are typical, all previous records being in those months (mostly September), and that in April unique. This last bird (Cork 1968) occurred at a time when there was an unusually early influx in Gibraltar.

The four records in our period compare with six prior to 1958 (1854, two in 1876 and two in 1951).

214

The two on the English east coast are atypical, for all the other eight up to 1972 were in English or Irish south coast counties—Cork (two), Wexford, Devon (3), Sussex and Kent.

1●

SPRING

AUTUMN

Cetti's Warbler
Cettia cetti

Breeds from Iberia and northwest Africa east to Sinkiang-Uigur; recent northwards spread in western part of range.

Very skulking, but has distinctive loud musical song which starts abruptly; dark rufous brown above and pale below, with rounded tail frequently cocked like Wren *Troglodytes troglodytes. Brit. Birds,* 57: 365, 366; *Cape Clear Bird Obs. Rep.,* 10: 41.

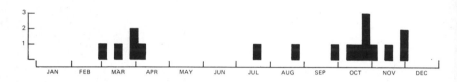

Though many individuals stayed for long periods, only first dates are shown here. It seems clear that movement occurs mainly in March to early April and July–November, especially October.

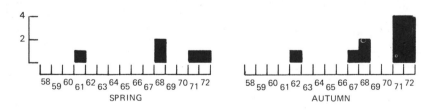

There were no records in Britain and Ireland prior to 1961, but this species has spread northwards through Europe (*Brit. Birds,* 57: 357) and since 1967 there have been increasing numbers and, since 1972, a breeding population has become established in Kent (1972 Kent records are omitted from this histogram). Since the end of our period, the colonisation has consolidated, with summering birds in several counties and breeding confirmed in Devon and Norfolk as well as Kent (*Brit. Birds,* 68: 393).

216

58% were in eastern south coast counties of England, from Hampshire to Kent, with vagrants north to Yorkshire (November 1972) and west to Cork (August 1968).

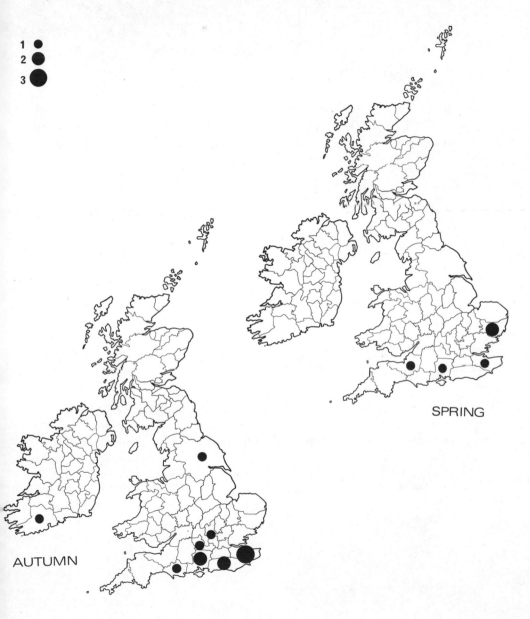

Lanceolated Warbler
Locustella lanceolata

Breeds from eastern-central Russia east to Kamchatka and Japan.

Like a tiny, drab-coloured Grasshopper Warbler *L. naevia* and even more skulking; often creeps on ground like a mouse; gorget of fine streaking on upper breast. *Brit. Birds*, 51: 243; 54: 142; *Scot. Birds*, 8: 34.

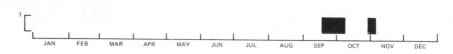

The records were all in autumn, from mid-September to early November. Previous records showed a similar pattern, but there was one in May (Shetland 1953).

The four records in our period compare with nine prior to 1958. The two in 1960 were both on Fair Isle (Shetland), on 30th September–4th October and 1st November. There is a pattern of short bursts of records—three in 1908–10, three in 1925–28, singles in 1938, 1953 and 1957 and then, in our period, three in 1960–61 and (with two in 1973) three in 1972–73. One cannot help but wonder whether periodic high population levels in central Russia are being reflected here. And, also, just how many individuals of this inconspicuous, skulking species go unrecorded in its 'invasion' years.

218

Apart from one in Lincolnshire (1909) and one in Orkney (1910), all records have been on Fair Isle (Shetland).

1
2
3
4

AUTUMN

Brown Thrasher

Toxostoma rufum

Breeds North America.

Size of slim, long-tailed Song Thrush *Turdus philomelos*, with rufous upperparts, two conspicuous pale wing-bars and white underparts with bold brown streaks; long tail is frequently cocked, jerked and flicked. *Brit. Birds,* 61: 550.

One record in the period:
Dorset: Durlston Head on 18th November 1966 to 5th February 1967
   There are no other records.

Red-flanked Bluetail

Tarsiger cyanurus

Breeds from Finland eastwards to Japan.

Adult males unmistakable with blue-grey upperparts—cobalt-blue shoulders, rump and sides to tail—and white underparts with orange flanks; females are olive-brown above, with blue rump and blue-grey tail, with white throat demarcated by olive-grey wash on breast; young males resemble females but have greyer backs. *Brit. Birds,* 54: 73; 66: 3; *Scot. Birds,* 7: 57.

Two records in the period:
Northumberland: Hartley on 16th October 1960
Shetland: Fetlar on 31st May to 1st June 1971
and one since:
Fife: Isle of May on 14th October 1975
   The three previous records were all in late autumn: Kent (October 1956), Lincoln (September 1903) and Shetland (October 1947).

220

Siberian Rubythroat
Luscinia calliope

Breeds in Siberia from the Urals eastwards.

In size and shape resembles long-legged Bluethroat *L. svecica*, with wings drooped and tail cocked in the same way; upperparts brown, more rufous on rump and wings; underparts pale buff with whitish belly, supercilia and moustaches; throat bright red in adult male, white in female and young.

None in the period, but one since:
Shetland: Fair Isle on 9th–11th October 1975

This is the only record; it is still under review for admission to the British and Irish list.

River Warbler
Locustella fluviatilis

Breeds from Poland and the Balkans eastwards to western Siberia.

Differs from Grasshopper Warbler *L. naevia* by dark olive-brown upperparts being unstreaked, and whitish underparts having indistinct grey-brown streaking on throat and upper breast. *Brit. Birds,* 55: 137; 66: 312.

Three records in the period:
Caernarvon: Bardsey on 17th September 1969
Shetland: Fair Isle on 24th–25th September 1961
Fair Isle on 16th September 1969
These are the only records.

Savi's Warbler

Locustella luscinioides

Breeds from Low Countries, France, Iberia and northwest Africa east to Kazakhstan.

Shape of Grasshopper Warbler *L. naevia* with general colouring of Reed Warbler *Acrocephalus scirpaceus*, though less rufous above and less creamy below, with satin-white chin and throat; trilling song is louder, slower, lower pitched and briefer than that of Grasshopper Warbler. *Brit. Birds,* 60: 349.

The records of migrants extend from April to August (with 74% in April–May), apart from one very late bird (31st October 1968, Pembrokeshire). Records from the counties where breeding occurs (Kent and Suffolk) are omitted from this histogram. The mean arrival date at the breeding stations is 19th April, and they are usually last noted in late July or early August.

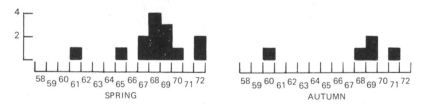

Again excluding the Kent and Suffolk records, there is a clear increase in vagrancy since the mid-1960s. Savi's Warblers bred in the Fens until the middle of the 19th century but between 1856 and the discovery of a breeding population in Kent in 1960 (perhaps present earlier) (*Brit. Birds,* 60: 349–355) there were only three individuals (two on Fair Isle, Shetland, on 14th May 1908 and a singing bird at Wicken Fen, Cambridge, in June–August 1954). More recently, two areas of Suffolk (*Brit. Birds,* 65: 229–232) and perhaps another in Kent have been colonised, though the total British breeding population was only about a dozen pairs even by 1972.

Apart from those in which breeding occurred, no county recorded more than three birds in the 15 years, though the scatter in nine counties in spring points to the possibility of future spread. In autumn, when the birds are silent, vagrant records are naturally very few. Outside the breeding stations, Savi's Warblers remain rare vagrants.

Minimum number of singing males at localities in Kent and Suffolk

	1958	59	60	61	62	63	64	65	66	67	68	69	70	71	72	73	74
Stodmarsh (K)			3	1	2	3	4	12	8	4	3	3	3	5	6	3	2
'North Kent'												2	2				
Minsmere (S)							1				1		1	2	3	6	3
Walberswick (S)											1	2	4	2	4	3	1

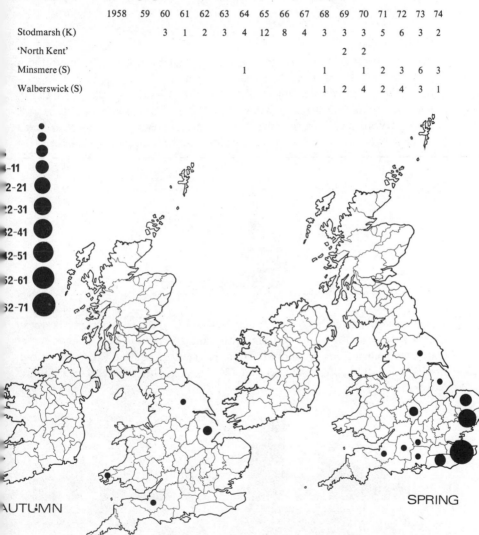

Moustached Warbler *Acrocephalus melanopogon*, see page 226.
Thick-billed Warbler *Acrocephalus aedon*, see page 226.

Great Reed Warbler
Acrocephalus arundinaceus

Breeds northwest Africa and most of Continental Europe, north to southern Sweden and Finland and east to Sinkiang-Uigur.

Europe's largest warbler, bigger than Skylark *Alauda arvensis*; long-tailed, rather rufous, with marked supercilia; strident song from reed-beds may attract attention before bird is seen; very similar to more eastern Clamorous Reed Warbler *A. stentoreus*, which looks marginally paler, longer and slimmer in the field. *Brit. Birds,* 66: 382.

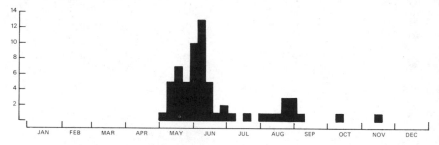

Though records extended from May to November, 71% were in just six weeks from 7th May to 17th June; the small autumn peak was in late August, but at that season silent birds are more likely to be overlooked than the vocal ones in spring. The late records were both at Thurlestone, Devon (October 1969 and November 1972).

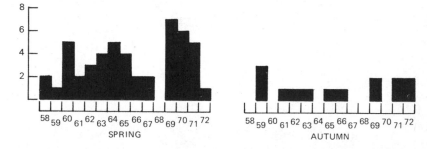

The 63 records in our period compare with only about 23 prior to 1958. Great Reed Warblers occurred at an average of four per year, but spring numbers varied from none (1968) to seven (1969).

224

Though there were records north to Shetland and west to Cork, 43% of those in spring were in the four coastal counties from Suffolk to Sussex, with most in Kent. Males have temporarily taken up territories in large reed-beds on several occasions, but none has yet paired and stayed to breed. Apart from the Lancashire bird (which was on 17th July in 1963 and may be better regarded as a late spring record), autumn occurrences were less widespread than those in spring—all in southern England.

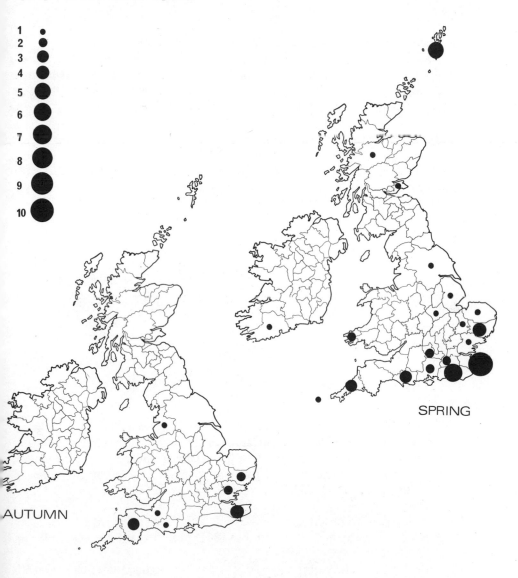

1
2
3
4
5
6
7
8
9
10

SPRING

AUTUMN

Moustached Warbler
Acrocephalus melanopogon

Breeds Mediterranean region, eastern Europe and southwest Asia.

Same size as and resembles Sedge Warbler *A. schoenobaenus*, but crown black, supercilia white and square-ended, underparts whiter and less creamy and upperparts more rufous; tail-cocking is said to be characteristic, but this habit is not invariable. *Brit. Birds,* 45: 219, 412; 47: 15.

One record in the period:
Buckingham: Wendover on 31st July 1965

The three previous records included the extraordinary but thoroughly well-documented case of confirmed breeding at Cambridge in 1946; also two together in Hampshire (August 1951) and one in Kent (April 1952).

Thick-billed Warbler
Acrocephalus aedon

Breeds southern Siberia, Mongolia, Manchuria, northeast China and Japan.

Size of Great Reed Warbler but lacks supercilia and black throat streaks and bill is much shorter and deeper; also has relatively shorter wings and longer, more rounded tail; shape and colour resemble Garden Warbler *Sylvia borin*. *Brit. Birds,* 49: 89; 60: 239.

One record in the period:
Shetland: Whalsay on 23rd September 1971; taken to Lerwick, where died on 25th.

The only previous record was also in late autumn in Shetland: Fair Isle on 6th October 1955.

Blyth's Reed Warbler
Acrocephalus dumetorum

Breeds from Finland eastwards through central and southern Asia.

Similar to Marsh Warbler *A. palustris* and Reed Warbler *A. scirpaceus* but upperparts cold earth-brown (not olive-brown or rufous-brown) in autumn, greyer in spring; has virtually no supercilia, relatively shorter wings and longer tail and a longer, more slender bill. *Brit. Birds,* 63: 214; 66: 385; *Cape Clear Bird Obs. Rep.,* 11: 34.

One record in the period:
Cork: Cape Clear Island on 13th–19th October 1969
and one since:
Yorkshire: Filey Brigg on 30th August 1975

The nine or ten previous records were all between 20th September and 21st October and all but two were in 1912: Norfolk, Northumberland, Shetland (four or five) and Yorkshire; also Shetland 1910 and 1928.

Paddyfield Warbler
Acrocephalus agricola

Breeds from southern Russia eastwards to Mongolia.

Bright and rather rufous, with striking creamy or off-white supercilia, more prominent than in other species of unstreaked *Acrocephali*; tail even longer and wings even shorter than Blyth's Reed Warbler, and bill much shorter and stouter. *Brit. Birds,* 47: 297; 66: 385.

One record in the period:
Durham: Hartlepool on 18th–21st September 1969
and two since:
Northumberland: Low Hauxley on 12th October 1974
Scilly: St. Mary's on 30th September to 15th October 1974

The two previous records were both in autumn on Fair Isle, Shetland: 1st October 1925 and 16th September 1953.

227

Aquatic Warbler
Acrocephalus paludicola

Breeds from Germany eastwards through European Russia; also northern Italy, Hungary.

Resembles sandy-coloured Sedge Warbler *A. schoenobaenus* but back more heavily streaked black, giving greater contrast, and streaking extends on to rump; prominent central crown stripe which together with long buff supercilia give head a very stripy appearance; even more skulking than Sedge Warbler; young Sedge Warblers with crown stripe are a trap for the unwary. *Brit. Birds,* 48: 514.

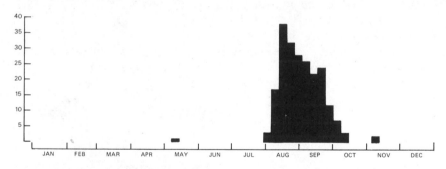

The records were highly concentrated, with 94% in August and September, peaking during 13th–19th August. The two November records were in Devon (1960) and Yorkshire (1967).

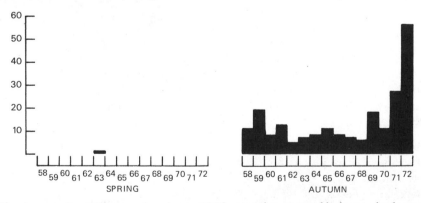

There were about 50 records prior to 1958, a total surpassed in just a single year (1972) of our period; during 1958–72 there were 215. The recent increase, which perhaps started in 1969, has been maintained, with about 48 in 1973.

228

In autumn, 70% were on the English coast, with 46% in Dorset and adjoining counties, but only 9% in Sussex and Kent, and only 6% in the five eastern counties from Yorkshire to Essex. This pattern strongly suggests arrival with a greater southerly than easterly element. The records are discussed in detail in *Scarce Migrant Birds in Britain and Ireland* and *Brit. Birds*, 67: 443.

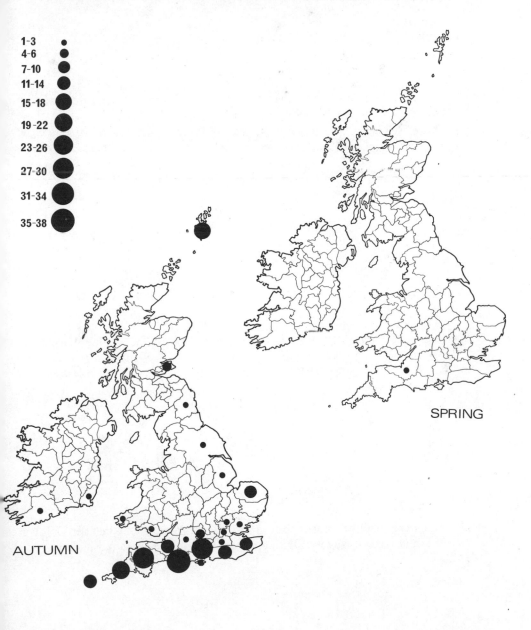

1-3
4-6
7-10
11-14
15-18
19-22
23-26
27-30
31-34
35-38

SPRING

AUTUMN

Olivaceous Warbler
Hippolais pallida

Breeds Iberia, northwest Africa and locally south through north Africa; also Balkans and Egypt east to Pakistan and Kazakhstan.

Like Melodious Warbler *H. polyglotta*, with short wings, but bill much longer and more dagger-like, with yellowish base, and plumage lacks green or yellow; somewhat resembles greyish-brown Reed Warbler *Acrocephalus scirpaceus*, with flat crown and very long bill. *Brit. Birds*, 53: 311; 57: 282; 59: 195, 197.

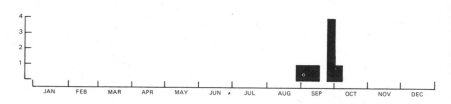

All records were between late August and early October, half of them in the last week of September. The timing is much later than that of Icterine Warbler *H. icterina* (which peaks during 27th August–9th September) or Melodious Warbler (27th August–16th September) (*Scarce Migrant Birds in Britain and Ireland*).

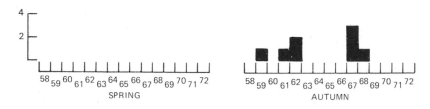

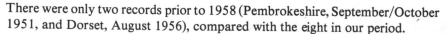

There were only two records prior to 1958 (Pembrokeshire, September/October 1951, and Dorset, August 1956), compared with the eight in our period.

230

Six of the eight in our period (and seven of the ten up to 1972) were in English south coast counties from Scilly to Kent. The Donegal and Fife birds were of the eastern race *H. p. elaeica*, as was the 1956 bird, while that in 1951 was of the southern race *H. p. opaca*.

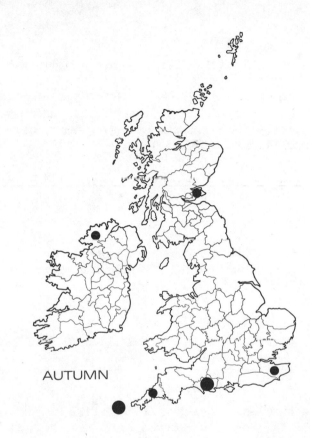

1 ●
2 ●

AUTUMN

Booted Warbler
Hippolais caligata

Breeds from northwestern Russia east to western Mongolia and south to southern Iran.

Small, short-winged *Hippolais* only slightly larger than Chiffchaff *Phylloscopus collybita* with, for *Hippolais*, small weak bill; uniform grey-brown upperparts, indistinct supercilia, thin pale eye-ring and thin pale outer margins to tail. *Brit. Birds,* 53: 123; 57: 282; 65: 170.

Three of the four records (and also the only one prior to 1958) were on Fair Isle between 28th August and 8th September. The other, in late October, was in Scilly, where eastern vagrants typically appear late in the year.

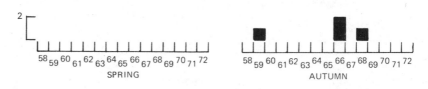

Prior to the four in our period, the only record was on Fair Isle, Shetland on 3rd September 1936. The two in 1966 included the October Scilly bird.

232

The four early autumn birds up to 1972 were all on Fair Isle, Shetland; the fifth was in Scilly in October.

AUTUMN

Orphean Warbler *Sylvia hortensis*, see page 236.
Sardinian Warbler *Sylvia melanocephala*, see page 236.

233

Subalpine Warbler

Sylvia cantillans

Breeds Mediterranean basin.

Small, neat, delicate *Sylvia* warbler, resembling Lesser Whitethroat *S. curruca* but lacks dark ear-coverts; tail often cocked, like Red-breasted Flycatcher *Ficedula parva*, and resemblance enhanced by white undertail coverts; may have pale buff patch, but lacks rufous in wing of Spectacled Warbler; males have blue-grey upperparts and pink underparts with white moustaches. *Brit. Birds,* 55: 90; 60: 123.

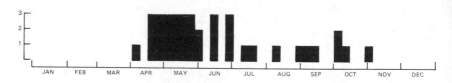

Though 54% occurred in the seven weeks from 16th April to 3rd June, there were records in every month from April to November: an unusual scatter for a Mediterranean species. Spring arrivals have tended to become earlier, there being no April records before 1964: those prior to 1958 were all in May–June (8) or September–October (4).

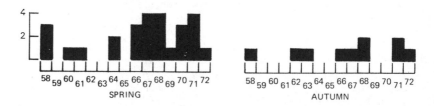

The 37 records in our period compare with only 12 prior to 1958, and in recent years Subalpine Warblers have become annual in spring (though none was reported in 1973). Remarkably, 'pairs' have been recorded on three occasions: ♂ 12th June, ♀ 13th–14th June on Fair Isle in 1958; ♂ 25th–27th June, ♀ 26th June on Fair Isle in 1967; ♂ 22nd April–5th May, probable ♀ 5th May on Whalsay, Shetland in 1968.

234

Though there was a scatter in coastal counties elsewhere, 52% were in the Northern Isles in spring. The possibility that these were as likely to be eastern *S. c. albistriata* as southern *S. c. cantillans* has been suggested (Kenneth Williamson (1974): *Identification for Ringers. 3. The Genus Sylvia*). The distribution of autumn records (60% on the British east coast, not one on the south coast of the English mainland and three of the four western records in October) also tends to point to a south-eastern rather than southern origin at that season.

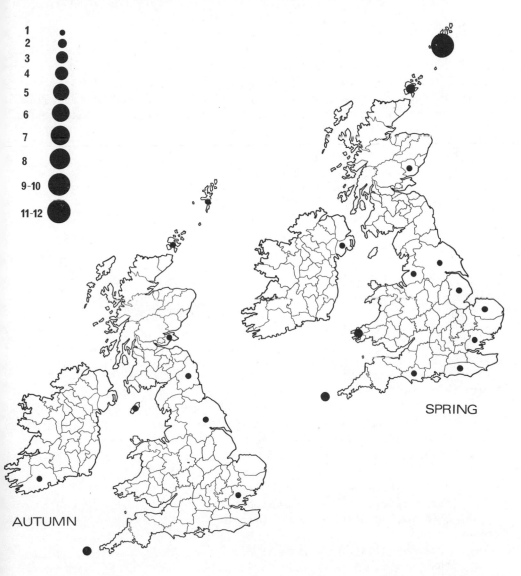

Orphean Warbler

Sylvia hortensis

Breeds from Iberia and northwest Africa eastwards to northwest India.

    Distinguished from other black-capped warblers by large size, dull cap extending below eye and merging with grey mantle, white throat and white in outer tail feathers; may resemble large Lesser Whitethroat *S. curruca*, due to ear-coverts being blacker than crown; usually has pale eyes. *Brit. Birds*, 63: 178; 64: 68.

One record in the period:
Cornwall: Porthgwarra on 22nd October 1967

    The two previous records were in Dorset (20th September 1955) and Yorkshire (6th July 1848).

Sardinian Warbler

Sylvia melanocephala

Breeds Mediterranean basin and eastwards to Afghanistan.

    Resembles plump Whitethroat *S. communis* in shape, but has heavier bill, no rufous in wing and often cocks tail; smaller size not always apparent in field. Male has glossy black cap extending below eye, grey upperparts and conspicuous red eye-ring; female is browner, with cap like upperparts and rufous-brown eye-ring. *Brit. Birds,* 55: 90; 60: 480, 483.

Two records in the period:
Pembroke: Skokholm on 28th October 1968
Shetland: Fair Isle on 26th–27th May 1967
and two since:
Kent: Dungeness on 17th April 1973
Norfolk: Waxham on 28th–29th April 1973

    The only previous record was on Lundy, Devon on 10th May 1955.

Spectacled Warbler

Sylvia conspicillata

Breeds Mediterranean basin.

    Resembles small volatile Whitethroat *S. communis*, but white throat even more distinct from dark head and pinkish breast; sleekness recalls Lesser Whitethroat *S. curruca* or Subalpine Warbler (differs from former by lack of dark ear-coverts and from latter by rufous in wings); legs yellow; pale eye-ring not always a good field-character. *Brit. Birds,* 55: 90.

Two records in the period:
Cornwall: Porthgwarra on 17th October 1969
Yorkshire: Spurn on 21st–31st October 1968
    These are the only records.

Desert Warbler

Sylvia nana

Breeds northwest Sahara and central Asia.

    Small greyish-brown or pale sandy *Sylvia* with pale legs; yellow, black-tipped bill; otherwise very uniform. *Brit. Birds,* 65: 460.

One record in the period:
Dorset: Portland on 16th December 1970 to 2nd January 1971
and two since:
Essex: Frinton-on-Sea on 20th–21st November 1975
Yorkshire: Spurn on 20th–24th October 1975
    These are the only records.

Fan-tailed Warbler *Cisticola juncidis*, see page 270.

Greenish Warbler

Phylloscopus trochiloides

Breeds from northeast Germany and Finland east to Sea of Okhotsk; also Himalayas.

Resembles greyish Chiffchaff *P. collybita* with single narrow wing-bar and long supercilium; legs dark; bill weaker than Arctic Warbler, which is larger, has pale legs, longer bill and, often, two wing-bars. Eastern races of Chiffchaff with faint wing-bars have been mistaken for Greenish Warblers and care is needed. *Brit. Birds*, 48: 499.

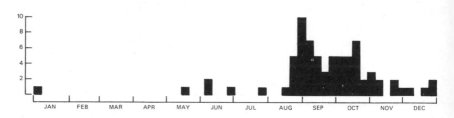

Though a few occurred in spring (May–June) and there was one in July (1962, Isle of Man), the majority occurred in autumn and winter (August–January). There was a suggestion of a double autumn peak—20th August to 16th September and 24th September to 21st October. The winter records (five in December–January) are particularly surprising for a species which usually winters in India.

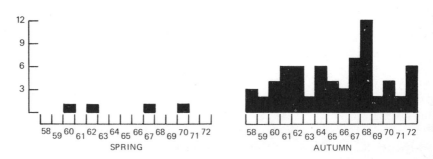

The 73 records in our period compare with only 12 prior to 1958 (which included two in June and one in July). Spring records have not increased as greatly as those in autumn, though there has been a decrease in the latter since the record 12 in 1968.

The spring records, all in the east, presumably derive from overshooting by the north European population. The autumn records were spread through coastal counties north to Shetland and west to Cork. 59% of the east coast birds occurred in the three weeks from 20th August to 9th September, while 58% of those in the west occurred in the five weeks from 1st October to 4th November. The two autumn peaks (see first histogram), therefore, were made up of 81% east coast and 72% west coast birds, respectively. This pattern, suggesting that the western birds in late autumn have a more southerly and easterly origin, is discussed in detail in *Scarce Migrant Birds in Britain and Ireland.*

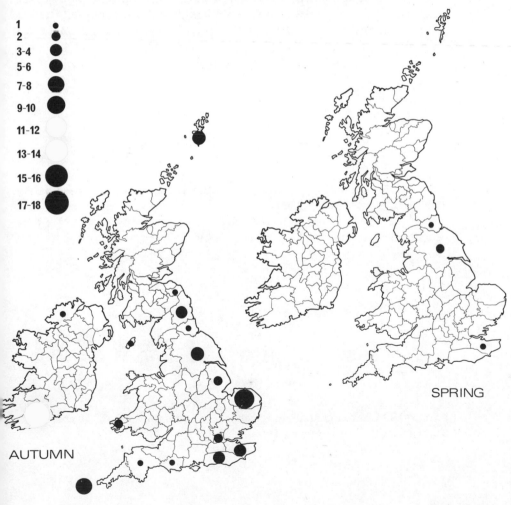

1
2
3-4
5-6
7-8
9-10
11-12
13-14
15-16
17-18

SPRING

AUTUMN

239

Bonelli's Warbler

Phylloscopus bonelli

Breeds central and southern Europe, north to central France and southern Germany, east to Near East; also northwest Africa.

Large-headed, pale *Phylloscopus* warbler, dark eye contrasting with greyish head and nape; bright greenish-yellowish panel in wing, edges to tail feathers and patch at carpal joint; underparts gleaming white; pale rump not always obvious in the field. *Brit. Birds,* 53: 276; 54: 395; 55: 92, 277, 278.

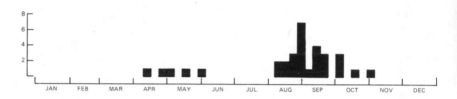

84% were in autumn (August to early November), with a distinct peak during 27th August to 2nd September (which is also the period when the three previous records occurred). There were only five in spring, but two stayed for long periods: male singing 19th May to 9th June 1963 (Cheshire) and 3rd–29th June 1967 (Kent).

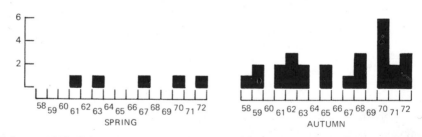

Prior to 1958 there were only three records (all autumn, 1948, 1954 and 1955), compared with 32 in our period.

240

The spring records were mostly in southeast England, suggesting overshooting by west European birds. Autumn records were widespread, north to Shetland, but most were in Cork (all Cape Clear Island) and Caernarvon. One (Yorkshire, 15th October 1970) has been referred to *P. b. orientalis* and others of the late birds (Cork, Northumberland and two Scilly) may also have been of this eastern race, rather than *P. b. bonelli*.

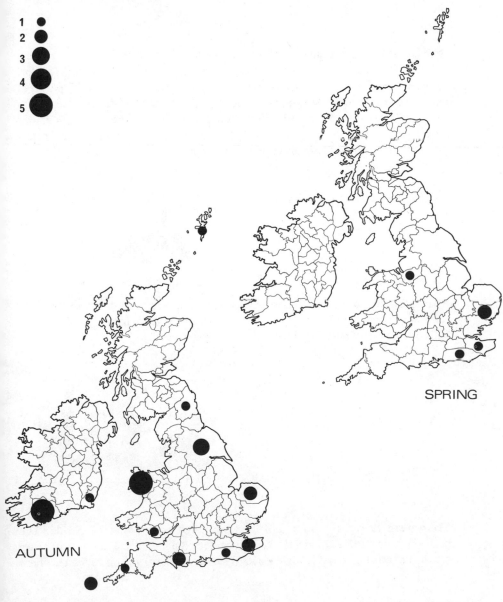

Arctic Warbler
Phylloscopus borealis

Breeds northern Scandinavia east to Alaska.

Largely greenish above and white below; larger than Greenish Warbler, between Bonelli's Warbler and Wood Warbler *P. sibilatrix* in size, with pale legs and one or two narrow wing-bars on each wing; bill long and dagger-like which, together with flat forehead, gives head-shape recalling Reed Warbler *Acrocephalus scirpaceus,* but crown sometimes ruffled to give shaggy crest; supercilia exceedingly long and upcurved at rear. *Brit. Birds,* 46: 330; 48: 132.

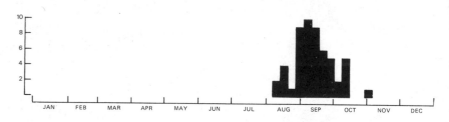

Apart from one on 30th October (Scilly 1971), all occurred in ten weeks from early August to mid-October, with 52% in just three weeks from 27th August to 16th September. There has never been a spring record.

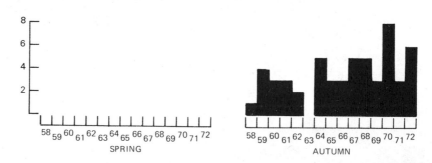

There were 19 records prior to 1958, compared with 54 in our period. The number during 1958–72 merely kept pace with the increase in records of other rare birds (attributed to the increase in observer-activity) and on Fair Isle, where

242

the bird observatory has maintained a steady high recording level throughout our period, there were six in 1958–62, six in 1963–67 and ten in 1968–72. The latter, however, included an exceptional six in 1970, without which the average of about one per year would have been maintained.

Most occurred in Shetland (56%), especially on Fair Isle (41%), with a mere 19% south of Yorkshire. The pattern of records is discussed in more detail in *Scarce Migrant Birds in Britain and Ireland*.

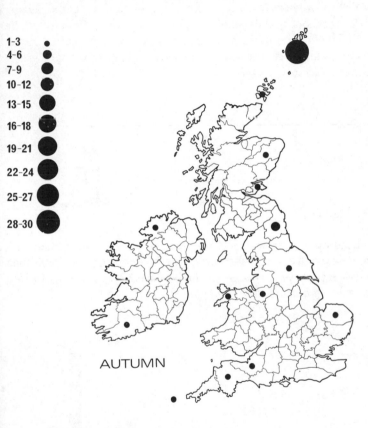

1-3
4-6
7-9
10-12
13-15
16-18
19-21
22-24
25-27
28-30

AUTUMN

Pallas's Warbler

Phylloscopus proregulus

Breeds from southern central Siberia east to Sea of Okhotsk.

Resembles Yellow-browed Warbler *P. inornatus* with prominent supercilia and double wing-bars, but is even smaller and more active, constantly on the move and with habit of hovering like hummingbird when feeding; central crown-stripe and square pale yellow/creamy rump patch; upperparts bright green, recalling Firecrest *Regulus ignicapillus. Brit. Birds,* 57: 508; *Cape Clear Bird Obs. Rep.,* 10: 46.

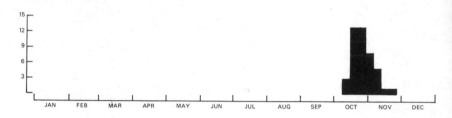

All records (including those prior to 1958) were in October–November, with 77% in the three weeks from 15th October to 4th November (much later than Yellow-browed Warblers, with 58% in the three weeks 24th September to 14th October: *Scarce Migrant Birds in Britain and Ireland*).

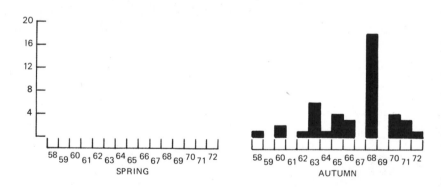

With only three records prior to 1958 (1896, 1951 and 1957), the six in 1963 were regarded as quite extraordinary (*Brit. Birds,* 57: 508–513) but were eclipsed by the influx of 18 in 1968, and another of 13 in 1974. There was a total of 44 during 1958–72.

244

Though there were singles north to Fair Isle (Shetland) and west to Cape Clear Island (Cork), 70% were in the seven counties from Yorkshire to Sussex, with no fewer than nine at Spurn Point (Yorkshire)—a much more southerly distribution than Yellow-browed Warblers, which have a breeding distribution which extends farther north in Siberia (*Brit. Birds,* 62: 89–92).

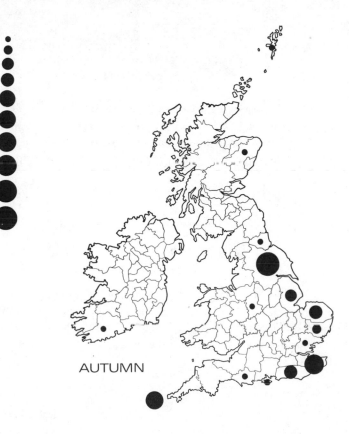

AUTUMN

Dusky Warbler
Phylloscopus fuscatus

Breeds from west-central Siberia eastwards to northeast Siberia.

Apart from ground-feeding and skulking, actions recall Chiffchaff *P. collybita*, but has uniform dark brown upperparts and greyish-white underparts, with fairly long rusty-white supercilia; rather nondescript. *Brit. Birds*, 65: 497.

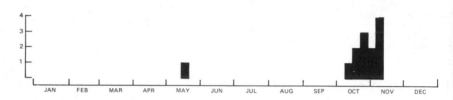

Twelve of the 13 records were in just 28 days, from 14th October to 10th November. The spring bird was ringed on Calf of Man on 14th May 1970 and was found dying in Limerick on about 5th December 1970: the circumstances suggest that it had probably overwintered in western Europe after westwards vagrancy in autumn 1969.

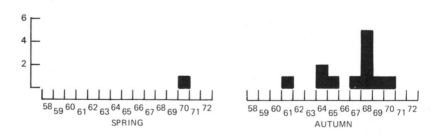

There was only one record prior to 1958 (1st October 1913, Orkney), compared with the 13 in our period. The five in 1968, coinciding with the large influx of Pallas's Warblers, included two at Holkham and two at Holme (both Norfolk), the former on overlapping dates and the latter on successive days (26th October–6th November, 29th October–2nd November; 9th November, 10th November).

246

The distribution is similar to that of Pallas's Warbler, with most on the southern east coast of England, from Yorkshire to Kent, and in Scilly. The four in Norfolk were all in 1968. The spring record in the Isle of Man and the autumn (December) record in Limerick concern the same individual.

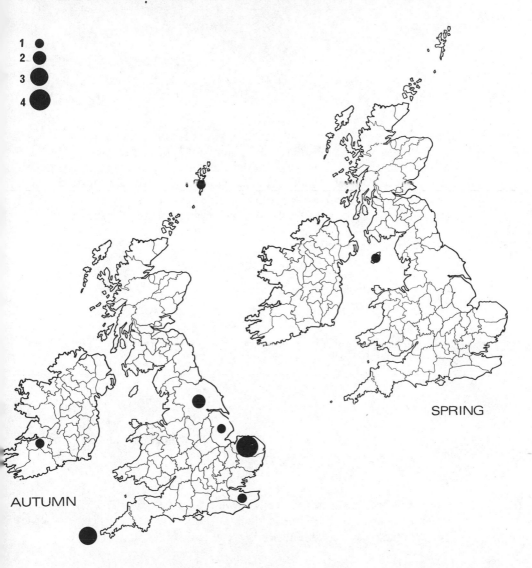

1

2

3

4

SPRING

AUTUMN

Radde's Warbler

Phylloscopus schwarzi

Breeds from south-central Siberia eastwards to Sea of Okhotsk.

Skulking, ground-feeding, dark, heavy *Phylloscopus* with deliberate movements; long creamy supercilia bordered black above and below; underparts yellowish-white or buff; legs long, stout, yellowish; long thick bill with pinkish-orange base to lower mandible; large eyes; frequently calls; distinctive shape and plumage, unlike Dusky Warbler. *Brit. Birds*, 53: 117; 65: 497.

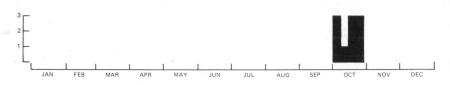

All records were concentrated within a period of 22 days, from 3rd–24th October, slightly earlier than the Dusky Warblers.

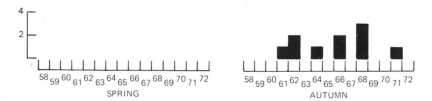

The ten records in our period compare with just one prior to 1958 (1st October 1898, Lincolnshire). The three in 1968 (all 20th–22nd October) coincided with peaks in that year of both Pallas's Warbler and Dusky Warbler.

The distribution of records is the most southerly of all Siberian species here, with 80% south of 53°N.

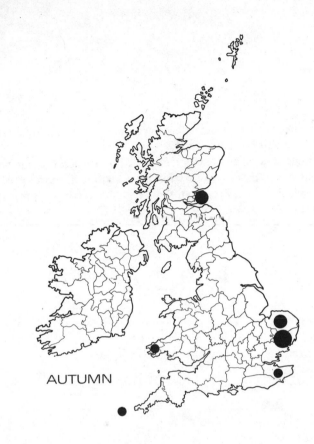

1 ●
2 ●
3 ●

AUTUMN

Collared Flycatcher
Ficedula albicollis

Breeds from eastern France through central and southeastern Europe east to European Russia and northern Iran.

Breeding male resembles Pied Flycatcher *F. hypoleuca* but has broad white collar, whitish rump, more white on forehead and much more white on wings (but less on tail); female greyer than female Pied, usually with traces of collar and rump patch. *Brit. Birds*, 47: 302; 51: 36; 69: 20.

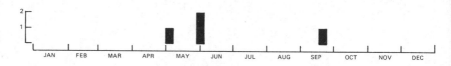

Three of the four in our period and both prior to 1958 were in May to early June. Autumn birds are less distinctive, so might be overlooked more easily among Pied Flycatchers, and only one has been discovered.

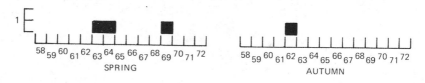

The two prior to 1958 were in 1947 (Shetland) and 1957 (Caernarvonshire). With only four in our 15 years, this very attractive species remains a very rare vagrant here.

There was a wide scatter, with spring records up to 1972 in Norfolk, Caernarvon, Cumberland, Orkney and Shetland, and the only autumn one in Essex.

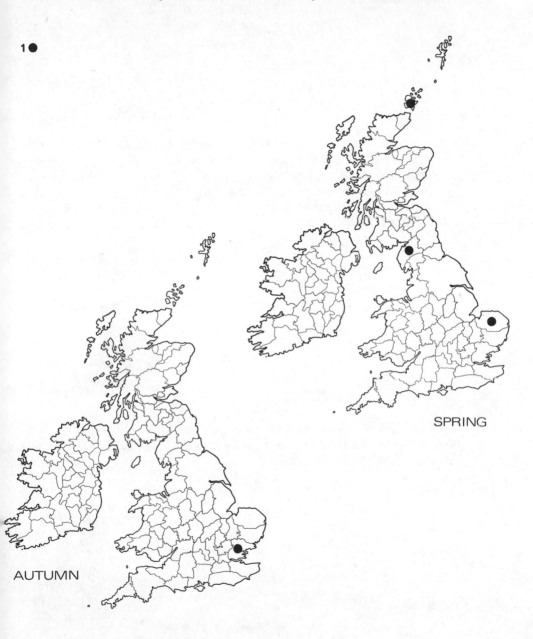

1●

SPRING

AUTUMN

Alpine Accentor *Prunella collaris*, see page 270.

Richard's Pipit
Anthus novaeseelandiae

iw

Breeds from western Siberia east to Manchuria and south to Malaysia, Australia and New Zealand; also Ethiopian region.

Large, heavily-streaked pipit, recalling Skylark *Alauda arvensis* in brownish colour, bulkiness, bold upright stance and habit of hovering prior to landing; long stout legs with large feet; call explosive, rasping 'schreep'. *Brit. Birds,* 56: 285, 292; 65: 287.

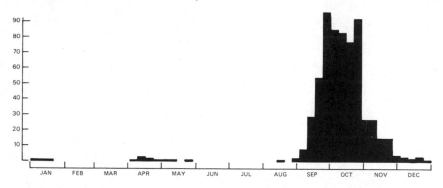

Most records were in August–January, with 75% in just six weeks from 17th September to 28th October, but there were also signs of a spring passage, with ten records (1.5%) in April–May.

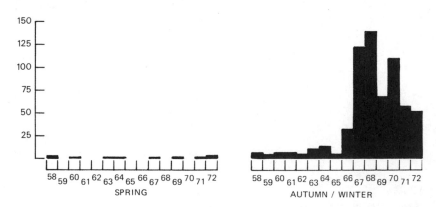

252

There were about 140 records prior to 1958, compared with 647 in our period, but during 1958–65 there was an average of only seven Richard's Pipits per year. The numbers during 1966–72 (an average of 84 per year) thus consitute an extraordinary upsurge in what was formerly a rare vagrant.

Four of the ten April–May records were in Kent, and two more were in the adjoining counties of London and Surrey: presumably these were birds which had wintered in western Europe or Africa. In autumn, the relative lack of records from counties between the main concentrations in Shetland (13%), Yorkshire to Norfolk (31%), Kent and Sussex (4%) and Devon to Scilly and Pembroke (35%) may point to arrival of coasting birds leaving Continental headlands (see fuller discussion in *Scarce Migrant Birds in Britain and Ireland*).

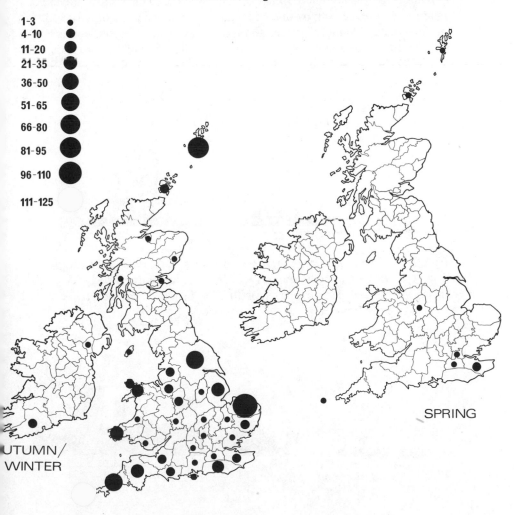

1-3

4-10

11-20

21-35

36-50

51-65

66-80

81-95

96-110

111-125

AUTUMN/
WINTER

SPRING

Tawny Pipit

Anthus campestris

Breeds from northwest Africa, Iberia, southern and eastern France and southern Sweden eastwards to Mongolia.

Wagtail-like pipit; adult has uniform sandy-coloured upperparts and creamy underparts, relieved only by fine streaking on breast and line of dark spots on median coverts; immature greyer and more heavily streaked, but not as brown as Richard's Pipit and distinguished by more delicate build, more horizontal stance, less heavy legs and feet, and soft, less explosive call. *Brit. Birds,* 46: 439; 65: 287.

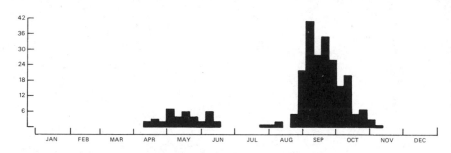

Though 15% were in spring, there was no clear peak, records extending from 12th April to 15th June. Autumn records, from late July to early November, showed a marked peak, however, with 88% in just seven weeks, from 27th August to 14th October.

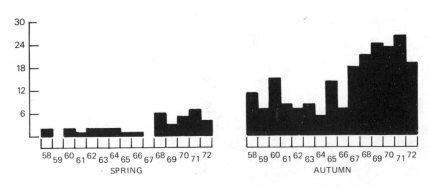

254

Though there is an impression of an increase since about 1968 (spring) or 1967 (autumn), this may merely reflect increasing observer-activity. The 251 records in our period compare with about 110 prior to 1958.

Only two counties (Kent and Norfolk) recorded more than four birds in spring in the 15 years. In autumn, 87% of the records were in coastal counties from Norfolk to Scilly, with 25% in Sussex alone. Most Tawny Pipits clearly reach us by a short crossing of the English Channel. The patterns are discussed at greater length in *Scarce Migrant Birds in Britain and Ireland*.

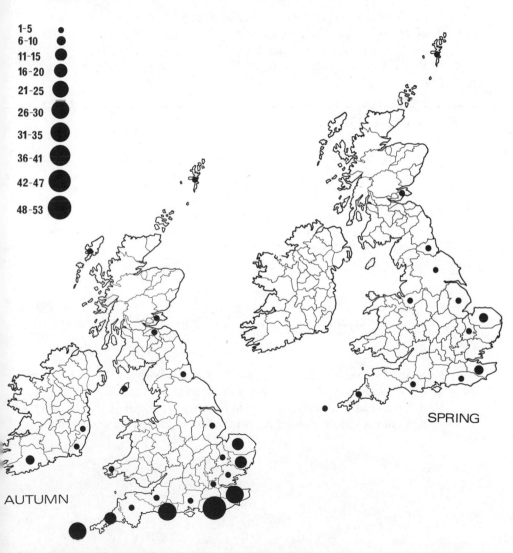

1-5
6-10
11-15
16-20
21-25
26-30
31-35
36-41
42-47
48-53

SPRING

AUTUMN

Olive-backed Pipit *Anthus hodgsoni*, see page 271.

Pechora Pipit
Anthus gustavi

Breeds from northeastern Russia eastwards to northeastern Siberia.

Exceptionally skulking pipit, with pair of white lines on back, forming 'braces'; underparts very white, boldly streaked; call clear, loud 'pwit'. *Brit. Birds,* 46: 210; 47: 299; *Scot. Birds,* 7: 263; *Fair Isle Bird Obs. Bull.,* 4: 70; 5: 234.

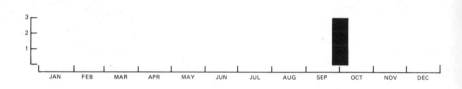

The six records in our period all occurred within a ten-day period, from 26th September to 5th October. Previous records were between late August and mid-November, but mostly late September/early October.

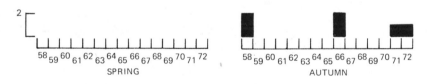

There were 13 records during 1925–57, compared with the six in our period. This is an elusive species, but it has a distinctive call-note, once this is known. More have been suspected (at its main British haunt, Fair Isle, Shetland) than have been seen well enough for documentation as authenticated records.

256

All but two of the 19 records up to 1972 were on Fair Isle, Shetland; the others were at Spurn, Yorkshire (1966) and Whalsay, Shetland (1972).

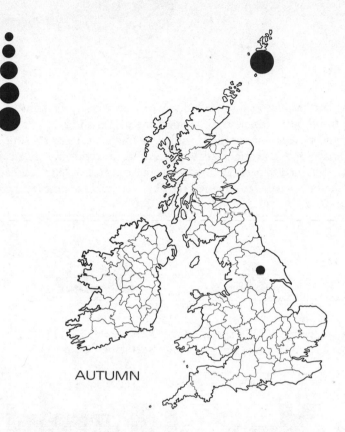

1
2
3
4
5

AUTUMN

Red-throated Pipit

Anthus cervinus

Breeds extreme northern Eurasia, from Norway to northeastern Siberia.

Size as Meadow Pipit *A. pratensis,* but upperparts darker and greyer, with no greenish tinge, and more heavily streaked with black (including rump and upper-tail coverts); underparts also more heavily streaked; in summer, throat and usually breast, lores and supercilia, brick-red; calls explosive 'chup', hoarse 'psss' or 'tzeez', latter vaguely resembling Tree Pipit *A. trivialis* but more hissing, and soft 'teu'. *Brit. Birds,* 46: 210; 47: 443; 62: 110.

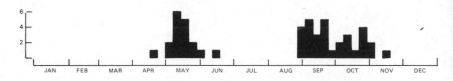

The records were divided 37% in spring (April–June, mainly May) and 63% in autumn (late August to mid-November, mainly September–October).

The 49 records in our period compare with about 29 prior to 1958. During 1958–72 the average of about one per year in spring and two per year in autumn has remained fairly steady which, with the increase in observer-activity in this time, suggests a recent—though perhaps only temporary—decrease.

258

More were recorded in Shetland than any other county in both spring and autumn. The majority were on the British east coast (Norfolk to Shetland) in spring, but in autumn there were approximately equal numbers there and in the south and west (Kent to Scilly and Wexford).

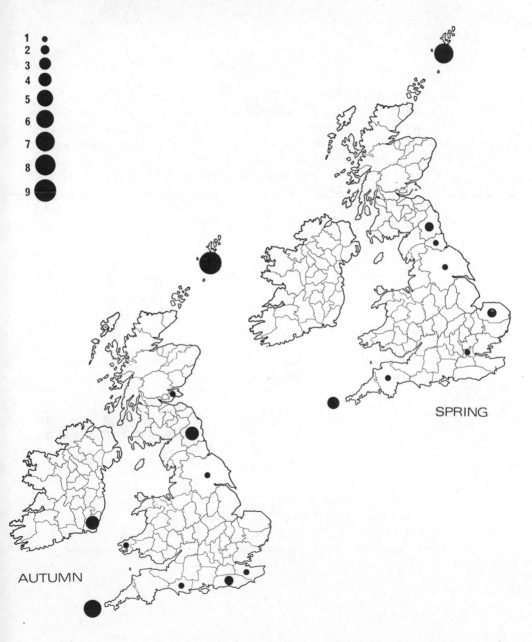

1
2
3
4
5
6
7
8
9

SPRING

AUTUMN

259

Citrine Wagtail
Motacilla citreola

Breeds from eastern Russia eastwards to Amurland and south to Iran.

Combines characters of Yellow and White Wagtails *M. flava flavissima* and *M. alba alba*; immatures have uniform soft grey upperparts, short white-edged black tail, white supercilia, double white wing-bars, prominent white edges to tertials and white underparts; no olive and often no yellow in plumage; summer male has bright yellow head and underparts and black half-collar on nape; female and winter male have reduced yellow; call louder and shriller than that of Yellow Wagtail, intermediate between calls of Yellow and Grey Wagtail *M. cinerea. Brit. Birds,* 48: 358; 54: 125; 56: 30; 58: 344.

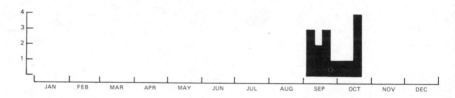

All arrival dates have been within a seven-week period from 3rd September to 17th October, but the latest bird (Suffolk 1964) stayed until 14th November.

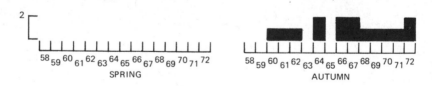

This species was not recorded here until 1954, when two occurred (Fair Isle, 20th–24th September and 1st–5th October), the only ones prior to 1958. This compares with the total of 15 in our period. With records in 1973 and 1974, Citrine Wagtails have now been recorded annually for nine consecutive years.

260

Ten of the 17 records up to 1972 were on Fair Isle (Shetland) but, though the first six were on Fair Isle, the latest 11 have included seven away from there, all in eastern Britain apart from two (together on 15th October 1966) in Hampshire.

AUTUMN

Lesser Grey Shrike

Lanius minor

Breeds from France and Germany eastwards to Zaisan Nor and Afghanistan.

Resembles Great Grey Shrike *L. excubitor* but has black forehead and very little white on scapulars; relatively shorter tail, longer wings, shorter and stubbier bill, and more upright, less thrush-like stance. *Brit. Birds,* 53: 397 (compare 50: 250); *Cape Clear Bird Obs. Rep.,* 9: 77.

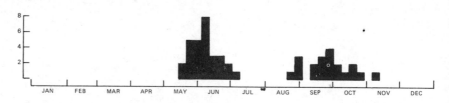

60% occurred in spring (mid-May to early July, peaking during 4th–10th June) and 40% in autumn (late August to early November, mostly September).

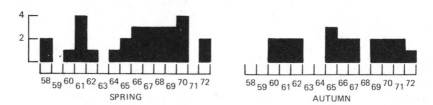

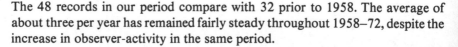

The 48 records in our period compare with 32 prior to 1958. The average of about three per year has remained fairly steady throughout 1958–72, despite the increase in observer-activity in the same period.

At both seasons, most occurred in Shetland and on the British east coast, and very few on the English south coast (14% in spring and 11% in autumn), with none in well-watched Scilly, and just one ever in Ireland (1962). This suggests that most derive from eastern Europe rather than the closest parts of the breeding range.

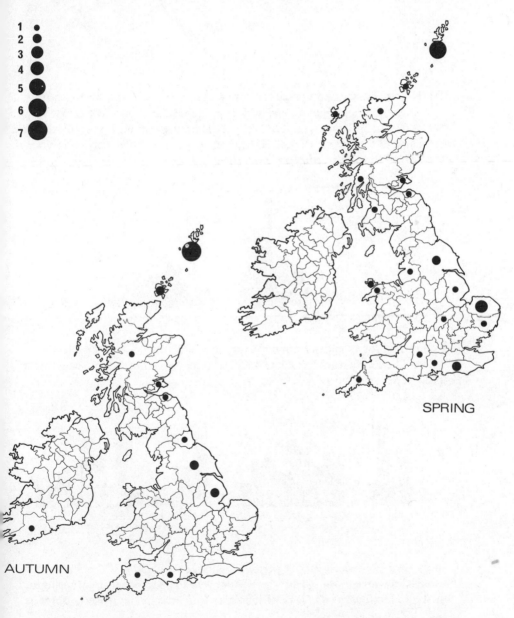

263

Woodchat Shrike
Lanius senator

Breeds from France and northwest Africa east to Ukraine and southern Iran.

Strikingly-patterned black and white, with chestnut crown and nape; white underparts conspicuous at long range; immatures show traces of adults' scapular and rump patches and are greyer, paler and more scaly than young Red-backed Shrikes *L. collurio. Brit. Birds,* 58: 461.

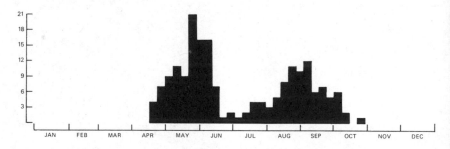

Though records extended from mid-April to late October, there were clear peaks in late May/early June and late August/early September. 55% occurred in spring (up to 8th July).

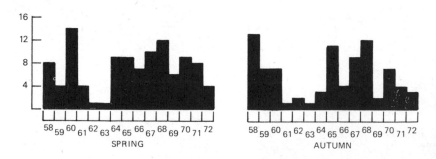

There were 192 records in our period, compared with about 101 prior to 1958. Though the numbers varied strikingly from year to year (one to 14 in spring and one to 13 in autumn), the lack of increases to match the increase in observer-

264

activity (five-year totals of 61, 64 and 67) suggests a steady or recent decrease, though not so severe as was suggested by the slump between autumn 1961 and autumn 1963. The peak numbers early in our period (spring 1960 and autumn 1958) have not been exceeded recently, despite the greater number of observers now.

In spring, there were more on the British east coast (44%) than in the west (40%), whereas in autumn the majority were in the west (70%) and very few (19%) on the east coast. The patterns are discussed at length in *Scarce Migrant Birds in Britain and Ireland*.

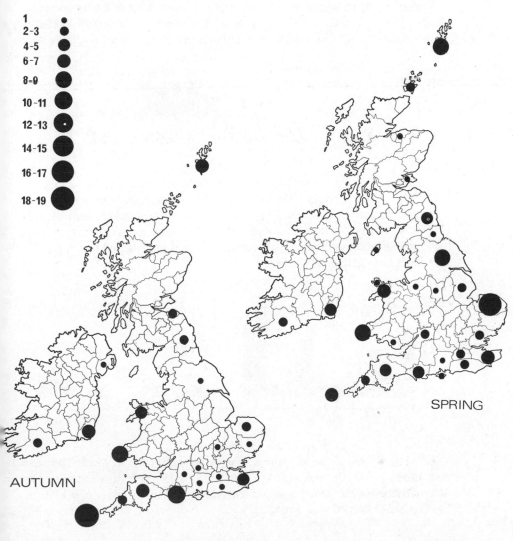

1
2-3
4-5
6-7
8-9
10-11
12-13
14-15
16-17
18-19

SPRING

AUTUMN

265

Rose-coloured Starling

Sturnus roseus

Breeds from Hungary and Balkans east to Kazakhstan and southern Iran.

Similar in shape to Starling *S. vulgaris* but adult conspicuously patterned glossy black and pink, with shaggy crest; immature sandy-brown like some young Starlings, but with yellowish bill and darker wings. *Scot. Birds,* 7: 97.

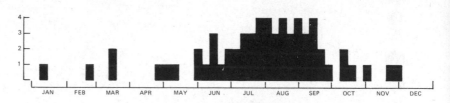

This species is a famous nomadic wanderer. Though birds in Britain and Ireland have in the past frequently been suspected of being escapes from captivity, the marked concentration of records (79%) in June–September accords with genuine vagrancy. (It should be noted that all records are included here, even those which, because of the bird's tameness, worn plumage or urban habitat, had doubt cast on them at the time.)

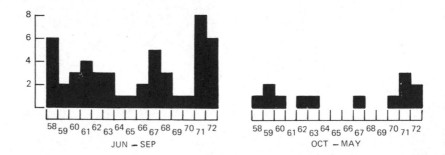

The 62 records in our period compare with over 160 prior to 1958. The years with June–September peaks (1958, 1967, 1971 and 1972) also accounted for 54% of those in October–May and it seems clear that the majority of British and Irish records relate to wild birds.

266

Though records in June–September were scattered throughout Britain and Ireland, almost half were in Scotland, with most in Shetland. During the rest of the year, the pattern was quite different, with 11 out of 13 in England south of a line from the Wash to Severn.

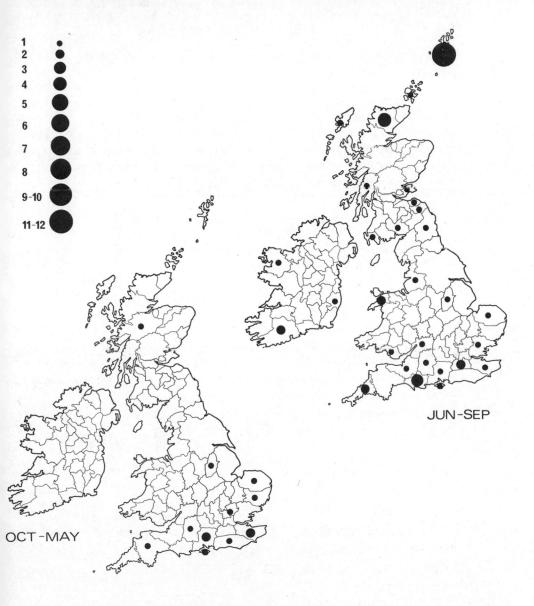

Red-eyed Vireo
Vireo olivaceus

PJG

Breeds North America.

About size of House Sparrow *Passer domesticus* with shape and actions of a short, square-tailed *Acrocephalus* warbler; crown blue-grey, striking white supercilia and black eye-stripe, green upperparts, silky-white underparts, thick blue legs and stout bill. *Brit. Birds,* 56: 462; 61: 176; 65: 400.

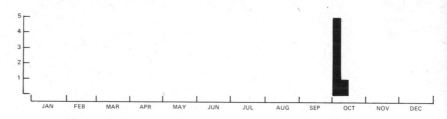

All records have fallen within an 11-day period, 4th–14th October (apart from one on 14th, all occurred within three days, 4th–6th October). Two (St Agnes, Scilly in 1962) were present from 4th–10th, one staying until 17th, but the others were seen on only one or two dates.

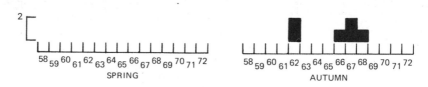

The only record prior to 1958 was one found dead on Tuskar Rock (Wexford) on 4th October 1951.

The pattern is typical of American passerines, with most in Scilly, southern Ireland and Wales (see pp. 310–311).

1
2
3
4

AUTUMN

Fan-tailed Warbler
Cisticola juncidis

Breeds in Mediterranean basin, Atlantic (and recently Channel) coasts of France, central and southern Africa, and southern Asia to Australia.

Resembles a tiny streaked *Acrocephalus*, with short, rounded, black-and-white tipped tail, which is often cocked, and short rounded wings; back and crown bright buff with dark streaks; rump tinged rufous; needs to be carefully distinguished from other species of grass-warbler. *Brit. Birds,* 65: 501; 68: 45.

One record in the period:
Cork: Cape Clear Island on 23rd April 1962
   This is the only record.

Alpine Accentor
Prunella collaris

Breeds mountains from Iberia and northwest Africa eastwards to Japan.

Larger than Dunnock *P. modularis* but longer-legged stance, more flighty, has lark-like flight and lark-like call-notes; soft-grey breast and flame-orange flank spots; greater coverts dark, forming dark bar between double wing-bars. *Brit. Birds,* 48: 267, 373.

One record in the period:
Shetland: Fair Isle on 27th–28th June 1959
   Formerly much more regular, with about 30 previous records, mostly in August–January (a few March–June), nearly all in southern England.

Olive-backed Pipit
Anthus hodgsoni

IW

Breeds northeast Russia to Japan.

Similar in size, shape and stance to Meadow Pipit *A. pratensis* but more contrasting plumage: underparts very white, with bold black spots on breast like Song Thrush *Turdus philomelos*, combining into dark smudge at sides of neck; upperparts greenish-olive, lightly streaked; striking supercilia, orange-buff in front of eye and white behind. *Brit. Birds,* 60: 161.

Three records in the period:
Dorset: Portland on 2nd–10th May 1970
Shetland: Fair Isle on 17th–19th October 1964
           Fair Isle on 29th September 1965
and three since:
Norfolk: Holkham on 10th October 1975
Shetland: Fair Isle on 24th September 1973
           Fair Isle on 24th–26th November 1974
These are the only records.

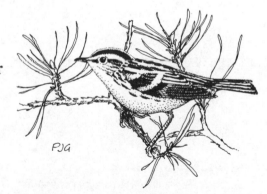

Black-and-White Warbler
Mniotilta varia

PJG

Breeds North America.

About size of Lesser Whitethroat *Sylvia curruca* with stripy black and white plumage; distinguished from Blackpoll Warbler by white stripe through crown and habit of searching bark of trunks and branches of trees for food by creeping like a treecreeper *Certhia sp.* or nuthatch *Sitta sp.*; female lacks male's black throat-patch and cheeks and has brownish flanks; immature also has browner black areas and the white areas tinged buff. *Brit. Birds,* 53: 97.

None in the period, but one since:

Scilly: St Mary's on 27th–30th September 1975

The only previous record was one found dead at Scalloway, Shetland in mid-October 1936.

271

Tennessee Warbler
Vermivora peregrina

RJG

Breeds North America.

Size similar to Willow Warbler *Phylloscopus trochilus*; in spring and summer, head grey with white supercilia, olive-green back and white underparts (female has less grey head and yellow tinge on underparts); in autumn, unstreaked dingy yellow underparts except for white under tail coverts, yellowish supercilia, and pale wing bar.

None in the period, but two since:
Shetland: Fair Isle on 6th–18th September 1975
            Fair Isle on 24th September 1975
    These are the only records; they are still under review for admission to the British and Irish list.

Parula Warbler
Parula americana

RJG

Breeds North America.

Size of Chiffchaff *Phylloscopus collybita* but more robust with heavier bill and more forked tail; upperparts bluish-grey; underparts yellow down to upper breast and then white (male has rufous breast band); two very prominent broad white wing-bars; white crescentic marks above and below eye. *Brit. Birds,* 63: 149.

Three records in the period:
Cornwall: St Ives on 26th November 1967
Dorset: Portland Bill on 9th October 1968
Scilly: Tresco on 16th–17th October 1966
    These are the only records.

272

Yellow Warbler
Dendroica petechia

Breeds North, Central and South America.
  Head and underparts primrose-yellow (with rusty streaks on breast of male); upperparts greenish, wing and tail feathers edged pale yellow; prominent black eye. *Brit. Birds,* 58: 457.

One record in the period:
Caernarvon: Bardsey on 29th August 1964
  This is the only record.

Myrtle Warbler
Dendroica coronata

Breeds northern North America.
  Bright yellow rump patch and (in all but juvenile plumage) yellow patches on crown and flanks; black tail with white patches near tips of outer feathers; incomplete orbital ring round large dark eye; two pale wing-bars; breeding male has black breast and cheeks, blue-grey upperparts streaked with black; frequently utters loud call-note, 'chick'. *Brit. Birds,* 48: 204, 216; 54: 250.

Two records in the period:
Devon: Lundy on 5th–14th November 1960
Scilly: St Mary's on 22nd–27th October 1968
and one since:
Scilly: Tresco on 16th–23rd October 1973
  The only previous record was one at Newton St. Cyres, Devon on 4th January to 10th February 1955.

273

Blackpoll Warbler

Dendroica striata

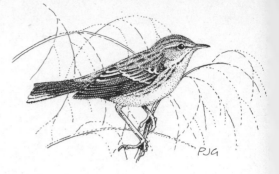

Breeds North America.

Larger and heavier than Willow Warbler *Phylloscopus trochilus*. Breeding male grey, striped with black, with white cheeks and underparts and black cap; in other plumages: olive-green upperparts, yellowish underparts (including throat), both faintly streaked; white under tail coverts; two white wing-bars; pale yellow legs. *Brit. Birds,* 63: 153.

Three records in the period:
Caernarvon: Bardsey on 22nd–23rd October 1968
Scilly: St Agnes on 12th–25th October 1968
       St Agnes on 20th–26th October 1970
and one since:
Scilly: St Agnes on 19th October to 1st November 1975
    These are the only records.

Ovenbird

Seiurus aurocapillus

Breeds North America.

Appearance of small thrush with striped rather than spotted underparts; olive-green or greenish-brown upperparts; white underparts with striking black spots, forming streaks on upper breast; prominent creamy-white eye-ring; dark coronal stripes with centre of crown pale orange; stance, with cocked tail and drooped wings, may resemble Nightingale *Luscinia megarhynchos*; plumage recalls giant Goldcrest *Regulus regulus*. *Brit. Birds*, 68: 453.

The only record in the period was of a wing found on the tide-line at Formby, Lancashire on 4th January 1969; the bird may never have reached Britain alive (perhaps dying at sea or on board a ship).

One record since:
Shetland: Out Skerries on 7th–8th October 1973
    These are the only records.

274

Northern Waterthrush

Seiurus noveboracensis

Breeds North America.

Shape like small Song Thrush *Turdus philomelos* but otherwise resembles a plump pipit, feeding on the ground and bobbing. Olive-brown above and wholly yellowish below, with clear-cut brown streaks and spots, throat usually yellowish or off-white; supercilia buffy yellow. *Brit. Birds*, 53: 513; 65. 484, 69: 27.

Two records in the period:

Scilly: St Agnes on 30th September to 12th October 1958

Tresco on 3rd–7th October 1968

These are the only records.

Hooded Warbler

Wilsonia citrina

Breeds North America.

Olive-green above and yellow below, with no streaks or wing-bars, but inner webs of outer three tail feathers white for two-thirds of their length from near the tip, forming distinctive patches when tail fanned; breeding male has black head with yellow mask. *Brit. Birds,* 65: 203.

One record in the period:

Scilly: St Agnes on 20th–23rd September 1970

This is the only record.

American Redstart *Setophaga ruticilla*, see page 278.

Bobolink *Dolichonyx oryzivorus*, see page 278.

Baltimore Oriole

Icterus galbula

Breeds North America.

About size of Starling *Sturnus vulgaris* with similar pointed bill; male has black head, upper back and throat contrasting with brilliant orange underparts, lower back, rump, sides to black tail and primary coverts; conspicuous white wing-bars and edges to secondaries; female duller, mainly olive above and orange-yellow below, with double white wing-bars. *Brit. Birds,* 56: 52, 464.

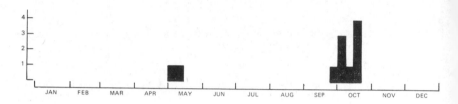

The records were concentrated into six days in spring (6th and 11th May) and 20 days in autumn (29th September to 18th October).

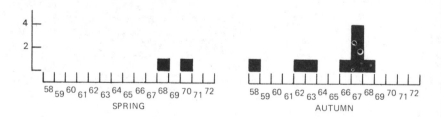

One in Shetland on 26th September 1890 is not generally regarded as having been a wild bird (though the date is a very likely one for a transatlantic vagrant), and the 11 in our period are the only accepted British and Irish records. The four in 1967 were during 5th–18th October, in Scilly, Pembroke and Devon (two on Lundy).

The patterns of both spring and autumn records suggest transatlantic vagrancy immediately prior to discovery, with all but one record (Sussex 1962) in western Britain. The relative paucity of observers probably explains the lack of Irish records.

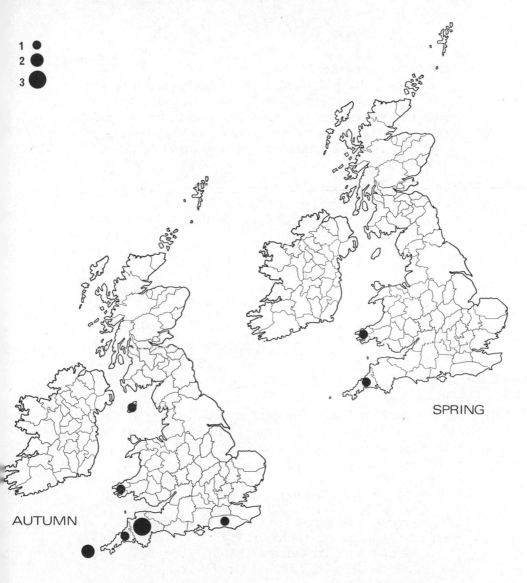

American Redstart

Setophaga ruticilla

Breeds North America.

Floating, butterfly-like flight; large tail usually fanned; black or grey-brown with a large primrose-yellow flash on each side; head smoky grey; upperparts greenish-olive; wide yellow wing-bar; off-white underparts (under tail coverts pure white) with yellow or orange patch on each side of breast; adult male has black upperparts and orange wing-bars, breast- and tail-patches. *Brit. Birds,* 63: 151; 66: 36.

Two records in the period:
Cork: Cape Clear Island on 13th–14th October 1968
Cornwall: Porthgwarra on 21st October 1967
These are the only records.

Bobolink

Dolichonyx oryzivorus

Breeds North America.

Recalls Reed Bunting *Emberiza schoeniclus* but generally yellowish with striped head pattern (yellow crown stripe and yellow supercilia, bordered by black coronal stripes and line behind eye), pointed tail and large conical pointed bill; breeding males have black head and underparts, yellow nape and white rump and shoulder patches; flight may recall Kingfisher *Alcedo atthis*. *Brit. Birds,* 58: 208; *Irish Bird Report,* 19: 53.

Three records in the period:
Scilly: St Agnes on 19th September 1962
        St Mary's on 10th October 1968
Wexford: Hook Head on 12th–14th October 1971
and two since:
Scilly: St Mary's on 9th October 1975
Shetland: Out Skerries on 18th September 1975
These are the only accepted records.

Evening Grosbeak
Hesperiphona vespertina

Breeds North America.

Size and shape of Hawfinch *Coccothraustes coccothraustes*, with heavy whitish or lime-green bill and predominantly yellowish plumage (duller in female) with black tail, primaries and wing coverts, and white secondaries and tertials. *Brit. Birds*, 64: 189.

One record in the period:
Outer Hebrides: St Kilda on 26th March 1969
    This is the only record.

Trumpeter Finch
Rhodopechys githaginea

Breeds North Africa (and recently southern Spain) eastwards through Iran to India.

Size of Linnet *Acanthis cannabina* but large heavy pink bill (with rounded tip), big head, plump body, upright stance on ground and short wings and tail; pale sandy-brown except for darker wings and tail; rump, wings and underparts often tinged pink, especially in breeding male. *Brit. Birds*, in prep.

Two records in the period:
Suffolk: Minsmere on 30th May to 15th June 1971
Sutherland: Handa Island on 8th–9th June 1971
    These are the only records.

Arctic Redpoll
Acanthis hornemanni

Breeds circumpolar Arctic.

Very similar to Redpoll *A. flammea* and some authorities consider them to be conspecific; distinguished by clear white rump; pale head; grey back; purer, less streaked underparts; two white wing-bars. *Brit. Birds,* 54: 238; *Scot. Birds,* 7: 97.

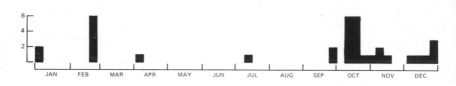

With arrival in late September to October, some remain to over-winter here (November–February).

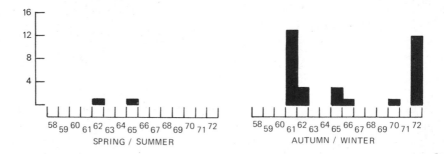

Treating January–February records as referring to the previous year, there were only two marked influxes in our period, in 1961 and 1972. The 35 records in our period compare with over 30 prior to 1958, but numbers are difficult to determine because of the identification problem.

280

With autumn and winter records strictly confined to the British east coast, from Shetland to Kent, it is clear that most originated from northern Eurasia rather than Greenland or Canada. Past specimens which have been racially assigned related to *A. h. hornemanni* (Ellesmere and Baffin Islands and Greenland) and *A. h. exilipes* (rest of species' range) in approximately equal numbers. Most records prior to 1958 were on Fair Isle, Shetland, mainly from mid-September to mid-November.

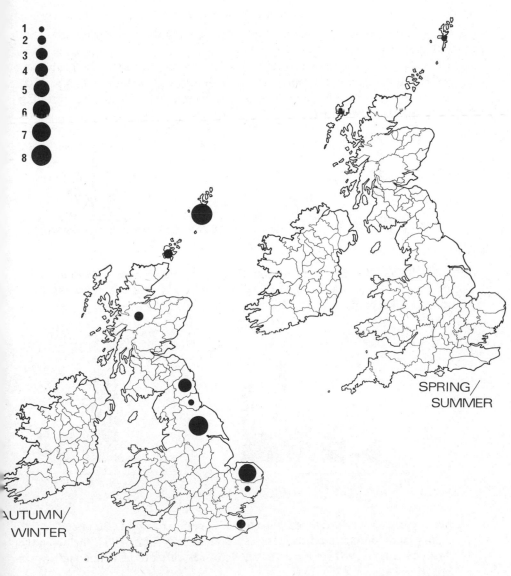

Serin

Serinus serinus

Breeds from southern Sweden, France, Iberia and northwest Africa eastwards to Ukraine and Near East.

Smaller and more compact than Siskin *Carduelis spinus,* with stubbier bill, no yellow tail-flashes, but a yellow rump; male has yellow forehead, supercilia, throat and breast, with brown flank stripes; female duller; distinctive twittering flight call. *Brit. Birds,* 64: 213.

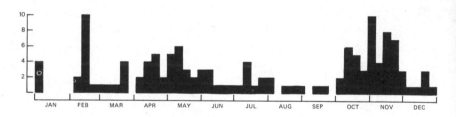

Though recorded almost throughout the year, there are clear indications of increases in April–May and October–November, which were also the peak months for records prior to 1958 (see *Brit. Birds,* 64: 213–223).

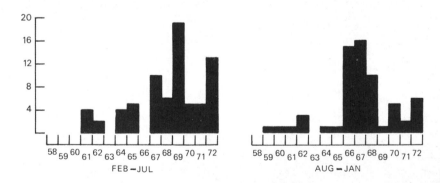

There were about 70 records prior to 1958, compared with 136 in our period. Spring and summer records increased dramatically from 1967, including the first breeding in 1967 (Dorset) and 1969 (Sussex), after large autumn influxes in

282

1966–68. It was confidently anticipated that Serins would colonise Britain as part of their northwards (and eastwards) spread through Europe during the past 200 years but, despite increased breeding season fieldwork by observers taking part in the BTO/IWC Atlas Project during 1968–72, the published records suggest instead a decline since the summer of 1969.

Records have almost all been in English east and south coast counties from Northumberland to Scilly, with the majority on the south coast (70% in spring/summer and 89% in autumn/winter).

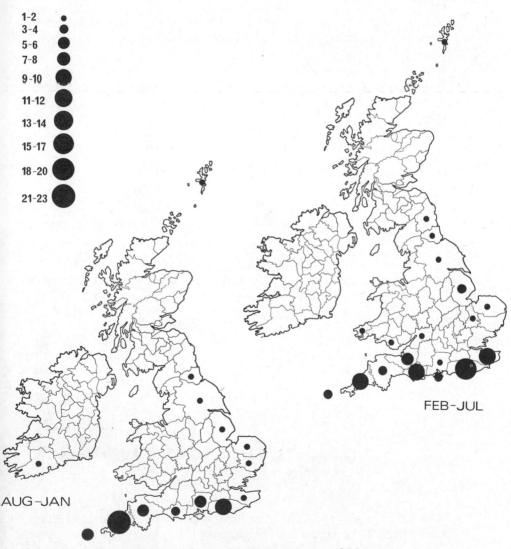

Trumpeter Finch *Rhodopechys githaginea*, see page 279.

283

Scarlet Rosefinch

Carpodacus erythrinus

Breeds from Germany and southern Sweden eastwards to Kamchatka, and from Georgia eastwards to central China.

Size of Bullfinch *Pyrrhula pyrrhula*; females and immatures nondescript, rather uniform yellowish- or greenish-brown above and greyish- or buffish-white below; double white wing-bars, heavy conical bill and beady black eye are most useful marks; dumpy shape; adult males have pink head, breast and rump. *Brit. Birds,* 55: 130; *Cape Clear Bird Obs. Rep.,* 12: 42; *Lundy Field Soc. Ann. Rep.,* 23: 27.

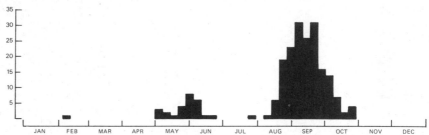

Apart from singles in February (Middlesex 1971) and July (Shetland 1970), all records were in May–June (13%) or August–October, with peaks during 28th May to 10th June and 3rd–23rd September.

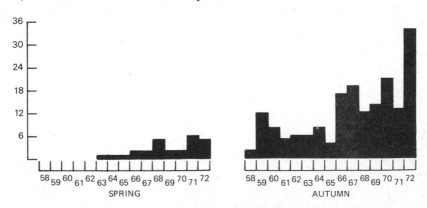

There were probably over 200 but less than 300 occurrences prior to 1958, compared with 208 in our period. There was only one spring record prior to 1958

(2nd April 1926 on Fair Isle), but five-year totals of none, seven and 20 during 1958–72. Autumn records similarly increased, with 33, 54 and 94. With the majority on Fair Isle, the increase in observer-activity will have had less effect on this species than on most, so genuine increases are indicated. The trend continued after 1972, with 40 in 1973 and about 35 in 1974 (including nine and five in spring). The increase in spring records makes one speculate about the possibility of breeding here in the future.

Though recorded in 12 counties in spring, half of these were on the British east coast and more than half of the records were in the Northern Isles. Though almost seven times as many were seen in autumn, records were in only 14 counties, with 74% in Shetland. The pattern is discussed in detail in *Scarce Migrant Birds in Britain and Ireland.*

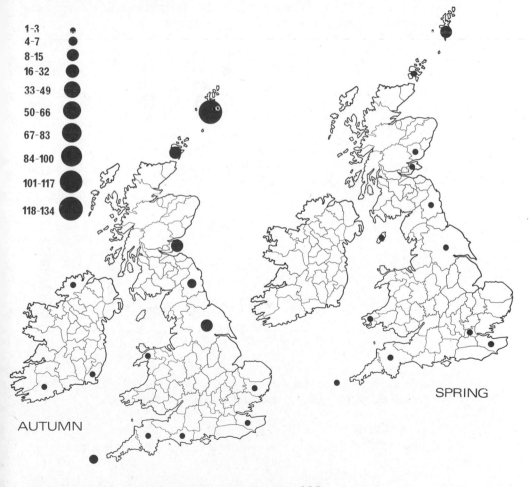

AUTUMN

SPRING

Pine Grosbeak *Pinicola enucleator*, see page 288.

285

Two-barred Crossbill

Loxia leucoptera

Breeds from northern Fenno-Scandia east to Amurland; also northern North America and Hispaniola.

Resembles small Crossbill *L. curvirostra* with prominent double white wing-bars recalling Chaffinch *Fringilla coelebs,* but male also brighter pink, and female yellower. *Lundy Field Soc. Ann. Rep.,* 23: 27.

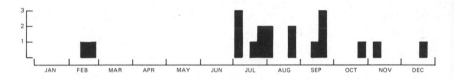

This species usually arrives here accompanying irrupting Crossbills, so the peak period of July–September is expected; the October–February records suggest that they sometimes remain to over-winter here.

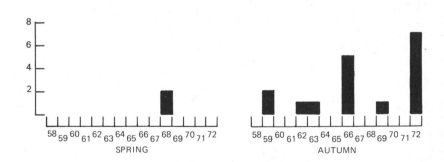

The 19 in our period compare with over 40 prior to 1958. The peaks in 1966 and 1972 coincided with large irruptions of Crossbills in those years.

Records were widespread in Britain, but the only county with more than two was Shetland with five (three of them in July 1972). Past records were mostly in eastern Britain from Shetland southwards, and Eurasian birds are clearly usually involved, but there have been four records in Ireland and one in Wales, and the Nearctic race *L. l. leucoptera* might have occurred.

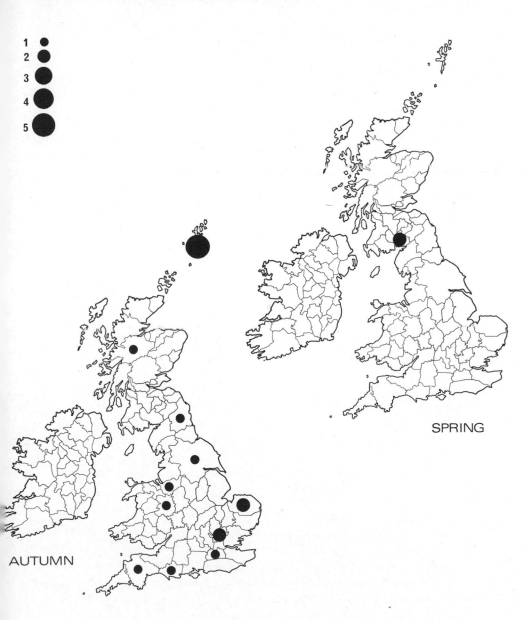

Pine Grosbeak
Pinicola enucleator

Breeds northern Europe, Asia and North America.

Almost as large as Redwing *Turdus iliacus* but in shape and colour resembles a massive elongated Crossbill *Loxia curvirostra* with long tail and bill like a Bullfinch *Pyrrhula pyrrhula*; double white wing-bars; pink areas of male are bronze in female. *Brit. Birds,* 48: 133.

One record in the period:
Kent: near Maidstone on 15th May 1971
and one since:
Northumberland: Holy Island on 11th–12th May 1975

The seven previous records were in Durham (prior to 1831), Fife (November 1954), Kent (April 1955, November 1957), Middlesex (prior to 1843), Nottingham (two in October 1890) and Yorkshire (about 1861).

Scarlet Tanager
Piranga olivacea

Breeds North America.   PJG

Nearly size of Corn Bunting *Emberiza calandra,* sometimes resembling a finch and sometimes a bulky warbler; colour of Greenfinch *Carduelis chloris,* with black lesser coverts contrasting with paler wings; greenish-olive head and back; underwing coverts white; breeding male is scarlet, apart from black wings and tail. *Brit. Birds,* 65: 155.

One record in the period:
Scilly: St Mary's on 4th October 1970
and one since:
Scilly: Tresco on 28th September to 3rd October 1975

These are the only certain records but an unidentified tanager at Copeland, Co. Down on 12th October 1963 was either this species or Summer Tanager (see p. 318).

288

Pine Bunting
Emberiza leucocephala

Breeds from eastern Russia through Asia and Siberia.

Male has complicated chestnut, black and white head pattern, with white crown; rump chestnut; lesser coverts brown; female like Yellowhammer *E. citrinella,* but with white replacing yellow. *Scot. Birds,* 5: 225.

One record in the period:
Orkney: North Ronaldsay on 7th–11th August 1967
and one since:
Dorset: Portland on 15th April 1975

The two previous records were both in the Northern Isles: Orkney (15th October 1943) and Shetland (30th October 1911).

Cretzschmar's Bunting
Emberiza caesia

Breeds southern Balkans, Asia Minor and south to northern Israel.

Closely resembles Ortolan Bunting *E. hortulana* but smaller and dumpier, with blue-grey head and breast, orange throat, brown wings and faint eye-ring; compared with young Ortolan Bunting, immature is more buffish-chestnut, chin is more orange; axillaries and underwing coverts dirty white (pale yellow in Ortolan Bunting). *Brit. Birds,* 62: 144.

One record in the period:
Shetland: Fair Isle on 10th–20th June 1967

This is the only record.

Black-headed Bunting
Emberiza melanocephala

Breeds Italy and southeast Europe eastwards to Iran.

Bulky bunting; male with black head, yellow underparts and collar, rufous back and no white in tail; female has unstreaked underparts, usually with yellow undertail coverts, and olive-brown upperparts. *Brit. Birds,* 45: 229.

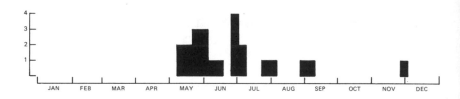

87% of the records were in spring/summer, between 11th May and 4th August (65% in May–June). Though this is a common cage-bird and occurrences often come under suspicion of being escapes, the timing accords with genuine vagrancy.

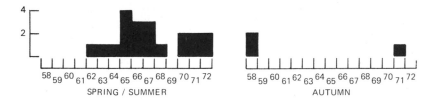

There were only nine records prior to 1958, compared with the 23 in our period. The surge of records in 1965–67 (43% in just three years) were, at the time, mostly regarded as probable escapes from captivity. With fewer since, despite continuing escape possibilities and a greater number of observers, their status deserves reconsideration.

The Northern Isles accounted for 40% of the spring/summer records, a pattern shared by other southeastern vagrants (but also by some obvious escaped cage-birds).

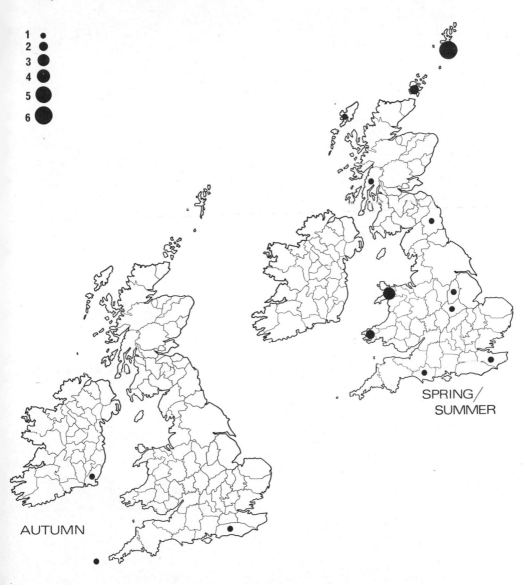

Yellow-breasted Bunting

Emberiza aureola

Breeds from Finland eastwards to Kamchatka and Japan.

Smaller, paler and with more contrasting plumage than Yellowhammer *E. citrinella,* females and immatures with pale yellow throat, breast and belly, almost unstreaked; yellowish supercilia and narrow buff crown stripe, recalling Aquatic Warbler; pale double wing-bars; summer males have black face and chin and narrow chestnut breast-band. *Brit. Birds,* 52: 161; 53: 229.

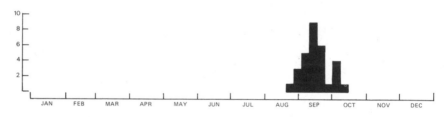

The records were all within eight weeks from late August to mid-October, with 73% in September, as were nine of the ten records prior to 1958 (the exception being an adult male on Fair Isle on 13th July 1951).

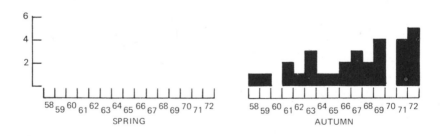

The 30 records in our period compare with ten prior to 1958. The five-year totals in 1958–72 (five, ten and 15) show a steady increase which is probably genuine, as most were on Fair Isle, which has been consistently well-watched.

The ten records prior to 1958 were in Shetland (4), Norfolk (3), Fife (2) and Outer Hebrides (1). The bias towards Shetland was even greater in our period, with singles in Cork, Donegal, Northumberland and Orkney, four in Fife and the other 22 (73%) in Shetland, 17 of them on Fair Isle.

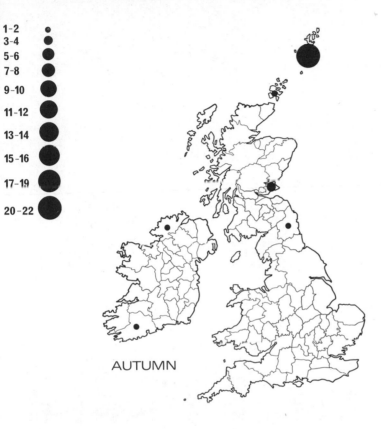

1-2
3-4
5-6
7-8
9-10
11-12
13-14
15-16
17-19
20-22

AUTUMN

Cretzschmar's Bunting *Emberiza caesia*, see page 289.
Rock Bunting *Emberiza cia*, see page 300.

293

Rustic Bunting
Emberiza rustica

Breeds from Fenno-Scandia eastwards to Kamchatka.

Recalls rufous Reed Bunting *E. schoeniclus* with white underparts and orange breast band and flank streaks; white stripe behind eye; crown feathers ruffled to form crest. *Cape Clear Bird Obs. Rep.,* 9: 82.

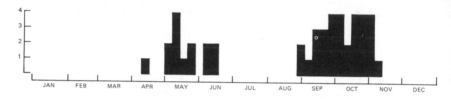

The records were all in April–June, mostly May, and September to early November, with 70% in autumn.

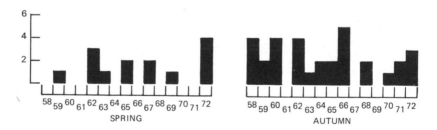

SPRING   AUTUMN

Rustic Buntings are irregular in their appearances and, despite the increased number of observers, occurrences have decreased recently (five-year totals during 1958–72 of 18, 15 and 13). These 46 records in our period compare with 34 prior to 1958.

Twelve of the 14 spring records were in Scotland (64% in Shetland), but autumn records were more widespread, mostly on the British east coast from Shetland (43%) to Essex, but also Scilly (22%) and Cork (the only Irish record: 1959).

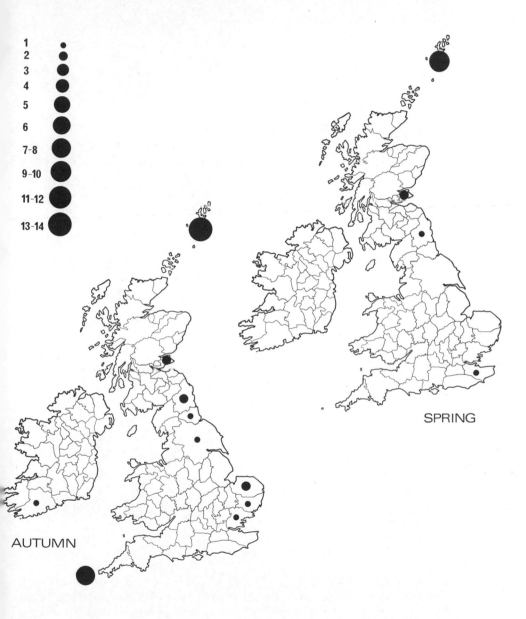

1
2
3
4
5
6
7-8
9-10
11-12
13-14

SPRING

AUTUMN

Yellow-browed Bunting *Emberiza chrysophrys*, see page 300.

Little Bunting

Emberiza pusilla

Breeds from northern Fenno-Scandia east to Sea of Okhotsk.

Like small neat compact Reed Bunting *E. schoeniclus* the size of Linnet *Acanthis cannabina,* but whitish underparts neatly marked with fine black streaks; crown and cheeks chestnut, outlined with black; short tail usually not fanned or flirted, so white far less conspicuous; ticking call-note. *Brit. Birds*, 50: 206, 208.

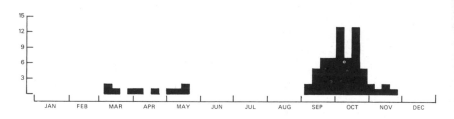

Both spring and autumn records were spread throughout three months—ten in March–May and 65 in September–November, with 60% of them in October.

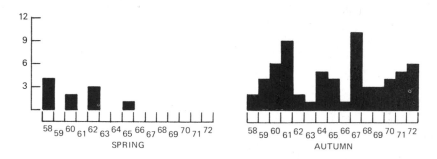

Spring records, which made up 31% during 1958–62, have become very rare, with none in our period since 1965. There was one in 1973, but none in 1974, so there were just two in the 12 years 1963–74, compared with nine in the five years 1958–62. Autumn records, though varying from one to ten annually, have not

296

kept pace with the increases shown by other rare species due to increased observer-activity (five-year totals of 23, 21 and 21). The 75 in our period compare with over 91 prior to 1958, again perhaps suggesting a decline in vagrancy.

The few spring records were scattered, apart from four in Shetland and three (together, 1962) in Cheshire. Autumn records were mostly in Shetland (66%) and, including these, 83% were on the British east coast south to Essex.

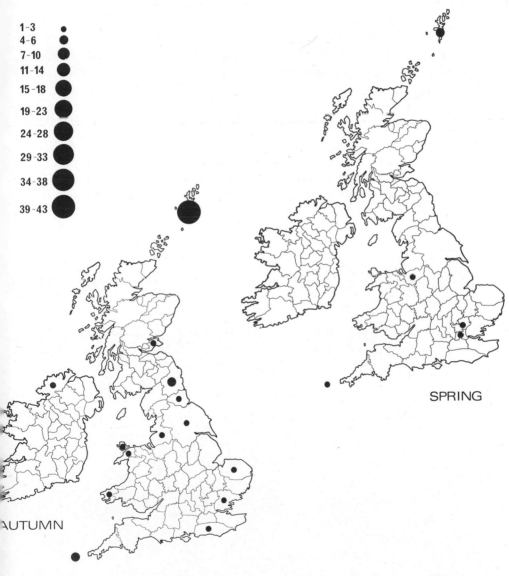

1-3
4-6
7-10
11-14
15-18
19-23
24-28
29-33
34-38
39-43

SPRING

AUTUMN

Song Sparrow
Melospiza melodia

Breeds North America.

Colour, shape and rather skulking habits resemble Dunnock *Prunella modularis,* but has bunting-like bill and striped head; heavily-streaked breast, with dark central spot; rounded tail. *Brit. Birds*, 52: 419; 59: 198; 65: 260.

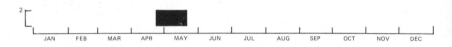

All four records were of birds first seen in a period of 22 days, from 27th April to 18th May. Though two were seen on only one and four dates (Yorkshire 1964 and Caernarvon 1970), two stayed for longer periods: 14 days (Shetland 1959) and 22 days (Isle of Man 1971).

The four records in our period are the only ones for Britain and Ireland.

Apart from the Yorkshire bird, the others show the typical western and northern bias of spring American passerines (see p. 310).

1●

SPRING

Rock Bunting

Emberiza cia

Breeds from Iberia and northwest Africa eastwards to China.

Head and breast cold grey; bold black head stripes; upperparts warm chestnut-brown, streaked with black; buffish-orange underparts (especially bright on flanks); chestnut rump unstreaked; often flicks tail, showing white outer tail feathers; often exceedingly flighty and difficult to approach; very thin call-note 'tsit'. *Brit. Birds,* 53: 35; 55: 158.

Three records in the period:
Caernarvon: Bardsey on 1st June 1967
Pembroke: Dale on 15th August 1958
Yorkshire: Spurn on 19th February to 10th March 1965

The previous records were in Kent (February 1905) and Sussex (two in October 1902).

Yellow-browed Bunting

Emberiza chrysophrys

Breeds central Siberia.

Size between Little Bunting and Reed Bunting *E. schoeniclus*; distinctive summer male has black head with rufous ear-coverts, white crown stripe and streak through ear-coverts, and yellow supercilia; upperparts brown, streaked black; underparts white, streaked dark brown on breast and flanks; male in winter and female duller, with black replaced by chestnut-brown, and white by buff.

None in the period, but one since:
Norfolk: Wells on 19th October 1975

This is the only record; it is still under review for admission to the British and Irish list.

Fox Sparrow

Passerella iliaca

Breeds North America.

Larger than House Sparrow *Passer domesticus*, with rump, upper tail coverts and tail bright chestnut, and white underparts very heavily streaked with large chestnut-brown spots. *Brit. Birds*, 55: 560.

One record in the period:
Down: Copeland on 3rd June 1961
This is the only record.

Rufous-sided Towhee

Pipilo erythrophthalmus

Breeds North and Central America.

Shape and stance recall huge Dartford Warbler *Sylvia undata* but bill finch-like; on ground resembles Song Thrush *Turdus philomelos* and in flight a shrike *Lanius sp.* Upperparts, chin and throat black (male) or reddish-brown (female); white breast and belly, with chestnut-red flanks; white tips to sides of tail; eye red (brown in immature). *Brit. Birds*, 63: 147.

One record in the period:
Devon: Lundy on 7th June 1966
and one since:
Yorkshire: Spurn from at least 5th September 1975, into 1976
These are the only records.

White-throated Sparrow
Zonotrichia albicollis

Breeds North America.

Shape, colour and actions recall Dunnock *Prunella modularis,* but has bunting-like bill; head boldly striped with black and white, with supercilia lemon-yellow in front of eye; throat white, bordered with black. *Brit. Birds,* 54: 366; 65: 222; 66: 449.

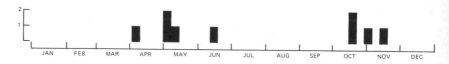

Records were divided between April–June and October–November, unusually for American buntings and sparrows, which usually occur mainly in spring on this side of the Atlantic.

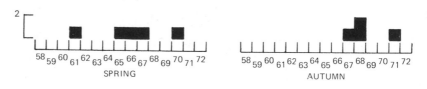

The nine in our period compare with only one prior to 1958 (18th May 1909 on Flannan Islands, Outer Hebrides). The 1961 bird almost certainly crossed the Atlantic on board ship (*Brit. Birds,* 54: 439), while others not included here are known to have done so (*Brit. Birds,* 58: 230).

The spring records suggest recent transatlantic arrivals (perhaps on ships). At least three of the four in autumn were first-year birds, so they too were newly arrived, despite the pattern atypical of Nearctic passerines.

1 ●

SPRING

AUTUMN

Slate-coloured Junco

Junco hyemalis

Breeds North America.

Mostly dark grey, with white lower breast, belly and outer tail feathers (very obvious when tail flicked); bill pinkish; immatures have browner plumage. *Scot. Birds,* 6: 53.

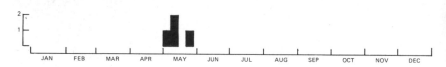

The records were all in May.

The only record before the four in our period was at Loop Head, Co. Clare on 30th May 1905.

Three of the four in our period were in Shetland, the other being in Kent (1960).

SPRING

Rufous-sided Towhee *Pipilo erythrophthalmus*, see page 301.

Rose-breasted Grosbeak
Pheucticus ludovicianus

Breeds North America.

Almost size of Song Thrush *Turdus philomelos* with build of Hawfinch *Coccothraustes coccothraustes*; plumage of female and immature bears resemblance to a huge Whinchat *Saxicola rubetra*; actions like shrike *Lanius sp.*, with upright stance, undulating flight and tail-wagging; underwing coverts crimson (male) or yellow (female); adult male largely black above and white below with red breast; female and young streaky brown with strikingly striped head; both sexes have white bars and patches in wing. *Brit. Birds,* 53: 149; 58: 440; 61: 176.

Three records in the period:
Cork: Cape Clear Island on 7th–8th October 1962
Pembroke: Skokholm on 5th October 1967
Scilly: St Agnes on 6th–11th October 1966
The only previous record was in Antrim (November 1957).

Spanish Sparrow
Passer hispaniolensis

Breeds Iberia and northwest Africa, Sardinia and the Balkans eastwards to southwest Asia.

Similar to House Sparrow *P. domesticus,* but male has chestnut crown and very extensive black breast and black-streaked flanks.

Two records in the period:
Devon: Lundy on 9th June 1966
Scilly: St Mary's on 21st October 1972
These are the only records.

American waders

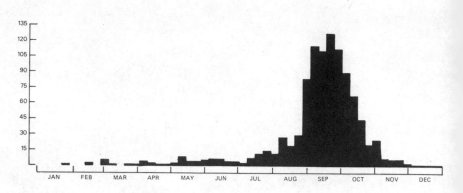

The records of all 18 species of American waders which have occurred in Britain and Ireland are combined here. Though there were records in every month of the year, the eight weeks from 27th August to 21st October accounted for 74%.

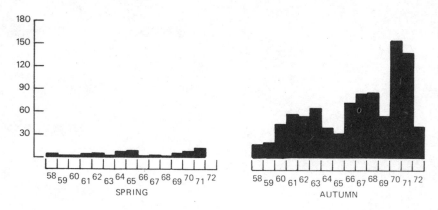

The spring records varied from none (1972) to 12 (1971), averaging less than four per year. The huge peaks in 1970 and 1971 dominate the autumn picture, but were followed in 1972 by the lowest total for seven years (1965, when there was far less observer-activity). The 1,013 records in our period compare with about 340 prior to 1958. Kenneth Williamson (in *The Changing Flora and Fauna of Britain:* 1974) postulated that changes in weather patterns (particularly a southerly shift by about 10° in the mean centre of the Icelandic low this century) have been an important factor in increased vagrancy by Nearctic birds. This may be so, but it must not be forgotten that observer-activity has increased enormously, nowhere more so than in the areas where most Nearctic birds are recorded nowadays (western Ireland and Scilly), which were almost unwatched in the past; and also that birdwatchers have only recently become fully aware of the likelihood of seeing American birds and made special efforts to look for them.

The expected westerly bias is very strong in autumn, with 68% in Ireland and western Britain (38% in just four counties—Cork, Cornwall, Kerry and Scilly), compared with 19% on the east coast of the British mainland. The early autumn (July and early August) records were mostly in eastern Britain and it is probable that these mainly related to birds which had crossed the Atlantic in a previous season and were migrating south after summering in northern Europe. The spring records, though many fewer, showed a very similar pattern, with 63% in the west and 19% on the British east coast. The conclusion, as with those in autumn, is that most birds are recent transatlantic arrivals. It may be significant in this context that none was seen in spring 1972, despite the second largest autumn arrival on record in 1971. The patterns are discussed at much greater length in *Scarce Migrant Birds in Britain and Ireland.*

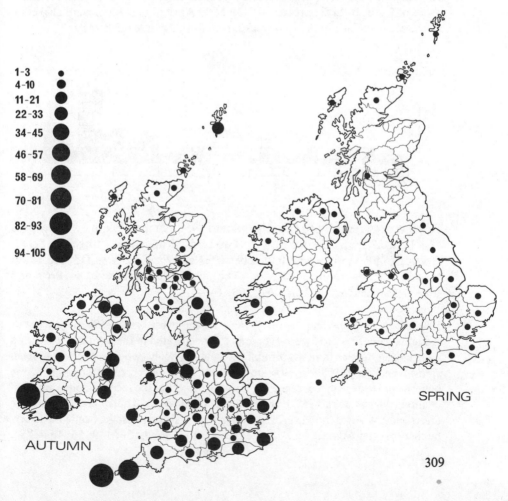

1-3
4-10
11-21
22-33
34-45
46-57
58-69
70-81
82-93
94-105

SPRING

AUTUMN

309

American landbirds

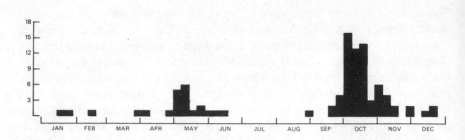

The records of all 27 American passerines and near-passerines which occurred during 1958–72 are combined here. 78% occurred in autumn and winter, between late August and mid-February, with 59% of them in the first three weeks of October. Spring records, from early April to mid-June, were also concentrated, with 55% in the two weeks from 30th April to 13th May.

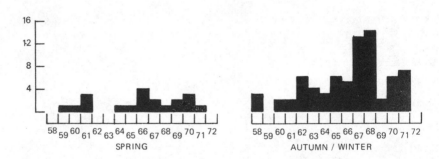

There were 46 records of 15 species prior to 1958, compared with the 93 records of at least 27 species in our period. (Two birds identified only to genus—*Dendroica sp.* in Pembroke on 5th October 1961 and *Piranga sp.* in Down on 12th October 1963—are included here.) The unprecedented influxes in 1967 and 1968 were discussed in *Brit. Birds,* 63: 145–147.

50% of the April–June records were in the west, and 25% in Shetland. Autumn/winter records were even more concentrated in the west (82%), with a more southerly bias than in spring, 30% being in Scilly (where there was none in spring) and only 10% in Scotland (where 45% occurred in spring). These patterns of westerly occurrence support the view that the records concern transatlantic vagrants rather than escaped cage-birds. There is considerable divergence of views, however, regarding ship-assisted passage. Some birds certainly cross the Atlantic on board ships (e.g. *Brit. Birds,* 54: 439; 56: 157–164;

310

58: 230) but the spectrum of species occurring here in autumn is not the same as that of birds landing on ships off the eastern seaboard of North America, and the species concerned (mainly insectivorous) are those which would have to cross quickly or die. In a more detailed discussion in *Scarce Migrant Birds in Britain and Ireland,* it was concluded that spring records (mostly of seed-eating birds) could result largely from ship-assisted passage but that it was most unlikely that this made a major contribution to autumn vagrancy. It is seldom that a firm conclusion can be reached in any individual case, however, and, for that reason, the possibility of ship-assistance is regarded by the B.O.U. Records Committee as no bar to admittance to the British and Irish list.

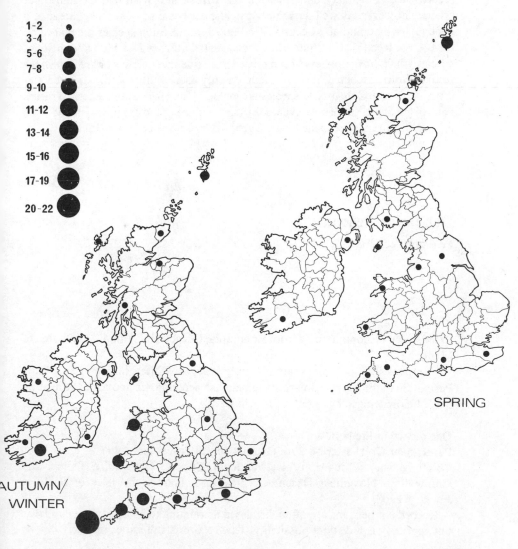

1-2
3-4
5-6
7-8
9-10
11-12
13-14
15-16
17-19
20-22

SPRING

AUTUMN/
WINTER

As stated in the Introduction (p. 11), the possibility must always be borne in mind that some of the records in this book refer to birds which have escaped from aviculturalists' collections. The escape likelihood is so high, and the chance of vagrancy so low, for some species (e.g. Orange-gorgeted Flycatcher *Ficedula strophiata,* recorded on Lundy, Devon on 17th November 1973) that the records are completely omitted from the British and Irish list. Certain other species, however, as well as being very suspect because of the likelihood of a captive origin, could also occur as genuine vagrants. Such species are placed by the B.O.U. Records Committee in a special list, Category D, which also includes species which have only ever been recorded as tide-line corpses or are *known* (as distinct from suspected) to have occurred only as a result of a ship-assisted sea-crossing. These Category D species are included here for completeness. If future records justify it, some may eventually earn a place in the main British and Irish list (as has already happened with Ovenbird and Slate-coloured Junco).

Dalmatian Pelican

Pelecanus crispus

Breeds very discontinuously from Roumania, Greece and Albania eastwards to Mongolia.

Unmistakable pelican shape; mainly greyish-white; larger than White Pelican; in flight, black primaries and blackish secondaries above but little or no black below wings; legs grey; eyes yellow.

One record in the period:
Essex: near Colchester on 29th October to 8th November 1967
This bird was subsequently seen in Kent, Sussex, Hampshire, Dorset and Cornwall in November/December 1967 and, finally, the Isles of Scilly in January 1968.

Records of pelicans are often dismissed as relating to escapes from captivity, but vagrancy is a distinct possibility. This record is still under review.

White Pelican

Pelecanus onocrotalus

Breeds very discontinuously from Roumania, Greece and Albania eastwards through Kazakhstan; also tropical east and south Africa.

Unmistakable pelican shape; mainly white, tinged pinkish; slightly smaller than Dalmatian Pelican; in flight, distinct black wing tips above and whole of rear of wing black beneath; legs pinkish or orange; eyes red.

One record in the period:
Norfolk: off Great Yarmouth and many other localities on 9th July 1964 to 20th February 1965
and one since:
Lincolnshire/Yorkshire: River Humber on 16th July 1975

Records of pelicans are often dismissed as relating to escapes from captivity, but vagrancy is a distinct possibility. These records are still under review.

Greater Flamingo

Phoenicopterus ruber

Breeds very locally in south France, south Spain, northwest Africa, from southeast Russia and Iraq eastwards to west India, and Kenya and South Africa (*P. r. roseus*); also Caribbean and South America (*P. r. ruber*).

Typical flamingo shape; distinguished from other species by pale pinkish-white plumage (apart from striking crimson and black wings); bill mostly pale pink with black tip.

Most, if not all, occurrences of flamingos in Britain and Ireland are now considered to relate to escapes from captivity. Various species are involved, the most common being Chilean Flamingo *P. chilensis*. Even the records of the Eurasian and African race of the Greater Flamingo *P. r. roseus*, the most likely to occur naturally, are so suspect, however, that they are probably often neither reported nor published. This species was included on the British and Irish list until 1971, but was then relegated to Category D. The status of this species in Britain and Ireland was discussed in *Brit. Birds*, 60: 423–426.

Baikal Teal

Anas formosa

Breeds central and eastern Siberia. (Many are kept in wildfowl collections.)

Male very distinctive, with complicated creamy, buff, black and green head-pattern; pink breast; grey flanks and black under-tail separated by vertical white lines; female like Teal *A. crecca*, but has white spot at base of bill. *Fair Isle Bird Obs. Bull.*, 2: 194.

Three records in the period:
Dorset: Brownsea Island on 1st January 1969
Fermanagh: Crom on 13th January 1967
Moray: Loch Spynie on 5th February 1958

The six previous records were in Essex (January 1906), Hampshire (about 1915), Norfolk (December 1929), Shetland (September 1954), Suffolk (November 1951) and Sussex (November 1927).

Yellow-shafted Flicker

Colaptes auratus

Breeds North America.

Woodpecker with barred brown back and white rump; boldly spotted underparts; yellow under wings and tail; grey crown, with red nape patch; black breast band.

One record in the period:
Cork: One flew ashore from RMS *Mauretania* at Cobh Harbour at dawn on 13th October 1962; it had been first seen aboard $2\frac{1}{2}$ hours out of New York at dusk on 7th October (*Brit. Birds,* 56: 157).

This is the only record.

Blue Rock Thrush
Monticola solitarius

Breeds southern Europe, northwest Africa and southern Asia.

Almost size of Redwing *Turdus iliacus* but plumper with short tail; male blue-grey with slaty wings and tail; female bluish-brown above and paler with barring below. *Brit. Birds,* 61: 303.

One record in the period:
Orkney: North Ronaldsay on 29th August to 6th September 1966
This is the only record.

Red-headed Bunting
Emberiza bruniceps

Breeds from southeast Russia eastwards to northwest China and southwards to Iran and Afghanistan.

Size and shape like a stocky Yellowhammer *E. citrinella*; male has chestnut or orange head and throat, greenish mantle and yellowish rump, nape and underparts; female closely resembles female Black-headed Bunting but usually has pale yellow (not pale chestnut) rump and a greenish tinge to upperparts. *Fair Isle Bird Obs. Bull.,* 1 (3): 34.

The record of one on North Ronaldsay (Orkney) on 19th June 1931 was formerly accepted as relating to a wild bird but it, and most, if not all, of the numerous records since, are now considered to be attributable to escaped cage-birds. A total of 33 was reported in 1958–61, between 20th April and 28th October, with seven in May, June, August and September, three in July and singles in April and October. Since 1961, records of this species have not been collected or assessed by the Rarities Committee and many occurrences are now probably neither reported nor published. Genuine vagrancy is possible, however, and despite the high escape likelihood, it is to be regretted that we are losing the current pattern. The British and Irish records were discussed in *Brit. Birds,* 60: 344–347, 423–426, 529; 61: 41–43.

Chestnut Bunting

Emberiza rutila

Breeds southern-central and southeastern Siberia.

Smaller than House Sparrow *Passer domesticus*; male has head, breast, wing-coverts and upperparts to rump bright chestnut; streaks on flanks dark olive or rich chestnut; underparts otherwise bright yellow; tail and flight feathers olive-grey; bill dark, eye black, legs pinkish; female browner and duller, with white throat; call similar to Reed Bunting *Emberiza schoeniclus* but more mellow.

None in the period, but one since:
Shetland: Foula on 9th–13th June 1974

This is the only record. This is a cheap cage-bird and the record is still under review.

Blue Grosbeak

Guiraca caerulea

Breeds North America.

Like a slim, long-tailed Corn Bunting *Emberiza calandra* with large bill like a Hawfinch *Coccothraustes coccothraustes*; both sexes have prominent double wing-bars, rusty (male) or buff (female); male dull blue apart from brownish wings and tail; female brown.

Two records in the period:
Inverness: Kiltarlity on 10th–11th March 1972
Shetland: Out Skerries from mid-August to 26th August 1970

These are the only records.

Indigo Bunting
Passerina cyanea

Breeds North America.

Size of Tree Sparrow *Passer montanus*; male almost wholly blue, with darker wings and tail; female similarly brown, paler below; upright stance, and Fair Isle bird had habit of expanding tail with nervous sideways twitch.

One record in the period:
Shetland: Fair Isle on 3rd–7th August 1964
and one since:
Essex: Walton-on-the-Naze on 8th September 1973
These are the only records.

Painted Bunting
Passerina ciris

Breeds North and Central America.

Male splendidly colourful, with blue head, yellow-green mantle and red eye-ring, underparts and rump; female brilliant yellow-green.

One record in the period:
Shetland: Voe on 28th May 1972
This is the only accepted record.

List of the 23 species on the British and Irish list which have not been recorded since 1957, with the total number of records and date of the most recent. In some cases (marked *), there have been records since the date shown, but these are not accepted as relating to birds of wild origin. Useful references are noted where possible.

Capped Petrel *Pterodroma hasitata* One; 1850.

Frigate Petrel *Pelagodroma marina* One; 1897. *Brit. Birds*, 51: 269.

Madeiran Petrel *Oceanodroma castro* Two; last 1931. *Sea Swallow*, 18: 69.

Green Heron *Butorides virescens* One; 1889. *Brit. Birds*, 65: 424.

Hooded Merganser *Mergus cucullatus* Four; last 1957*. *Brit. Birds*, 64: 385.

Egyptian Vulture *Neophron percnopterus* Two; last 1868*.

Griffon Vulture *Gyps fulvus* Two; last 1927. *Brit. Birds*, 39: 275.

Spotted Eagle *Aquila clanga* Twelve; last 1915.

Pallid Harrier *Circus macrourus* Three; last 1952.

Sandhill Crane *Grus canadensis* One; 1905. *Brit. Birds*, 65: 427.

Allen's Gallinule *Porphyrula alleni* One; 1902. *Brit. Birds*, 67: 405.

Caspian Plover *Charadrius asiaticus* One; 1890. *Brit. Birds*, 65: 124.

Eskimo Curlew *Numenius borealis* Seven; last 1887.

Eagle Owl *Bubo bubo* Probably less than 20; last 1883*. *Brit. Birds*, 50: 486.

Red-necked Nightjar *Caprimulgus ruficollis* One; 1856. *Brit. Birds*, 66: 390.

Egyptian Nightjar *Caprimulgus aegyptius* One; 1883.

Blue-cheeked Bee-eater *Merops superciliosus* Two; last 1951. *Brit. Birds*, 45: 225.

White-winged Lark *Melanocorypha leucoptera* Four; last 1955. *Brit. Birds*, 49: 41.

Siberian Thrush *Turdus sibiricus* One; 1954. *Brit. Birds*, 48: 21.

Pallas's Grasshopper Warbler *Locustella certhiola* Three; last 1956. *Brit. Birds*, 50: 395; 61: 269.

Yellowthroat *Geothlypis trichas* One; 1954. *Brit. Birds*, 48: 145, 170.

Citril Finch *Serinus citrinella* One; 1904. *Brit. Birds*, 49: 398.

Summer Tanager *Piranga rubra* One; 1957. *Brit. Birds*, 56: 49.

APPENDIX III : Geographical distribution of rarities

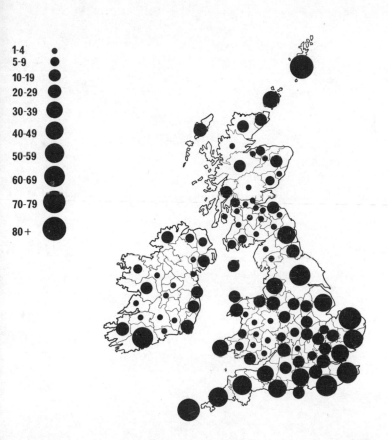

1-4
5-9
10-19
20-29
30-39
40-49
50-59
60-69
70-79
80+

Rivalries have long existed between counties—which is the 'best' birdwatching county? For rare birds, at least, the 1958–72 records show that Shetland tops the list with over 80 species, followed by the Isles of Scilly and Norfolk in the 70s and Kent, Sussex, Co. Cork and Yorkshire in the 60s. Bearing in mind the very uneven distribution of observers in Britain and Ireland, with very many fewer in Scotland and Ireland (especially the latter) than in England and Wales (see fig. 2 in the Introduction), the high position of Co. Cork is remarkable. The low number of rare species (sometimes none) in various other Irish counties suggests that these areas would greatly repay the attention of some active field ornithologists. Co. Waterford, with only two rare species in the 15 years, compared with the adjoining counties' totals of 61 in Cork and 26 in Wexford, is an obvious example and should surely soon be the target for observers wishing to break new ground.

319

SUMMARY

SHORT-TERM TRENDS

The number of rare birds seen annually in Britain and Ireland rose from ap-proximately 200 per year in the late 1950s to nearly 500 per year in the early 1970s (fig. 3). Records of Cory's Shearwaters, Cranes, Nutcrackers and Richard's Pipits are omitted from fig. 3, since the very large numbers which oc-curred in exceptional movements would create enormous bias. The overall up-ward trend is clearly indicated by the five-year totals of 1,125 birds in 1958–62, 1,521 birds in 1963–67 and 2,350 birds in 1968–72.

This upward trend is very unlikely to be due to rare birds (as a group) becoming commoner. Some species considered to be rare in 1958 have become so common that they have been dealt with in the companion volume *Scarce Migrant Birds in Britain and Ireland* rather than here (e.g. Mediterranean Gull

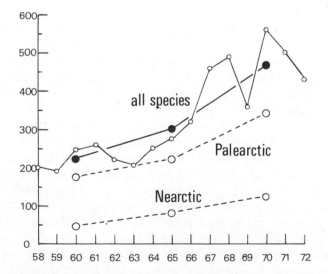

FIGURE 3. Number of rare birds seen in Britain and Ireland during 1958–72: annual totals and five-year means. The dotted lines show Palearctic species (upper) and Nearc-tic species (lower) separately.

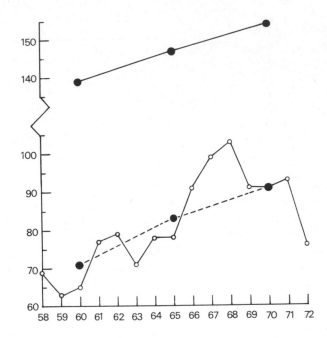

FIGURE 4. Number of rare species seen in Britain and Ireland during 1958–72. The two lower graphs show annual totals and five-year means; upper graph shows five-year totals.

Larus melanocephalus, Icterine Warbler *Hippolais icterina,* Melodious Warbler *H. polyglotta,* Yellow-browed Warbler *Phylloscopus inornatus*). These species certainly produced more records in the 15 years than could possibly have been compensated for by any reduction (to the point of rarity) of species not considered to be rare in 1958. Indeed, not one such species comes to mind. The actual increase in the number of records of rare birds may, therefore, have been even greater than that suggested by fig. 3.

The number of species of rare birds seen in Britain and Ireland also rose, from a mean of 71 per year during 1958–62 to a mean of 91 per year during 1968–72, and the actual five-yearly totals were 139 species during 1958–62, 147 during 1963–67 and 154 during 1968–72 (fig. 4). (These totals include the four species omitted from fig. 3.) Before passing on, it is worth drawing attention to the peak years for numbers of rare birds (1968 and, especially, 1970) and the peak year for variety of rare species (1968): many of us will have happy recollections of exciting days in the field in those years.

In the most recent period, the number of rare birds recorded in Britain and Ireland was more than double that of a decade earlier. This change is almost certainly merely a reflection of the larger number of observers nowadays and, to a degree perhaps, their greater field competence, their greater awareness of the likelihood of finding rare birds and (some would say) the greater emphasis which

322

a certain proportion of birdwatchers place upon rarities. The growth of ornithological interest in Britain may be indicated by the rise in the number of members of two of the national societies. Membership of the Royal Society for the Protection of Birds rose from about 7,500 in 1958 to almost 118,000 (1,573%) in 1972 and the comparable figures for the British Trust for Ornithology were 2,641 and 5,994 (227%). With such figures in mind, it no longer becomes surprising that the number of rare birds recorded doubled in the same period. The effects of an increase in the number of observers active in the field have already been shown in comparing the numbers of rare birds found at weekends with those on weekdays (*Brit. Birds*, 59: 556–558).

The trends shown by 67 of the 69 rare species which averaged one or more per year during 1958–72 (Crane and Nutcracker, with exceptional peaks in 1963 and 1968, respectively, are omitted), and three groups of American birds, can be determined by comparing their patterns during the three five-year periods with the overall pattern for the rare birds shown in fig. 3. The species are categorised within nine basic patterns in Table I. It must be stressed again that these categories show the trends after the elimination of increases due to extra observer-activity. Thus, to take one example, Alpine Swift is categorised as showing no change, even though 20 were seen in 1958–62, 26 in 1963–67 and 41 in 1968–72, *because this precisely fits the increase for all rare species* and it is concluded that the increase merely reflects the increase in the number of observers. Table I is the distillation of many hours of collation and will repay considerable study. Some facts, such as the recent increases in numbers of Cetti's and Savi's Warblers, are widely appreciated but others, such as the decrease in Bee-eaters, are not apparent until one calculates how many 'ought' to have been seen recently, in view of increased observer-activity. The lack of evidence for any significant change in the numbers of American waders (all species, as a group) reaching Britain and Ireland is another example of a conclusion that may surprise observers who are aware of the larger numbers *recorded* in recent years.

TABLE I. Trends shown by records of rare species recorded on 15 or more occasions in Britain and Ireland during 1958–72, analysed by five-year periods.1958–62 is termed 'early 1960s', 1963–67 is termed 'mid-1960s' and 1968–72 is termed 'recent'. Species listed in small capitals are unquestionably placed in the correct categories. Although the other species are probably also in the correct categories, this is less clear-cut and the possible alternative category is indicated within parentheses*.

●—●—● (a) *Static*

White-billed Diver *Gavia adamsii* (h)

Little Bittern *Ixobrychus minutus* (f)

Gyrfalcon *Falco rusticolus* (b)

Little Crake *Porzana parva* (e)

Lesser Yellowlegs *Tringa flavipes* (d)

White-rumped Sandpiper *Calidris fuscicollis* (h)

PECTORAL SANDPIPER *C. melanotos*

ALL AMERICAN WADERS (as a group)

American waders, excluding Pectoral (as a group) (f)

WILSON'S PHALAROPE *Phalaropus tricolor*

ALL AMERICAN SPECIES (as a group)

White-winged Black Tern *Chlidonias leucopterus* (d)

Whiskered Tern *C. hybrida* (f)

Caspian Tern *Hydroprogne caspia* (h)

ALPINE SWIFT *Apus melba*

Great Reed Warbler *Acrocephalus arundinaceus* (e)

SUBALPINE WARBLER *Sylvia cantillans*

Bonelli's Warbler *Phylloscopus bonelli* (i)

ARCTIC WARBLER *P. borealis*

Tawny Pipit *Anthus campestris* (d)

Citrine Wagtail *Motacilla citreola* (h)

Lesser Grey Shrike *Lanius minor* (e)

Two-barred Crossbill *Loxia leucoptera* (b)

* e.g. Caspian Tern numbers have probably remained relatively unchanged, though there is some evidence of a recent decrease; Woodchat Shrikes have decreased in recent years, but this could be part of a decline starting earlier.

(b) *Steady increase*
AMERICAN WIGEON *Anas americana*
RING-NECKED DUCK *Aythya collaris*
LESSER GOLDEN PLOVER *Pluvialis dominica*
SPOTTED SANDPIPER *Tringa macularia*
SEMIPALMATED SANDPIPER *Calidris pusilla*
BONAPARTE'S GULL *Larus philadelphia*
RED-RUMPED SWALLOW *Hirundo daurica*
THRUSH NIGHTINGALE *Luscinia luscinia*
PALLAS'S WARBLER *Phylloscopus proregulus*
RICHARD'S PIPIT *Anthus novaeseelandiae*
Scarlet Rosefinch *Carpodacus erythrinus* (a)

(c) *Steady decrease*
LESSER WHITE-FRONTED GOOSE *Anser erythropus*
RED-FOOTED FALCON *Falco vespertinus*
GREAT SNIPE *Gallinago media*
BROAD-BILLED SANDPIPER *Limicola falcinellus*
BEE-EATER *Merops apiaster*
Greenish Warbler *Phylloscopus trochiloides* (a)
RUSTIC BUNTING *Emberiza rustica*
LITTLE BUNTING *E. pusilla*

(d) *Recent increase*
Purple Heron *Ardea purpurea* (b)
LITTLE EGRET *Egretta garzetta*
BLUE-WINGED TEAL *Anas discors*
KING EIDER *Somateria spectabilis*
BUFF-BREASTED SANDPIPER *Tryngites subruficollis*
Short-toed Lark *Calandrella cinerea* (a)
CETTI'S WARBLER *Cettia cetti*
SAVI'S WARBLER *Locustella luscinioides*

(e) *Recent decrease*
BLACK-WINGED STILT *Himantopus himantopus*

325

GULL-BILLED TERN *Gelochelidon nilotica*
RED-THROATED PIPIT *Anthus cervinus*
Woodchat Shrike *Lanius senator* (c)

(f) *Increase since early 1960s*
ALBATROSSES *Diomedea spp.*
CORY'S SHEARWATER *Calonectris diomedea*
WHITE STORK *Ciconia ciconia*
SERIN *Serinus serinus*
Yellow-breasted Bunting *Emberiza aureola* (a)

(g) *Decrease since early 1960s*
ROLLER *Coracias garrulus*
ROSE-COLOURED STARLING *Sturnus roseus*
ARCTIC REDPOLL *Acanthis hornemanni*

(h) *Increase in mid-1960s*
LITTLE SHEARWATER *Puffinus assimilis*
Surf Scoter *Melanitta perspicillata* (e)
DOWITCHERS *Limnodromus spp.*
BAIRD'S SANDPIPER *Calidris bairdii*
SNOWY OWL *Nyctea scandiaca*
AMERICAN PASSERINES (as a group)
BLACK-HEADED BUNTING *Emberiza melanocephala*

(i) *Decrease in mid-1960s*
NIGHT HERON *Nycticorax nycticorax*
Aquatic Warbler *Acrocephalus paludicola* (d)

LONG-TERM TRENDS

Long-term trends are even more difficult to detect with certainty. Taking only the 210 species for which totals are available, however, there were 4,307 records (43%) up to 1957 and 5,794 (57%) during 1958–72. On the assumption that rare birds (as a group) have not in reality become either commoner or rarer, some idea of changing status can be obtained by calculating the percentage of the total records of each species which were in 1958–72, ranking them and then dividing the list into two equal halves. Species close to the dividing line could be placed in the wrong group by this method, so two extra marginal groups are distinguished. Species with very few records cannot justifiably be considered in this way, so any with less than ten records up tó 1972 are omitted. The resulting list is shown in Table II.

Even apart from the fact that the records for over 150 years (about 1800–1957) are compared with those for just 15 years (1958–72), this method of analysis is open to all sorts of bias, as illustrated by the following examples. Sea-watching is a recent innovation (most past records of seabirds relating to corpses on beaches), so it is not surprising to find albatrosses, Cory's and Little Shearwaters shown as 'increasing'. The small American waders are difficult to identify and occur mainly in Ireland and the west of Britain. It is, therefore, hardly surprising that they feature as 'increasing', since observers' competence at field identification has improved enormously and there is now far more watching done in Ireland and western Britain than was formerly the case. The opening of bird observatories (mostly since the late 1940s and early 1950s) and use of Heligoland traps, and later mist-nets, to catch birds has increased the chances of small birds which are difficult to identify (e.g. warblers) being recorded. On the other hand, large obvious birds, such as Little Egret, are much less likely to have been missed in the past. Knowledge of identification features has improved in such cases as autumn marsh terns. The shooting of Snipe *Gallinago gallinago* for sport was formerly more widespread: its decrease may have resulted in a lower proportion of the Great Snipe being noted. Indiscriminate shooting is far less now, so that the rarer of two very similar species may be less often discovered (e.g. American Bittern). The likelihood of escapes from captivity is increasing all the time, and some increases in rare birds may result from this.

Many further examples of potential bias could be quoted, and few species are not affected in some way. Constantly bearing this in mind, however, the list (Table II) gives us at least some indication of trends, especially when a conspicuous species is in the 'increasing' group or an inconspicuous one in the 'decreasing' group—in each case the opposite of what one would expect. Striking instances of this are the increased numbers of Little Egrets and Caspian Terns, and the decreased numbers of White's Thrushes and Alpine Accentors. It is worth noting that of the ten species showing a steady increase recently (*during* 1958–72), nine also show a long-term increase (1958–72 compared with prior to 1958) and the tenth (Bonaparte's Gull) possibly does, while of the seven species showing a steady recent decrease, two also show a long-term decline, four possibly do and only one (Rustic Bunting) shows a possible long-term increase. Broadly speaking, therefore, the trends which are evident in the short-term (during 1958–72, from Table I) can be detected as progressions of long-term trends (from Table II), providing confirmation of their reality.

Even after allowing for the various forms of bias in the data, interpretation of trends in vagrancy pattern can still be fraught with difficulties. While genetic change, a new migration pattern, alteration of wintering quarters or changing weather patterns are possible reasons for a change in vagrancy pattern, an increase in numbers or an expansion of the breeding range are the usual reasons given in explanation of an increase in the number of vagrants and, conversely, a diminution in numbers or a contraction of the breeding range are taken to explain a decrease in vagrants. A species can be regressing over most of its range, however, while the population (perhaps small or perhaps distant) from which our vagrants derive is expanding. Thus, records in Britain and Ireland can increase at a time when the species is regarded as being in regression. Similarly, adverse factors, such as drainage of a species' nesting area, could lead to the establishment of a colony nearer Britain and Ireland, resulting in a greater number of vagrants here, when reports from the main breeding area are indicating a catastrophic decline. A tiny portion of the population close to Britain could be carefully protected and be expanding, when the main population is rapidly declining. Despite anomalies of this sort, however, it is likely that a species which is increasing or expanding its range will occur more often as a vagrant and one decreasing or contracting its range will occur less often as a vagrant.

TABLE II. Species recorded more than ten times up to 1972, arranged in order of the percentage of total records which were during 1958–72. Thus, the sequence runs from those recorded up to 1957 but not in 1958–72, to those recorded in 1958–72 but not prior to 1958. The exact positions in the list have little significance because of the many sources of bias, but, in general, the nearer a species is to the start of the list the scarcer it is becoming here, and the nearer it is to the end of the list the commoner it is becoming here. The divisions of the list into four groups is arbitrary, except that the first and last and the two central groups contain equal numbers of species. (Ruddy Shelduck *Tadorna ferruginea*, Crane *Grus grus*, Semipalmated Sandpiper *Calidris pusilla*, Lesser Short-toed Lark *Calandrella rufescens*, Nutcracker *Nucifraga caryocatactes* and Savi's Warbler *Locustella luscinioides* are omitted, for reasons obvious in the species accounts.)

Decreasing

Great White Egret *Egretta alba*

Spotted Eagle *Aquila clanga*

Eagle Owl *Bubo bubo*

White-tailed Eagle *Haliaeetus albicilla*

Baillon's Crake *Porzana pusilla*

Great Bustard *Otis tarda*

- Pallas's Sandgrouse *Syrrhaptes paradoxus*

Alpine Accentor *Prunella collaris*

Tengmalm's Owl *Aegolius funereus*

American Bittern *Botaurus lentiginosus*
Squacco Heron *Ardeola ralloides*
Glossy Ibis *Plegadis falcinellus*
Little Bustard *Otis tetrax*
Scops Owl *Otus scops*
Blyth's Reed Warbler *Acrocephalus dumetorum*
Cream-coloured Courser *Cursorius cursor*
Ivory Gull *Pagophila eburnea*
Great Snipe *Gallinago media*
White's Thrush *Zoothera dauma*
Gyrfalcon *Falco rusticolus*
Little Crake *Porzana parva*
Hawk Owl *Surnia ulula*
Lesser Kestrel *Falco naumanni*
Black Stork *Ciconia nigra*
Crested Lark *Galerida cristata*
Surf Scoter *Melanitta perspicillata*
Sooty Tern *Sterna fuscata*
Roller *Coracias garrulus*
Rose-coloured Starling *Sturnus roseus*
Night Heron *Nycticorax nycticorax*
King Eider *Somateria spectabilis*
Yellow-billed Cuckoo *Coccyzus americanus*
Bee-eater *Merops apiaster*
pratincoles *Glareola spp.*
Lanceolated Warbler *Locustella lanceolata*
Pechora Pipit *Anthus gustavi*
Two-barred Crossbill *Loxia leucoptera*
Little Bittern *Ixobrychus minutus*
Black-winged Stilt *Himantopus himantopus*
Greater Yellowlegs *Tringa melanoleuca*
Marsh Sandpiper *Tringa stagnatilis*
Black-eared Wheatear *Oenanthe hispanica*
Desert Wheatear *Oenanthe deserti*
Rufous Bush Robin *Cercotrichas galactotes*

329

Red-breasted Goose *Branta ruficollis*
Upland Sandpiper *Bartramia longicauda*

Little change, perhaps decreasing
Broad-billed Sandpiper *Limicola falcinellus*
American Robin *Turdus migratorius*
Little Bunting *Emberiza pusilla*
Killdeer *Charadrius vociferus*
Scarlet Rosefinch *Carpodacus erythrinus*
Red-footed Falcon *Falco vespertinus*
Lesser White-fronted Goose *Anser erythropus*
White Stork *Ciconia ciconia*
Solitary Sandpiper *Tringa solitaria*
White-billed Diver *Gavia adamsii*

Little change, perhaps increasing
Arctic Redpoll *Acanthis hornemanni*
Blue-winged Teal *Anas discors*
Sociable Plover *Vanellus gregarius*
Rustic Bunting *Emberiza rustica*
Bonaparte's Gull *Larus philadelphia*
Whiskered Tern *Chlidonias hybrida*
Alpine Swift *Apus melba*
Great Spotted Cuckoo *Clamator glandarius*
Lesser Grey Shrike *Lanius minor*
Purple Heron *Ardea purpurea*

Increasing
Red-throated Pipit *Anthus cervinus*
Lesser Yellowlegs *Tringa flavipes*
Woodchat Shrike *Lanius senator*
Serin *Serinus serinus*
Least Sandpiper *Calidris minutilla*
Gull-billed Tern *Gelochelidon nilotica*

Caspian Tern *Hydroprogne caspia*
Tawny Pipit *Anthus campestris*
American Wigeon *Anas americana*
Black Kite *Milvus migrans*
Spotted Sandpiper *Tringa macularia*
Short-toed Lark *Calandrella cinerea*
dowitchers *Limnodromus spp.*
Black-headed Bunting *Emberiza melanocephala*
Great Reed Warbler *Acrocephalus arundinaceus*
Arctic Warbler *Phylloscopus borealis*
Yellow-breasted Bunting *Emberiza aureola*
Pectoral Sandpiper *Calidris melanotos*
Subalpine Warbler *Sylvia cantillans*
Lesser Golden Plover *Pluvialis dominica*
White-rumped Sandpiper *Calidris fuscicollis*
Buff-breasted Sandpiper *Tryngites subruficollis*
Red-rumped Swallow *Hirundo daurica*
Ross's Gull *Rhodostethia rosea*
White-winged Black Tern *Chlidonias leucopterus*
Olivaceous Warbler *Hippolais pallida*
Aquatic Warbler *Acrocephalus paludicola*
Richard's Pipit *Anthus novaeseelandiae*
Little Shearwater *Puffinus assimilis*
Little Egret *Egretta garzetta*
Greenish Warbler *Phylloscopus trochiloides*
Cattle Egret *Bubulcus ibis*
Baird's Sandpiper *Calidris bairdii*
Citrine Wagtail *Motacilla citreola*
albatrosses *Diomedea spp.*
Stilt Sandpiper *Micropalama himantopus*
Thrush Nightingale *Luscinia luscinia*
White-throated Sparrow *Zonotrichia albicollis*
Bonelli's Warbler *Phylloscopus bonelli*
Radde's Warbler *Phylloscopus schwarzi*
Dusky Warbler *Phylloscopus fuscatus*

Pallas's Warbler *Phylloscopus proregulus*

Ring-necked Duck *Aythya collaris*

Wilson's Phalarope *Phalaropus tricolor*

Baltimore Oriole *Icterus galbula*

Cetti's Warbler *Cettia cetti*

For the European species, L. J. Yeatman's excellent book *Histoire des Oiseaux d'Europe* (1971) has documented the known recent changes in numbers and range. Comparing these with the lists in Table II, there is a clear connection between changing status in Europe and the changing pattern of vagrancy in Britain and Ireland (see Table III). This is especially clear for

TABLE III. The connection between the trends in vagrancy pattern in Britain and Ireland (from Table II) and the changing status as breeding birds (from *Histoire des Oiseaux d'Europe*) of species which breed in Europe.

Vagrancy position in Britain and Ireland	Increasing or spreading in Europe	Decreasing or contracting in Europe	European status unchanging or not known
Increasing	48%	36%	16%
Decreasing	10%	77%	13%
Little change	23%	46%	31%

species which have decreased as vagrants here, 77% of which are known to have declined in Europe and only 10% of which are known to have increased.

In general, therefore, though the trends shown by the number of vagrants recorded in Britain and Ireland are modified by numerous forms of bias in the recording, they seem to reflect each species' changing status. For some, the vagrancy pattern here may give clues to changing status which are not apparent in the breeding areas (through difficulty of access or lack of observers). Has Alpine Accentor declined in the mountains of Europe? Have White's Thrushes declined or contracted in central Siberia? Are Pallas's, Dusky and Radde's Warblers currently on the increase in southern and western central Siberia? There is no direct information from these breeding areas, but the British and Irish records of vagrants indicate indirectly—and tantalisingly—that these changes may have occurred.

Index